DEEP (Development Experience Exchange Partnership)
for the Vision of Vietnam

Vol. 1

Advanced Human Resource Development (AHRD) for State Capacity and Sustainable Development in Vietnam

Written by M. Jae Moon, Ilhyun Jo, Sam Youl Lee,
Sung Min Park, Jung Wook Lee

YONSEI UNIVERSITY PRESS

DEEP (Development Experience Exchange Partnership) for the Vision of Vietnam

Volume 1

Advanced Human Resource Development (AHRD) for State Capacity and Sustainable Development in Vietnam

Written by M. Jae Moon, Ilhyun Jo, Sam Youl Lee, Sung Min Park, Jung Wook Lee

Published and Printed the Republic of Korea
by Yonsei University Press.
50 Yonsei-ro, Seodemun-gu, Seoul, 03722, Republic of Korea
Tel: (+82-2) 2123-3380~2 Fax: (+82-2) 2123-8673 E-mail: ysup@yonsei.ac.kr
ISBN 978-89-6850-372-6 (94300)
978-89-6850-371-9 (Set)

The National Library of Korea cataloging in Publication (CIP) data for this volume can be found at the library's e-CIP homepage(http://seoji.nl.go.kr). and in the Korean Library Information System Network(http://kolis-net.nl.go.kr).
CIP Control Number: 2019049814

Table of Contents

Abbreviation 10

Executive Summary 15

Author : M. Jae Moon

CHAPTER ONE:

Advanced Human Resource Development for Sustainable Growth

Author : Jung Wook Lee

Ⅰ. Why Advanced Human Resource Development (AHRD)? 34

1. Sustaining the momentum of growth ? 34
2. Productivity challenges 35
3. Problems in state effectiveness 37
4. What needs to be done? 39
5. AHRD: A critical enabler of long-term sustainable growth and development 43

Ⅱ. Issues and Imperatives 48

1. Government 49
2. SOEs 58
3. Science and Technology (S&T)/ Research and Development (R&D) 67

CHAPTER TWO:

Advanced Human Resource Development for The Government of Vietnam

Author : Sung Min Park

Ⅰ. Introduction 84

Ⅱ. HUMAN RESOURCE DEVELOPMENT IN VIETNAM 86

1. Overview of HRD Agencies and Institutions in Vietnam 86
2. SWOT Analysis of the Current Government System in Vietnam 89

Ⅲ. Specifications of the AHRD Agencies 91

1. HRD and AHRD Authorities 91
2. Agencies Providing AHRD Services (Training Institutions) 93
3. Issues in the AHRD Agencies 96

Ⅳ. Specifications of AHRD Programs 97

1. Training for Civil Servants and Public Servants (CCT) 97
2. The Development of Training Systems and Programs 98
3. Training Program for Director Generals (DG) and Deputy DGs 99
4. Training Programs for Potential National Strategic Leadership 100
5. Issues in the AHRD Program 107

Ⅴ. Specifications of the AHRD System 108

1. Evolution of HRD and AHRD System in Vietnam 108
2. Key Features of the AHRD System in Vietnam 112
3. Systems and Methods of AHRD 114
4. Overall Assessment of AHRD System 118

Ⅳ. Lessons from Korea's Experience and Policy Recommendations 124

1. Recommended AHRD Reform Paths 124
2. Vietnam 2030: Towards Prosperity, Creativity, Equality and Democracy 154

CHAPTER THREE:

Advanced Human Resource Development in State-Owned Enterprises

Author : Ilhyun Jo

Ⅰ. Introduction 160

Ⅱ. Status of AHRD Systems for SOEs in Vietnam 165

1. Issues of SOEs in Vietnam 165
2. General HR in Vietnam's SOEs 167
3. SOE-General Suggestions and Future Directions 171

Ⅲ. Case Studies on AHRD in Vietnamese SOEs 174

1. Coal and mining industry in Vietnam - VINACOMIN 175
2. ICT industry in Vietnam - VNPT 180
3. Agriculture Banking Industry in Vietnam - Agribank 183

Ⅳ. Lessons from the Korean Experience 188

1. Development of Economy and AHRD in Korea 189
2. Target Corporations in Korea 193
3. Productivity Organization in Korea: Korea Productivity Center (KPC) 217

Ⅴ. Policy Recommendations and Imperatives 225

1. Summary of suggestions 225
2. Promoting strategies by steps 227

CHAPTER FOUR:
Advanced Human Resource Development in Research and Development (R&D) in Vietnam

Author : Sam Youl Lee

Ⅰ. Introduction 238

Ⅱ. Human Resources in R&D in Vietnam 239

1. The General Status of R&D and Analysis in Vietnam 239
2. Detailed Statistics on R&D Organizations 243
3. National Strategy for Science and Technology Development 2011-2020 253

Ⅲ. Policy Issues Related to AHRD Systems for R&D in Vietnam 257

1. Issues with National Innovation System in Vietnam 257

2. Main Issues: What Are the problems? 258

Ⅵ. Korean HRD Policy for R&D 264

1. Korean HRD Policy in R&D 264

2. Environment Change and Problems in S&T Policy in Korea 276

Ⅴ. Policy Recommendations 284

CHAPTER FIVE:

The Way Forward for AHRD in Vietnam 291

Author : M. Jae Moon

Appendices 303

References 346

Index 362

Authors 367

List of Figures and Tables

Figures

Figure P-1. Four Policy Pillars of AHRD in Government, SOEs, and R&D Sectors 26

Figure 1-1 Productivity Problems 37

Figure 1-2 State effectiveness problems 39

Figure 1-3 Productivity and state effectiveness 40

Figure 1-4 Priorities for enhancing productivity 41

Figure 1-5 Priorities for improving state effectiveness 42

Figure 1-6 Comparison between SOEs and FOEs in terms of HRM 63

Figure 1-7 Imperatives at a glance 79

Figure 1-8 Summary of Issues and Imperatives 82

Figure 2-1 Cadres and Civil Servant Training (CCT) Agencies in Vietnam 94

Figure 2-2 AHRD Agency Model 125

Figure 2-3 Operational Framework of the National HRD Institute 128

Figure 2-4 Operational Framework of the LOGODI 130

Figure 2-5 A Process Model for AHRD Programs 133

Figure 2-6 Training Program for High Ranking Officials 137

Figure 2-7 AHRD System Model: Strategic and Analytical Processes 142

Figure 3-1 Shares of key employment groups by occupations (%) 170

Figure 3-2 Total employees and excavation workers of the Vietnamese coal mining industry (Synchronized data from VINACOMIN from 2003 to 2010) 178

Figure 3-3 Outline of Case Studies on AHRD in Vietnamese SOEs 187

Figure 3-4 Real economic growth rates between 1960 and 1980 189

Figure 3-5 Korea's Coal Production (million tons) 194

Figure 3-6 Program for Executives and Employees in KT 205

Figure 3-7 Organizational Structures of KPC 220

Figure 3-8 Co-evolutionary History of KPC and Korean Economic Development 224

Figure 3-9 Concept map of the proposed strategies related the direct and indirect effects 227
Figure 4-1 Vietnam real GDP Growth 239
Figure 4-2 Patents granted in Vietnam (1990~2014) 240
Figure 4-3 R&D Personnel in Korea (1981~2014) 265
Figure 4-4 Government R&D Budget in Korea 1998~2015 (Unit: Trillion Won) 278
Figure 4-5 Researchers in R&D per Million in Korea 279
Figure 4-6 Korean population forecast, 1970~2060 (unit: thousands) 282
Figure 4-7 Number of Graduate Students in Korea (1980~2015) 282
Figure 4-8 Engineering Science Degrees Awarded by Country (2010) 283

Tables

Table P-1 Participants of AHRD Research Team 18
Table P-2 Structure of the Study 20
Table 1-1. SEDP 2011-2015 Indicators that failed to meet the 5-year planned targets 35
Table 1-2 Global Competitiveness Index (GCI) of Vietnam for 2015-2016 68
Table 2-1 SWOT Analysis 90
Table 2-2 Responsibility of Cadres and Civil Servants Training 95
Table 2-3 Development of Korean Officials' Training System and Program 126
Table 2-4 The Process of Open Competitive Employment 144
Table 2-5 The Vietnam AHRD Recommendations: From a Strategic Perspective 153
Table 3-1 Issues related to AHR in VINACOMIN 179
Table 3-2 Current Issues of AHR in KOCOAL 198
Table 3-3 KT's Competitiveness in AHR 204
Table 3-4 Outcome of Extension Service for Training ACK staffs (1961~1980) 214

Table 3-5 Target Corporations in Korea 217

Table 3-6 History of Government's Policy and performance of KPC 221

Table 3-7 KPC's Educational Programs 223

Table 3-8 "3 Year X 3 Domain" AHRD Innovation model 226

Table 4-1 Gross expenditure for R&D in 2013 241

Table 4-2 R&D personnel in Vietnam 242

Table 4-3 Distribution of R&D personnel by organizations 243

Table 4-4 Number of S&T Organizations (Divided by Scientific Sectors) 244

Table 4-5 S&T Organizations divided by Central and Provincial/City 245

Table 4-6 Organizations of Research and Development under Government 246

Table 4-7 Quantity of Universities, Academies and Colleges (2012-2013) 247

Table 4-8 Human Resources of R&D by Performer and Gender in 2013 (unit: person) 248

Table 4-9 Human Resources in R&D by Working Sectors (unit: Person) 248

Table 4-10 Personnel in Tertiary Education by Degree (unit: person) 249

Table 4-11 Main Quantitative Objectives of the SSTD 254

Table 4-12 Increase in International Publications 2011-2015 255

Table 4-13 Korean S&T HRD Policy between 1960 and 2012 266

Table 4-14 Korean HRD Policy in S&T in the 1960s 267

Table 4-15 Korean HRD Policy in S&T in the 1970s 269

Table 4-16 Korean HRD Policy in S&T in the 1980s 271

Table 4-17 Korean HRD Policy in S&T in 1990s 273

Table 4-18 Korean HRD Policy in S&T between 2000 and 2004 274

Table 4-19 Korean HRD Plans in S&T since 2004 276

Table 4-20 R&D Expenditure by Institutions, 2009~2013 (Unit: 100 million won) 280

Abbreviations

General

AHRD	Advanced Human Resource Development
FDI	Foreign Direct Investments
HCMA	Ho Chi Minh National Academy of Politics
HR	Human Resources
HRD	Human Resource Development
HRM	Human Resource Management
PAR	Public Administration Reform
R&D	Research and Development
SEDP	Socio-Economic Development Plan
SEDS	Socio-Economic Development Strategy
SMEs	Small and Medium-sized Enterprises
SOEs	State-Owned Enterprises

Part One:

Advanced Human Resource Development for Sustainable Growth

ADB	Asian Development Bank
ASEAN	Association of Southeast Asian Nations
FOEs	Foreign Owned Enterprises
GCI	Global Competitiveness Index
GDP	Gross Domestic Products
GRI	Government Research Institutes
HRST	Human Resources for S&T and Innovation

ILO	International Labour Organization
IMF	International Monetary Fund
MNCs	Multinational Corporations
MNEs	Multinational Enterprises
MoST	Ministry of Science and Technology
NIS	National Innovation Systems
PM	Performance Management
PPPs	Public-Private Partnerships
QS	Quacquarelli Symonds
S&T	Science and Technology
STEM	Science, Technology, Engineering, and Mathematics
STI	Science, Technology, and Innovation
T&D	Training and Development
TFP	Total Factor Productivity
TPP	Trans-Pacific Partnership
VCCI	Vietnam Chamber of Commerce and Industry

Part Two: Advanced Human Resource Development for the Government of Vietnam

CCO	The Central Committee for Organization
CCS	The Cadres and Civil Servants
CCT	The Cadres and Civil Servants Training
CPV	Communist Party of Vietnam
DG	Director general
DHRM	Department of Organization and Human Resource Management
DoET	Department of Education and Training
DOHA	The Provincial Department of Home Affairs
DoLISA	Department of Labour, Invalids and Social Affairs

GCOP	The Government Committee on Organization and Personnel
GOV	Government of Vietnam
KSA	Knowledge, Skill, and Ability
LNA	Learning Needs Analysis
LOGODI	Local Government Officials Development Institute
MOET	The Ministry of Education and Training
MOHA	The Ministry of Home Affairs
MOLISA	The Ministry of Labour, Invalids and Social Affairs
MOPI	The Ministry of Planning and Investment
NAPA	National Academy of Public Administration
NHI	National Human Resources Development Institute
PRP	Performance-related pay
PSPs	Provincial School of Politics
SCS	Senior Civil Service

Part Three:

Advanced Human Resource Development in State-Owned Enterprises

Agribank	Vietnam Bank for Agriculture and Rural Development
AHR	Advanced Human Resources
APO	Asian Productivity Organization
ARPU	Average Revenue Per Unit
BIDV	Bank for Investment and Development of Vietnam
CDP	Career Development Program
GSO	General Statistics Office
ICT	Information and Communications Technologies
IPCAS	Internal Payment and Customer Accounting System
ISD	Instructional Systems Design
IT	Information Technology
JPC	Japan Productivity Center

KISDI	Korea Information Society Development Institute
KMA	Korea Management Association
KOCOAL	Korea Coal Corporation
KPC	Korea Productivity Center
KT	Korea Telecom
MOET	Ministry of Education and Training
MOLISA	Ministry of Labour and Social Affairs
MOOC	Massive Open Online Course
MTP	Management Training Program
OCW	Open Course Ware
PMS	Productivity Management System
SBV	State Bank of Vietnam
SMU	Saemaul Undong
TM	Talent Market
TVET	Technical-Vocational Education and Training
VBA	Vietnam Bank for Agriculture
VBS	VINACOMIN Business School
VINACOMIN	The Vietnam National Coal and Mineral Industries group
VNPT	Vietnam Posts and Telecommunications
VPCS	Vietnam Productivity for SOEs
VPC	Vietnam Productivity Center

Part Four:

Advanced Human Resource Development in R&D in Vietnam

BK	Brain Korea
FTE	Full-Time Equivalent
GFRI	Government Funded Research Institute
GOE	Government-Owned Enterprise
GRI	Government R&D Institute

HAN	Highly Advanced National
HCI	Heavy and Chemical Industry
IGTDP	Industrial Generic Technology Development Project
IPR	Intellectual Property Right
KAIS	Korean Advanced Institute of Science
KAIST	Korea Advanced Institute of Science and Technology
KCIA	Korean Central Intelligence Agency
KIST	Korea Institute of Science and Technology
MNC	Multinational Corporation
MoST	Ministry of Science and Technology
NISTPASS	National Institute for Science and Technology Policy and Strategy Studies
SATI	State Agency for Technological Innovation
SSTD	Strategy for Science and Technology Development
STI	Science and Technology Institute
TFP	Total Factor Productivity
VNU-HCM	Vietnam National University - Ho Chi Minh city
VUSTA	Vietnam Union of Science and Technology Association
WIPO	World Intellectual Property Organization

EXECUTIVE SUMMARY:

ADVANCED HUMAN RESOURCE DEVELOPMENT STRATEGIES FOR VIET NAM

M. Jae Moon

Professor, Department of Public Administration, Yonsei University

EXECUTIVE SUMMARY:

ADVANCED HUMAN RESOURCE DEVELOPMENT STRATEGIES FOR VIET NAM

This publication is the result of three-year long KOICA-funded joint research project by both HCMA and University Industry Foundation of Yonsei University called "DEEP (Development Experience Exchange Partnership) for the Vision of Vietnam". Professor Doowon Lee of Yonsei University served as the project leader (PL) of this three-year project along with a project manager (PM) assigned for each year's project. Dr. Kwang Woo Jun, the former Chairman of the Financial Services Commission of the Korean government also served as the Chairman of the Coordination Committee of this project. We appreciate Dr. Jun a lot for his valuable advices and considerate supervision. Also, we appreciate Dr. Nguyen Xuan Thang, President of HCMA, for his devoted cooperation and support.

As the first year part of this project, this report aims to diagnose the current status of advanced human resource development in three key areas such as government, state-owned enterprises, and R&D which are arguably most compelling pillars to sustainable development of Vietnam. Vietnam has been recognized as one of most dynamic, fastest growing developing countries particularly since the Doi Moi reforms were introduced in 1986. While Vietnam still faces various challenges, the country has demonstrated high performing economic growth as one of the major middle-income countries and continued to build a springboard to leap forward a high-income country by accelerating pace of economic growth, promoting inclusive growth, and enhancing quality of government.

The research team is comprised of five Korean researchers and seventeen Vietnamese researchers. Korean researchers include M. Jae Moon (Yonsei University), Jung Wook Lee (Yonsei University), Sung Min Park (Sungkyunkwan University), Sam Youl Lee (Yonsei University), and Il-Hyun Jo (Ewha Womans University). The Vietnamese research team led by team leader Nguyen Tat Giap (HCMA) and Hoang Van Nghia (HCMA) is comprised of both HCMA researchers and external experts. Do Thi Thach, Luong Thu Hien, Tuong Duy Kien, Tran Thi Thanh Thuy, Bui Van Huyen, Nguyen Ngoc Toan, Ngo Tuan Nghia, and Dao Thi Nguyet Hang are HCMA researchers. There are seven external experts including Truong Duc Thang (Office of Government), Nguyen Cong My (DSI), Nguyen Xuan Son (The Central Organizing Committee), Ta Quang Tuan (Ministry of Home Affairs), Vu Xuan Nguyet Hong (Central Institute for Economic Management), Nguyen Thanh Trung (Ministry of Research and Development), and Nguyen Quang Tuan(NISTPASS). The research team is organized as summarized below.

The research team believe that the advancement of human resource development is a key foundation for sustainable development in Vietnam. The research team examines the advanced human resource development (AHRD) at three different dimensions such as level of competencies (advancement of competencies), level of management (middle and top managers), and level of HRD system (advancement of competencies). The first dimension refers to promotion of various competencies which enable human resources of government, public corporation, and R&D sectors. We will identify and assess different competencies which are in need in Vietnamese government officials,

Table P-1 Participants of AHRD Research Team

		Korea	Vietnam
Project Leader		Doo Won Lee (Yonsei University)	Nguyen Xuan Thang (HCMA)
AHRD Team Leader		M. Jae Moon (Yonsei University)	Nguyen Tat Giap (HCMA) Hoang Van Nghia (HCMA)
Research Theme	**Sustainable Growth**	Jung Wook Lee (Yonsei University)	Do Thi Thach (HCMA) Luong Thu Hien (HCMA) Truong Duc Thang (Office of Government) Nguyen Cong My (DSI)
	Government	Sung Min Park (Sungkyunkwan University)	Tran Thi Thanh Thuy (HCMA) Tuong Duy Kien (HCMA) Nguyen Xuan Son (The Central Organizing Committee) Ta Quang Tuan (Ministry of Home Affairs)
	SOEs	Il-Hyun Jo (Ewha Womans University)	Bui Van Huyen (HCMA) Nguyen Ngoc Toan (HCMA) Vu Xuan Nguyet Hong (Central Institute for Economic Management)
	R&D	Sam Youl Lee (Yonsei University)	Ngo Tuan Nghia (HCMA) Dao Thi Nguyet Hang (HCMA) Nguyen Thanh Trung (Ministry of Research and Development) Nguyen Quang Tuan (NISTPASS)

public corporation employees, and R&D personnel and then develop a roadmap for promoting and developing competencies which contribute to realize SEDS 2016-2020 and Vietnam Vision 2035. The second dimension refers to target of AHRD. We will particularly focus on middle and top managers as advanced-level target level of management. The third dimension refers to the advancement of HRD system in the government, public corporation, and R&D sector. The system level dimension is basically related to the advancement of training methods and strategies.

While AHRD focuses on human resource development, the research team will examine human resource management which is a key foundation and function designed to maximize individual performances in organizations. Human resource management is composed of various elements including job design and analysis, employment planning, recruitment and selection, training and development, performance management, and compensation among others. HRD as one of the key elements in human resource management will be further investigated in this research.

This study will be composed of different parts in addition to preface and conclusion: 1) Social Economic Development Strategy and Significance if AHRD; 2) Advancing High Level Government Officials for State Capacity Building; 3) Advancing High Level Management for Economic Prosperity; and 4) Advancing R&D Personnel for Economic Prosperity. Preface will offer general background of the research along with the scope of the research and method. Part 1 is the brief overview of SEDS and human imperatives which is a groundwork for various issues and imperatives of AHRD in government, SOEs, and R&D areas. Part 2 deals with AHRD for government officials by identifying major AHRD issues in governments based on both advancements and drawbacks and draws policy recommendations based on the lessons learnt from selected Korean cases. Part 3 examines the current status of AHRD in SOEs based on selected cases of Vietnamese SOEs including VINACOMIN and AGRIBANK. The part also reviews various aspects of AHRD system in comparable Korea's SOEs and draws lessons and policy implications for the advancement of AHRD in Vietnamese SOEs. Part 4 investigates AHRD in R&D in Vietnam. The part identifies key issues regarding training and development of R&D personnel in Vietnam. Based on the current status of R&D personnel development in Vietnam and Korean case studies, the part will offer various policy recommendations for the future AHRD in R&D in Vietnam. The part will be followed by concluding remarks which highlight critical issues and policy guidelines for future AHRD in Vietnam.

Table P-2 Structure of the Study

Part 1: Human Resources in Sustainable Growth - Issues - Imperatives		
Part 2: AHRD in Government - Status of AHRD for government officials - Korean Cases - Lessons and Policy Recommendation	Part 3: AHRD in SOEs - Status of AHRD for SOEs Personnel - Korean Cases - Lessons and Policy Recommendation	Part 4: AHRD in R&D - Status of AHRD for government officials - Korean Cases - Lessons and Policy Recommendation

Summary of Research

Chapter 1 written by Jungwook Lee offers a comprehensive framework of the advanced human resource development (AHRD) for long-term sustainable growth and development based on various official documents prepared by the Vietnamese government including Social Economic Development Strategy (SEDS) 2011-2020, SEDS 2011-2015, and Social Economic Development Plan (SEDP) 2016-2020 as well as selected development reports prepared by international organizations.

Vietnam is attempting at a major leap from low-middle income to high-middle income status by 2035. Two critical challenges are ahead: the country is seeing an economy-wide decline in productivity; and its state capacity barely matches demands from an increasingly sophisticated and complicated economy, contributing further to the productivity decline. Addressing these problems requires a whole variety of steps and measures, among which improving the quality of human resources is a top priority. Three areas call for immediate attention: state-owned enterprises (SOE), the science and technology (S&T) field, and government. High-quality human resources would help SOEs—widely perceived as a root cause for the country's productivity problems—better deal with their performance issues. Spurring innovation, and hence accelerating productivity growth, would be possible only when high-quality S&T human resources are more readily available across the economy. Effective government, a foundational condition for sustainable economic growth, would be in place only when the civil service is staffed with people with high levels of competencies for policy-making and implementation.

In order to achieve long-term sustainable growth and development, supporting each area to overcome its HR challenges, and thereby improving the capacity to attract, develop, and retain high-quality human resources, should be a top priority. This requires, most of all, delineating the most serious constraints and challenges facing each area today. For this purpose, this study conducted a review of official documents issued by the Government of Vietnam, such as SEDS 2011-2020, SEDP 2011-2015 and SEDP 2016-2020 as well as major development reports recently published by international donor organizations such as World Bank, OECD and ADB; academic and policy studies on HR in Vietnam were also included in the review. The figure below provides a picture of what are the most serious issues for each area. This study suggests a set of HR 'imperatives' that should be seriously considered in dealing with the major issues challenging each area.

Chapter 2written by Sungmin Park addresses a comprehensive set of AHRD issues in government organizations. Reform initiatives in Vietnam public sector over the last 20 years have delivered remarkable economic growth. The demands and challenges for sustainable development requires the government of Vietnam to carry out various initiatives to strengthen public sector developmental orientations; and advance strategic policy plans appropriate for national industrialization and modernization by 2020 and beyond. As a critical and integral component in achieving the vision 2020 for national development and modernization of the Vietnamese government, a well-entrenched and strategic public human resource development needs to be in place.

Therefore, this study suggests an "Advanced Human Resource Development" strategy drawing from applicable theoretical and practical experiences of the Korean public HRD, The AHRD philosophy is a visionary and strategic management of training, development interventions on human resource to ensure that the organization can adapt and take advantage of opportunities, realizing the objectives while providing the best opportunities for individual development.

In an effort to establish a workable and customized Vietnamese AHRD model, this study draws from the theoretical and practical experiences of the Korean public sector organizations. Especially, this study details a contextual and environmental (i.e., external and internal conditions) scanning of the Vietnam public sector that may influence the AHRD planning, implementation, and evaluation.

The recommended Vietnamese AHRD strategy was based on system, agency, and program models which were developed considering the contextual and environmental realities of the country. The Vietnamese AHRD system may adopt a distinct HRM/HRD system for high ranking officials, systematic civil service examination, and competitive recruitment system. In terms of AHRD agency, Vietnam government may establish a central human resource training and development agency. Finally, the AHRD programs may adopt a training and development interventions based on the rank and position and/or competency-based approaches.

Chapter 3written by Ilhyun Cho discusses AHRD issues in the Vietnamese state-owned enterprises. This part assesses advanced human resources development (AHRD) system in Vietnamese SOEs and provides systematic suggestions for the enhancement of it. To pursue for the goal, current states of AHRD activities of three key SOEs, VINACOMIN, VNPT, Agribank, each representing primary, secondary, and tertiary industries respectively, are analyzed and compared with benchmark Korean SOEs, KOCOAL, KT and Nonghyup. In addition to the comparative analyses of the 3 pair-wise comparisons of SOEs from both countries, KPC (Korea Productivity Center), who played strategic roles as facilitator and developer in Korea, is benchmarked and suggested as a key initiative.

Analyses indicate, for the sustainable AHRD system with maximum return on investment; 1) limited development resources should be strategically allotted to the three key parameters (institution, contents, and expertise in HRDers) of Vietnamese AHRD system, 2) the investment should serve as “Majungmul” (or priming water) for vertical trick-down effects and horizontal ripple effects across entire community of Vietnamese SOEs in the long run, and 3) long-term and step-wise approaches are required for this challenging and strategic initiative.

Suggestions are made based on the analyses above and discussions among Vietnamese and Korean researchers as a form of the “3 X 3 Model” (3-parameter by 3-stage). The "3 X 3 Model" stresses that a long-term partnership between Vietnam and Korea is a must-imperative. Further research, development, and reflections should lead both countries' mutual benefits in the development of HR and, ultimately, socio-economic statuses.

Chapter 4 written by Samyoul Lee discusses AHRD Issues in research and development in Vietnam. This chapter is to investigate the current status of personnel development and supply in research and development in Vietnam and implement diagnosis on the current advanced human resource development in research and development. Since the role of human capital especially in R&D is quite important and essential for Vietnam to catch up with developed countries, it is meaningful to understand the current status and problems in Vietnam. This chapter analyzes the advanced human resource policy in R&D in Korea and come up with the characteristics of Korean policies which can be referred to for Vietnam. Based on the analysis on Vietnam and Korea, this chapter suggests actionable items on advanced human resource development policy for Vietnam.

The policy recommendations are as follows;

1. Vietnam government needs to restructure the role and capacity of government-affiliated R&D organizations.
2. Vietnam government needs to renovate the economic growth model.
3. Vietnam government needs to invest in empowering the research capacity of GRIs and universities and change the salary to attract more competent researchers.
4. Vietnam government needs to strengthen collaboration among GRIs, Universities, and Business.
5. Vietnam government needs to bringing more competition to domestic market in order to make business be more innovative and thus supply

with more attractive jobs for R&D workers.

6. Vietnam government need to make technology transfer more efficient by promoting brain circulation and using strategic FDI policy. The main driver of technology transfer is the talent movement.
7. Vietnam government needs to strengthen implementation and evaluation capacity by creating a new R&D governing system including HRD and setting up a policy-learning mechanism
8. Vietnam government need to recommend and facilitate entrepreneurship at GRIs as well as Universities by streamlining laws, regulations, and incentives.

The recommendations have practical meanings since they are formulated with the collaboration between Vietnamese experts and Korean experts.

The Way Forward for AHRD in Viet Nam

While the Government of Vietnam has been making progress in improving its AHRD by introducing a position-based system and cultivating a performance culture in various sectors, this progress has been somewhat slow and limited. Based on various policy recommendations and suggestions by priority and urgency presented in four different parts of this report, we propose four key policy pillars that need to be considered by the Government of Vietnam to modernize the state and particularly to improve AHRD in the government, SOE, and R&D sectors in order to build a foundation for sustainable and inclusive economic and social development. The policy pillars of AHRD include the following: 1) promoting meritocracy in AHRD; 2) establishing new institutional arrangements to strategically promote AHRD; 3) enhancing institutional capacities of AHRD organizations; and 3) integrating fragmented AHRD systems.

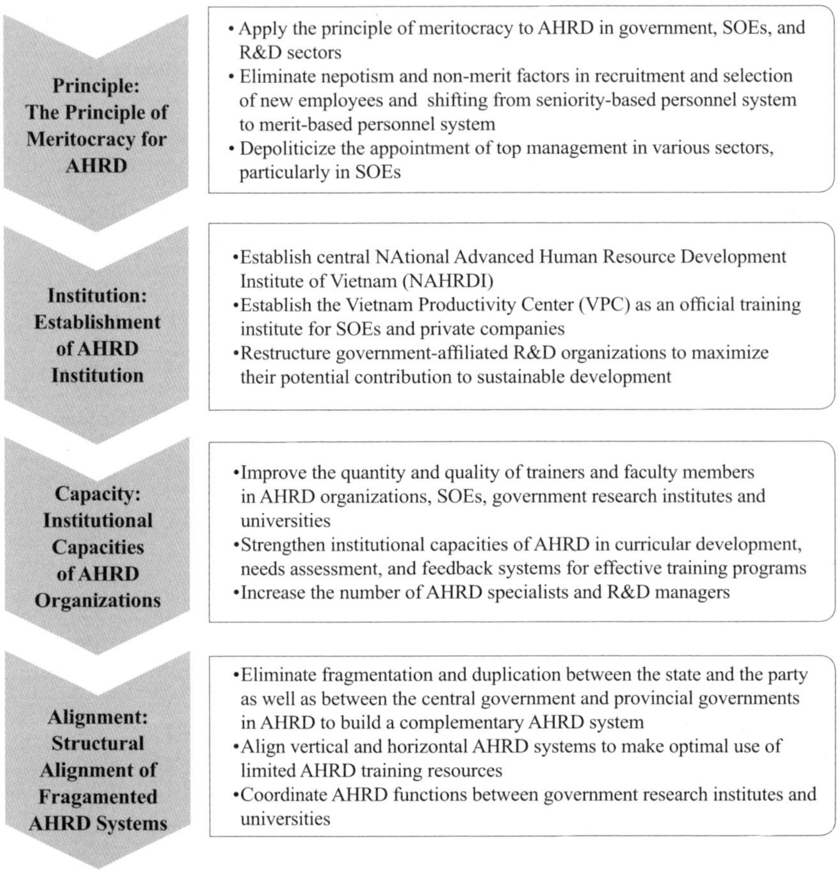

Figure P-1 Four Policy Pillars of AHRD in Government, SOEs, and R&D Sectors

Promoting Meritocracy in AHRD

First of all, the Government of Vietnam needs to strengthen and apply the principle of meritocracy to various stages of human resource management and development. In order to attract talented and competitive personnel to government, SOEs, and R&D, recruitment and selection of new personnel should be administered based on merit rather than nepotism or any other non-merit factors such as political, family or other personal and relational background. Key human resource decisions (i.e., promotion, job assignments, performance evaluation) need to be made based on performance and merit and move away from seniority-based and nepotism-based HR decisions. In SOEs, the intervention and influence of government and party often hampers a merit-based human resource system. The board of directors in SOEs also need to be reconstituted to ensure long-term planning and professional management. Short-term and often non-merit-based appointment of board members weakens the meritocratic and professional foundation of SOEs and eventually damages competitiveness in the global market. Meritocracy also helps to attract talented youth to the R&D area

- *Apply the principle of meritocracy to AHRD in government, SOEs, and R&D sectors*
- *Eliminate nepotism and non-merit factors in recruitment and selection of new employees and shifting from seniority-based personnel system to merit-based personnel system*
- *Depoliticize the appointment of top management in various sectors particularly in SOEs*

Building New Institutional Arrangements for AHRD by Establishing New AHRD Institutes to Supply Competitive Human Resources to Various Sectors

Vietnam is at a crossroads. The quality of human resources in various sectors determines success or failure in pursuing and realizing the strategic goals of SEDP 2016-2020 and Vietnam 2035. Despite partial and slow improvement of existing HRD institutes, they are not ready to be fully transformed into new AHRD institutes which can not only provide various training programs to meet the current demand for human resources in various sectors but also supply high-quality human resources in the future. While the Vietnamese government needs to conduct comprehensive evaluation of existing HRD institutes and find ways to transform them into innovative and comprehensive AHRD institutes, it also needs to consider establishing new AHRD institutes for government, SOEs, and R&D.

- *Establish the National Advanced Human Resource Development Institute of Vietnam (NAHRDI) for central government officials and later AHRD Institutes for provincial and local government officials*
- *Establish the Vietnam Productivity Center for SOEs (VPCS) as an official training institute for SOEs and possibly private companies to strategically meet their training needs in various areas then strengthen its research capacity and maximize spin-off effect to various organizations*
- *Establish a central R&D institute such as V-KIST (Vietnam version of Korean Institute of Science and Technology) to supply high-quality advanced R&D personnel to R&D institutes and private companies to enhance the potential and competiveness of the Vietnamese economy while restructuring existing government research institutes (GRI) to maximize*

their potential contribution to the sustainable development of Vietnam

Enhancing Training Capacities of AHRD Organizations by Developing Quality of Trainers, Training Curricula, and HR Professionals

Given the increasing future demand for competitive human resources in government, SOEs, and R&D in the next two decades, strengthening the institutional capacity of AHRD organizations is surely critical. Despite continued progress in AHRD organizations in the three selected areas, their institutional capacity has been limited due to lack of competitive trainers, effective training curricula, learning needs analysis and post-training feedback, among other issues. The Government of Vietnam needs to enhance both the quantity and quality of trainers as well as improve training curricula and training capacity of various training institutions under the Central Committee for Organizations (CCO), Ministry of Home Affairs (MOHA), Provincial Department of Home Affairs, and Department of Organization and Human Resource Management (DHRM). Dealing with the labor shortage in SOEs and R&D, enhancing the institutional capacity of AHRD organizations is not optional but required to supply skilled employees and competent high-quality R&D personnel. While each SOE needs to increase the number of AHRD managers and strengthen the institutional capacity of its own AHRD organization, it is also critical to supply enough skilled labor through a general skill training organization such as VNPT. Weak performance and teaching capacity in research institutions and universities are also problematic and have constrained the innovativeness and competitiveness of the Vietnamese economy. The quality of government research institutions as well as vocational and tertiary education will need to be increased in order to meet the demand for more competent and talented personnel in R&D. A sufficient supply of qualified faculty members in universities and R&D managers in government research institutes is critical.

- *Improve the quantity and quality of trainers in AHRD institutions in government and SOEs as well as ensuring qualified and competent faculty members in government research institutes and universities*
- *Strengthen institutional capacities of AHRD in curriculum development, training needs assessment, and feedback mechanisms for effective training programs*
- *Increase the number of AHRD specialists for governments and SOEs and R&D managers for R&D sectors as well as bridging the gap between talents needed and talents supplied*

Alignment of Fragmented AHRD Systems

It has been argued that state institutions are highly fragmented. Overlap and confusion in rules and roles between the State and the Party, between the central government and provincial governments, and even among central agencies are presented as one of the major obstacles to building a stronger state (World Bank and the MPI, 2016). Fragmentation and duplication are also common in AHRD when the center of the AHRD system is not strong and capable enough. The fragmented AHRD systems need to be unified and the overlaps and confusion which often pose obstacles to timely deployment of capable personnel in the right place need to be eliminated. The main targets for NAPA and HCMA need to be coordinated and various AHRD organizations for

SOEs also need to be strategically aligned and coordinated for various skill-based and problem-based training programs. The division of labor between government research institutes and universities in training and educating R&D personnel needs to be coordinated and strategically aligned.

- *Eliminate fragmentation and duplication between the Party and the state and between the central and provincial governments to build complementary AHRD systems*
- *Align horizontal and vertical AHRD systems among various AHRD organizations and skills-based training programs for optimal use of limited training resources in the nation*
- *Coordinate division of labor between government research institutes and universities in recruiting and educating competent R&D personnel*

As the government enacts these recommendations, AHRD systems will be put in place that will ensure a more capable and accountable state which will drive a post Doi Moi reform for continued realization of modernity, industrialization, and a high quality of life envisioned in the Vietnam 2035.

CHAPTER ONE:

Advanced Human Resource Development for Sustainable Growth

Jung Wook Lee
Professor, Department of Public Administration, Yonsei University

Ⅰ. Why Advanced Human Resource Development (AHRD)?

Ⅱ. Issues and Imperatives

CHAPTER ONE:

ADVANCED HUMAN RESOURCE DEVELOPMENT FOR SUSTAINABLE GROWTH

I. Why Advanced Human Resource Development (AHRD)?

1. Sustaining the momentum of growth – A tremendous challenge that requires a paradigm shift

As the economies of middle-income countries continue to grow fast, the gap between middle and high-income countries becomes narrower. However, as the country's income grows, the advantage of backwardness, which once acted as the most important economic growth driver, generally becomes smaller, demanding new approaches with clear blueprints for action. Vietnam, a country now attempting a major leap from low-middle income to high-middle income status within two decades, is no exception. Trends suggest that the key drivers that powered past growth, such as cheap labor, expansion of capital, and the exploitation of exhaustible natural resources, are beginning to show a diminished impact (Breu *et al*. 2012).

An assessment of the implementation of the Socio-Economic Development Plan 2011-2015 also reveals that sustaining the momentum of growth will be a huge challenge for the country. Out of the total 26 key development indicators, only 17 met their planned targets (see Table 1-1;refer to Appendix 1 for a complete list of the development indicators). Particularly worrisome is that more than half of those nine negative indicators are economic ones, and the two social indicators are closely concerned with economic development. These results provide yet another piece of evidence that avoiding the middle-income trap and thereby successfully transitioning to a high-middle income economy will not be an easy undertaking for Vietnam.

Table 1-1 SEDP 2011-2015 Indicators that failed to meet the 5-year planned targets

Economic indicators
- Five-year CAGR of gross domestic products (GDP)
- Five-year average proportion of total investment of the entire society over GDP
- State budget deficit in the ending year of the five-year planning period
- Ratio of high-tech products to total industrial production value
- Five-year average rate of technology renovation
- Social labor productivity growth rate
Social indicators
- Jobs created in the five-year period 2011-2015
- Proportion of trained workers of total working labor in the economy
Environmental indicators
- Forest coverage in the ending year of the five-year planning period

2. Productivity challenges

What should be the first priority in order for Vietnam not to fall into the middle-income trap? What should be done to realize the country's long-term aspiration to achieve a high-middle income status in the world economy? The results of the implementation of SEDP 2011-2015, as well as an increasingly challenging economic environment, clearly indicate that productivity should be the starting point for such discussions. The World Bank (2016: 32-33) points to productivity growth as the most critical issue for the country's sustainable growth, calling for immediate attention and action to the issue:

> *What will determine Vietnam's path? Productivity is fundamental ... Countries' inability to break out of the middle-income trap (whether or not they have been growing fast) is almost entirely attributable to stagnating productivity ... Paul Krugman notes, "Productivity isn't everything, but in the long run it is almost everything. A country's ability to improve its standard of living over time depends almost entire on its ability to raise its output per worker."*

International organizations warn that Vietnam is in a precarious situation. The World Bank (2016) notes that the country's productivity growth has been on a long-term declining trajectory stemming from broad reasons. According to the International Labour Organization (ILO; 2014), Vietnam's labour productivity was one of the lowest among the countries in the Asia-Pacific region due to a mismatch between the demand and supply in skills. To be more specific, ILO research indicates that productivity of Singapore, which is the leading country in the ASEAN region, was almost 15 times that of Vietnam in 2013; moreover, Malaysia and Thailand, two other middle-income countries in the region, showed 5 times and 2.5 times higher productivity than Vietnam, respectively. In an International Monetary Fund working paper, Anand, Cheng, Rehman, and Zhang (2014) report that Vietnam's total factor productivity (TFP) growth, which reflects the contribution to output as a result of efficiency improvement in the use of inputs, is much lower compared to those of the major countries in the region (Refer to Figure 1-1).

Turning the declining trend in productivity around requires more than

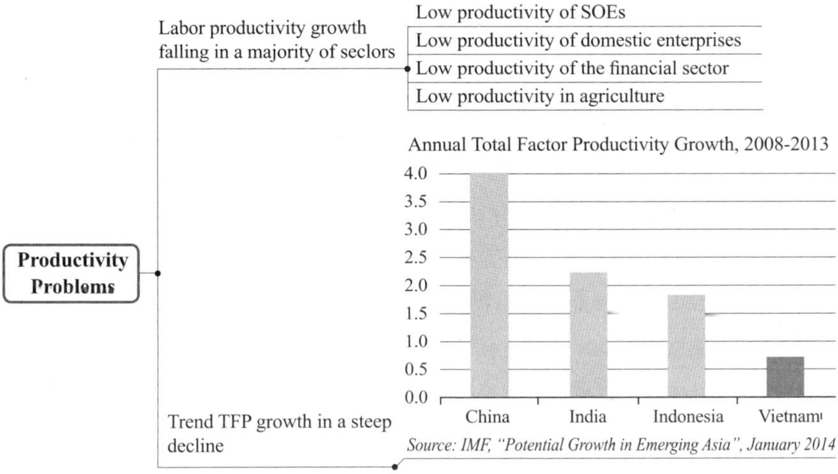

Source: Adapted from World Bank (2016) and Anh (2015)

Figure 1-1 Productivity Problems

incremental changes; rather it requires long-term strategies including fundamental structural reforms of the Vietnamese economy, with active participation from both the public and private sectors including not only Vietnamese private enterprises but also State Owned Enterprises (SOEs) and Multinational Enterprises (MNEs) as well.

3. Problems in state effectiveness

An important axiom in the development community is that state effectiveness matters. The International Bank for Reconstruction and Development/The World Bank (1997: 1) notes:

An effective state is vital for the provision of the goods and services—and the rules and institutions—that allow markets to flourish and people to lead healthier, happier life. Without it, sustainable development, both economic and social, is impossible ... The state is central to economic and social development, not as a direct provider of growth but as a partner, catalyst, and facilitator.

State effectiveness is a critical condition for economic growth and development. An economy cannot prosper when market institutions are not properly developed and implemented and will suffer from various distortions when an effective system of checks and balances is not in place. The quality of economic development is significantly affected by the policy-making and implementation capacity of the government. The Commission on Growth and Development (2008: 4) succinctly illustrates the importance of state effectiveness, particularly in relation to this last point:

Government is not the proximate cause of growth. That role falls to the private sector, to investment and entrepreneurship responding to price signals and market forces. But stable, honest, and effective government is critical in the long run. The remit of the government, for example, includes maintaining price stability and fiscal responsibility, both of which influence the risks and returns faced by private investors.

However, state effectiveness is a serious issue for Vietnam: the country's growth and development are hampered by its shortcomings in market institutions, checks and balances, and bureaucratic capacity. A recent Global Competitiveness Index (2015-2016) is illustrative in this regard: out of the 140 countries assessed, Vietnam ranks 93rd in property rights, 86th in judicial independence, and 80th in public-sector performance. The World Bank (2016) provides a comprehensive assessment of its state effectiveness problems. Figure 1-2 provides a summary of these problems.

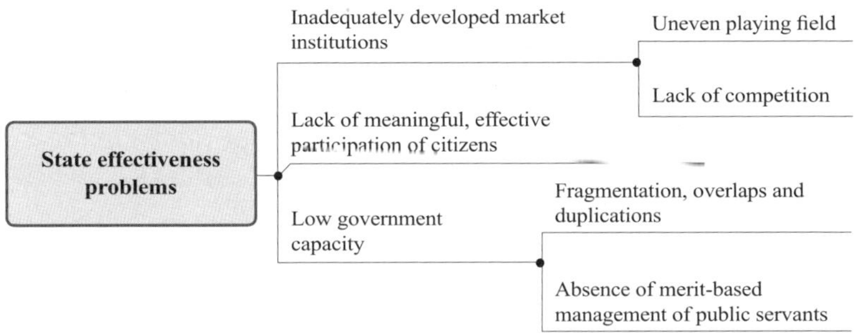

Source: Adapted from World Bank (2016)

Figure 1-2 State effectiveness problems

4. What needs to be done?

Vietnam has an ambitious goal of achieving a high-middle income status within a relatively short period of time, sustaining a 7% growth rate. In order to achieve this, the country should successfully address a series of demanding challenges. These can be categorized into two groups: one concerns productivity problems, while the other is about state effectiveness issues. First, Vietnam has to enhance productivity across sectors in the economy. Given the rapid weakening of past growth drivers, its growth strategies should focus on elevating productivity across the economy. Improving state effectiveness is yet another priority for Vietnam. As Figure 1-3 indicates, state effectiveness is a critical condition for a long-term, sustainable productivity-driven economy. Of course, an effective state is in and of itself important.

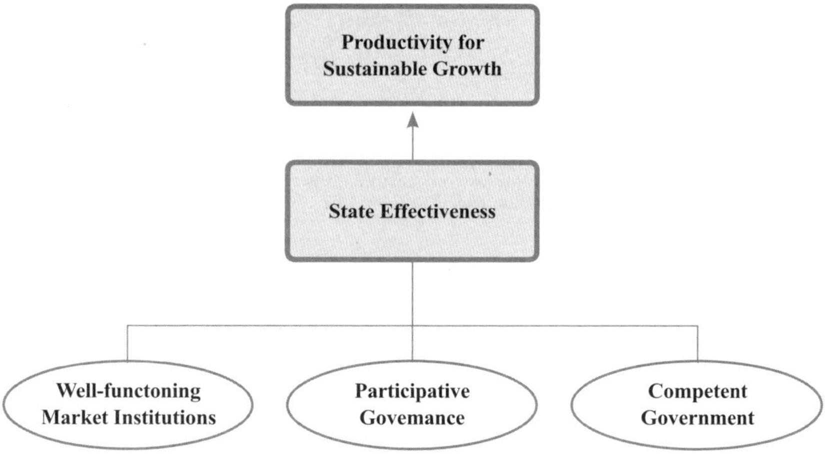

Figure 1-3 Productivity and state effectiveness

What tasks should Vietnam undertake? What options does it have? Answering these questions requires, most of all, a thorough review of two critical documents. First, the *Socio-Economic Development Plan (SEDP) 2016-2020*, based on a critical review of the implementation of the *SEDP 2011-2015*, suggests a series of tasks for improving productivity and state effectiveness. *Vision 2035*, a report prepared and published by the World Bank in close collaboration with the Government of Vietnam early this year, also includes a variety of discussions related to the issues of productivity and state effectiveness; the purpose of this World Bank report was to provide recommendations to the Government of Vietnam for the development of SEDP 2016-2020 and the Socio-Economic Development Strategy (SEDS) 2021-2030. Figures 1-4 and 1-5 provide a brief summary of priority tasks as suggested in the two documents.

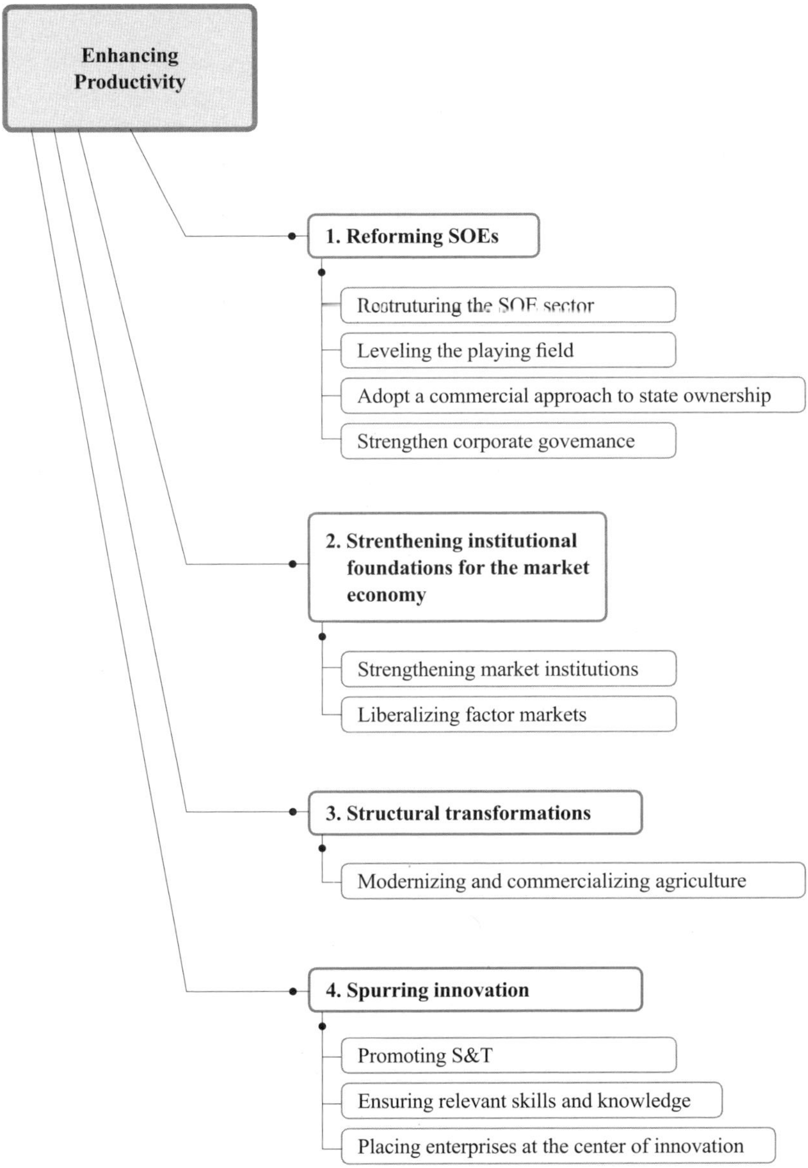

Figure 1-4 Priorities for enhancing productivity

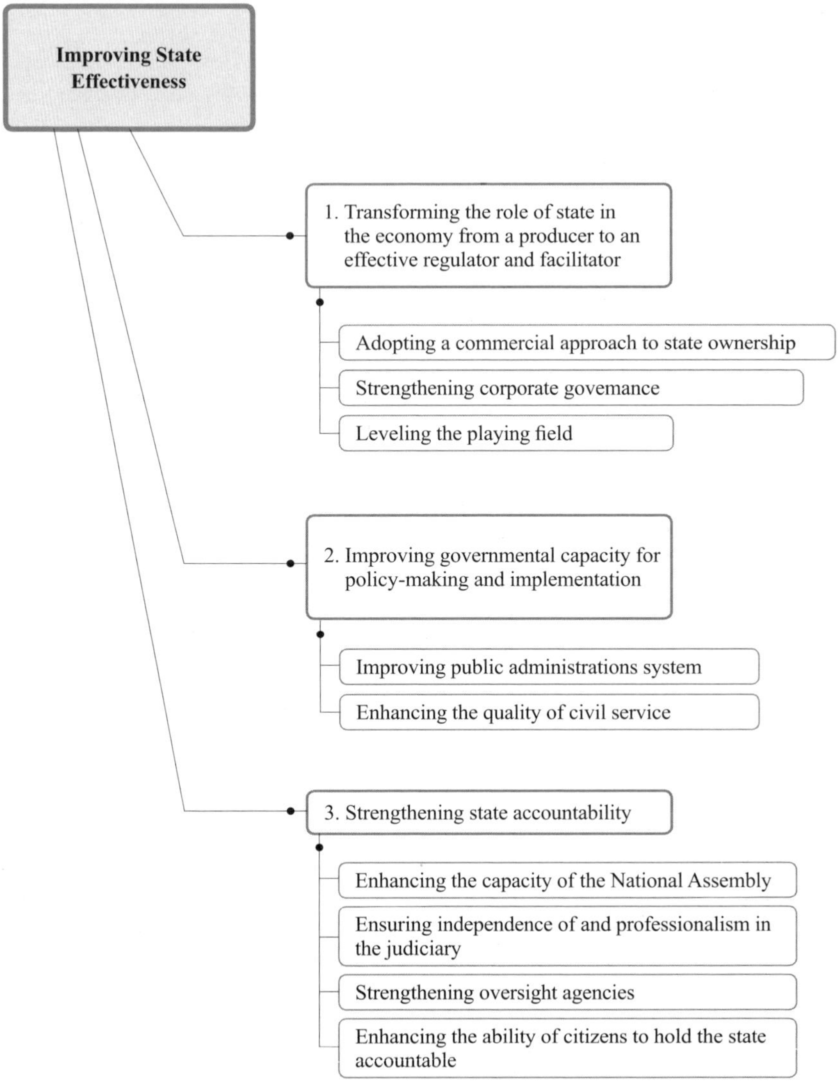

Figure 1-5 Priorities for improving state effectiveness

5. AHRD: A critical enabler of long-term sustainable growth and development

Addressing the issues of productivity and state effectiveness, as Figures 1.4 and 1.5 indicate, will be not only a demanding but also a tremendously complicated initiative. Given the scope and diversity of tasks as presented in these figures, a cross-cutting perspective is required in order to develop a coherent set of strategies and ideas. This study takes a human resources (HR) perspective for two reasons. First, as demonstrated in development success stories, the quality of human resources is a critical performance predictor in all sectors. Having the right people to do the appropriate jobs at the appropriate time makes a significant difference. Second, the seriousness of HR problems in Vietnam makes this perspective more relevant. Like most middle-income countries with rapid economic growth and emerging industry transformation, Vietnam is currently experiencing consequential challenges in overcoming a talent shortage, especially in the managerial and professional fields (Nankervis *et al.*, 2016; Warner, 2013). Strategic Risk (2014:14) called this HR shortage "the war for talent, part of the risk landscape in Vietnam." A most recent Global Competitive Index and Creativity Index substantiate this point: out of the total 140 countries assessed, Vietnam ranked 109th in reliance on professional management, 87th in country capacity to retain talent, and 75th in availability of scientists and engineers (World Economic Forum, 2015), while scoring 27.2 out of 100 in human capital (The Economist Intelligence Unit & Asian Development Bank, 2014). Recognizing the seriousness of the talent shortage, the Vietnamese government has included developing high-quality human resources as a national top priority in its Socio-Economic Development Strategy (SEDS) for 2011-2020.

Three areas call for more immediate and serious attention than others: the state-owned enterprises (SOEs), the science and technology (S&T)/research and development (R&D) field, and the civil service. Given their size and strategic importance, these sectors have huge impact on the country's growth and development potential. However, these are also the sectors where a shortage of high-quality human resources causes serious performance problems.

SOEs are probably one of the hottest topics in the discussions of Vietnam's economy. For example, in 2013, even though they only represented about 1% of the total number of enterprises and employed 13.5% of total workforces, they still exerted great influence in Vietnam's economy in that their share in Vietnam's GDP was around 32.2%; moreover, their proportion of total investment accounted 40.4% in 2013 as well (Hiep, 2015). As such, their performance matters for the overall growth potential of the economy. However, SOEs are widely known as one of the root causes of productivity problems in the country. As seen in the example, despite the slightly decreasing number of SOEs, they still consume a large amount of scarce resources by receiving a large amount from the State as investment, but produce lower output levels compared to their competitors in the private sector, dragging the economic growth (Asian Development Bank (ADB), 2015).

Many factors contribute to the productivity problems of SOEs, and HR problems are one of those factors. Studies show that SOEs' capacity for HRM/HRD has much room for improvement (e.g., Pham 2011; Warner 2013). An SOE would be better able to improve its productivity when it has the capacity to determine how to fulfill its workforce needs, to acquire the necessary personnel, to develop their skills, to motivate them to work harder and smarter, to reward them for this behavior, and to impose remedial actions to improve the performance of those who fail. This report will discuss strategies that would help SOEs to develop such capacity.

Enhancing the quality of human resources becomes more critical for SOEs as the demand for a more complete transition to a market economy is increasing. Vietnam's integration into the world economy does not come cheap; it is constantly being asked to correct various types of distortions such as an uneven playing field and lack of competition. In the long run, SOEs may have to compete with private enterprises and foreign invested enterprises without privileges they have long enjoyed. Vietnam is moving deeper into international economic integration. Such a circumstance requires that SOEs recognize shortages in talent and recruit advanced human resources from foreign countries to transfer necessary knowledge and skills in their transformation to internationally competitive enterprises (Breu *et al.*, 2012). SOEs need high-quality human resources more than ever.

Innovation is the key to Vietnam's long-term sustainable growth, and it is only when there is a strong foundation of S&T/R&D that makes innovation possible. As the World Bank (2014: 1) notes, "one key differential that will determine the trajectory of [its] growth path is the growth in productivity, and the single most important driver of productivity is innovation." Spurring innovation is a daunting task for developing countries since they typically do not have a solid S&T/R&D foundation. Unfortunately, Vietnam is no exception, and it is suffering from its weak S&T capacity. Vietnam lags behind its South-East Asian neighbors, and the gap with those neighboring countries is widening. For example, while Thailand has seven and Malaysia has four institutions included in the Quacquarelli Symonds (QS) ranking of the top 200 Asian universities in 2016, none of Vietnam's schools feature in this list or in the list of 500 top universities in the world in the QS rankings in 2015. The Global Competitiveness Index (2015-2016) also shows the country's weak innovation and S&T/R&D capacity: it ranks 75th in innovation and 92nd in technological readiness out of 140 countries surveyed. At the root of these problems lies a critical issue: Vietnam is suffering from a serious shortage of high-quality S&T/R&D human resources. In discussing science, technology and innovation (STI) reform in Vietnam, the World Bank (2014) and Anh (2015) suggest enhancing its human capital as a top priority area of focus in that success of STI reform ultimately depends on skills of responsible human resources. Upgrading innovation capacity is critical in jumping to the next level of growth and development. Without high-quality human resources that will vault the S&T/R&D to a more advanced level, Vietnam will not be able to transition to the innovation-driven economy it desperately aspires to.

This report also includes government as a primary target for HR interventions. As the World Bank (2016) says, when economies in countries moving up from lower to upper-middle-income become more complex and diversified, the role of government becomes more important, so its quality and capability to work with various economic actors is necessary. This quality and capability of government depend on the human resources working in the public sector, and an adequately designed incentive system can foster their competencies. In fact, some fast-growing economies attribute their growth to those highly trained and well-paid civil servants recruited by competitive processes (Commission on Growth and Development, 2008). Without those advanced human resources who possess essential high quality for carrying out public policies, it will be impossible for the nation to achieve sustainable growth and satisfy the increasing demands of the society (ADB, 2014). Recognizing the importance of effective government for its sustainable growth and development, Vietnam has implemented serious efforts at improving its human resources in government. After more than a decade of implementation of HR reforms in the context of public administration reform (PAR), however, little evidence is found that such reforms have made a significant difference.

On the contrary, Vietnam's public service faces complex and interrelated HR problems such as "overstaffing, low salary, prevalence of second and third jobs, rigidity, nepotism, corruption, [and] relation-oriented promotions" that all threaten sound productivity of employees (Ohno, 2014: 258). The government is losing its current and future talent to other sectors. For Vietnam, it is the right time to conduct a critical review of the current HR reform strategies and their implementation in order to come up with better solutions. In order to not be caught in the middle-income trap, an effective pubic administration system operated by equally effective workforces is not an option, but a necessity. It should be remembered that "an elite civil service may not come cheap. But poorly motivated, ill-prepared civil servants are tremendously costly" (Commission on Growth and Development 2008: 66).

Indeed, the three areas—SOEs, S&T/R&D, and government—are critical in accomplishing the national goal of transitioning to an upper-middle income status within two decades. Without properly addressing these HR problems, Vietnam will not be able to enhance the productivity of its economy. Thus, supporting each area to overcome HR challenges and to develop the capacity to attract, develop, and retain high-quality human resources should be a top priority in the pursuit of long-term sustainable growth and development.

II. Issues and Imperatives

Vietnam is attempting a major leap from a low-middle income status to a high-middle income status by 2035. Two critical challenges are ahead: the country is seeing an economy-wide decline in productivity, and its state capacity barely matches demands from an increasingly sophisticated and complicated economy, contributing further to the productivity decline. Addressing these problems requires a whole variety of steps and measures, among which improving the quality of human resources is a top priority. Three types of entities call for immediate attention: state-owned enterprises (SOE), science and technology (S&T)/research and development (R&D) bodies, and government. High-quality human resources will help SOEs—a root cause of low productivity—better deal with their efficiency issues. Spurring innovation, and thereby accelerating productivity growth, will be possible only when firms have more access to high-quality S&T/R&D human resources. Effective government, a framework condition for sustainable economic growth, is possible only when the civil service is staffed with people with high levels of understanding of the market economy and competencies for policy-making and implementation.

In order to achieve long-term sustainable growth and development, supporting each area to overcome its HR challenges and thereby improving the capacity to attract, develop, and retain high-quality human resources should be a top priority. This requires, most of all, delineating the most serious constraints and challenges facing each area today. For this purpose, this study conducted a review of official documents issued by the Government of Vietnam, such as SEDS 2011-2020, SEDP 2011-2015 and SEDP 2016-2020 as well as major development reports recently published by international donor organizations such as the World Bank, OECD and ADB. Academic and policy studies on HR in Vietnam were also included in the review. This study suggests a set of HR imperatives that should be seriously considered in dealing with the major issues challenging each area.

1. Government

1.1. Situation

When the Public Administration Reform (PAR) Index was introduced in 2013 in order to take a further step toward a better government, many HR-related problems had already frustrated previous reform efforts. For example, government had a hard time dealing with turnover problems of those who quit their jobs for better options at private or foreign corporations. However, a bigger problem lay in the capacity of civil servants and public employees: the director of the PAR department said in public media that evaluation of leaders indicated that only 30% of them were working well, 30% were working with limited results, and 40% with no results (Can, 2013).

In the years since PAR implementation, the situation seems no different: ineffectiveness and inefficiency of state management mostly caused by HR reasons is still prevalent in the country. The World Bank's World Governance Indicators 2014 substantiate this point: Vietnam ranked 72nd (lower 37.3 percentile) in government effectiveness, which indicates perceptions of the quality of public and civil service as well as policy-competence and 103rd (lower 30.1 percentile) in regulatory quality, which demonstrates perceptions of government's ability in policy-making and implementation of effective policies. The SEDP 2016-2020 specifically mentions that "capacities, qualities, sense of discipline of part of officials and public servants have not met the demand," and points out the limitations of qualification and competency among them. Moreover, difficulties in hiring and retaining highly-qualified and motivated people as well as losing them to other growing sectors are further aggravating the current problematic situation (Lan, 2016).

1.2. Issues

Issue 1. Limited progress in promoting the principle of meritocracy

a. Seniority rather than merit still plays a greater role in every stage of the Human Resource Management (HRM)process.

b. Progress in implementing performance management (PM) has been slow due to a lack of capacity and interest.

Issue 2. Slow progress in strengthening elements of a position-based system

a. Reforms were enacted but not properly implemented.

Issue 3. No significant improvement in salary and incentives

a. Wages are still too low and can only cover only a portion of basic needs.

b. Overstaffing remains unsolved, making salary reform slow.

Issue 4. Upgrading training has been slow

a. Training and retraining methods have much room for improvement in terms of scope and quality.

b. Donor-funded training programs are not managed in a systematic way.

Issue 5. A dual subordination system constrains effective talent management

a. Duplication between party and government rules makes developing technically competent human resources more challenging.

As briefly mentioned, limited progress of government reforms can be attributed to chronic HR-related problems in the Vietnamese government. While there are numerous problems that cause the current low capacity of government, five major problems are worth further analysis.

First, there has been only limited progress in promoting the principle of meritocracy. To begin with, seniority is still more valued in the process of recruitment and promotion than merit. A large gap between the actual grade of civil servants and their competence levels continues partly because the promotion examinations only require knowledge generic to the grade rather than the actual competencies required. With such lifelong employment and seniority-based promotion systems, civil servants and public employees have little incentive to improve their performances, resulting in an ineffective HR management system (ADB, 2014). Moreover, a performance management system, which is an effective tool for promoting meritocracy, has showed slow progress in its implementation mainly due to lack of capacity for and interest in it. According to SEDP 2016-2020, the Vietnamese government is still facing hardships in replacing poorly performing, incompetent, unqualified, and irresponsible officials in a timely manner. Unclear job descriptions, performance indicators, and personal authority and responsibilities of officials in addition to low focus on work results in the current performance appraisal system make all these matters worse.

Along this line, the second problem can be discussed: there has been slow progress in strengthening the elements of a position-based system. While there were some government-wide reform efforts in 2008, they were not properly implemented (World Bank, 2016). Previous government reform efforts around the world as well as in Vietnam yielded one important lesson in the advanced human resource development (AHRD) context: there must be an institutionalized system for job analysis, description, and performance measurement and management in order to coordinate and carry out various HRM activities more effectively. However, the Vietnamese government has had only moderate success in setting these systematic elements as preconditions for a strong position-based system. For example, there are still unclear and generic job descriptions, and conflicts in performance evaluation system are still observed quite often.

Third, there have been no significant improvements in salary and incentives of public officials and civil servants[1]. Although this problem has been constantly pointed out in previous studies and reports (Acuna-Alfaro, 2012; Commission on Growth and Development, 2008; Kim *et al*., 2012; Lan, 2016; Ohno, 2014), there have not been many significant movements to solve it. As a result, wages are still low and can only cover about one-third of basic needs ("Vietnam's Public Wages Too Low," 2015). Leaving out the incomparable salary level of the public sector to the private sector from discussion, a great number of civil servants and office-holders are struggling to maintain good quality of life due to the mismatch between their current level of salary and the cost of living (Lan, 2016). However, this weak salary and incentive system brings other serious problems as well. Many high-quality officials leave the government to work in the private sector, causing brain drain, and incumbent officials rely on other informal income sources that distract them from their original duties (Acuna-Alfaro, 2012). In the end, the public sector attracts those who want mere stability, or those who want to take advantage of official privileges (Ohno, 2014), rather than motivated new entrants to the job marketwho genuinely believe in public service despite the low salary.

1 Public perception of the current incentives system in the public sector also demonstrates the importance and seriousness of this issue. Please refer to Appendix 2 for further information.

In addition, overstaffing makes salary reform slow. Without cutting off a significant number of incumbent civil servants, it would be hard to guarantee the success of salary reform (Can, 2013).

Fourth, upgrading training has been slow as well. Any training and retraining methods still have much room for improvement in terms of scope and quality, and donor-funded training programs are not managed in a systematic way. Many training courses and programs overlap and are designed to meet the general requirements of HR policies, resulting in theory- and legal-based contents rather than practical information (ADB, 2014; Can, 2013).

Lastly, a dual subordination system largely constrains effective talent management in government. In reality, civil service management is currently carried out by both government and the Party, especially the Central Commission on Organization and Personnel (CCOP). This management duplication actually makes developing technically competent human resources more challenging in that disadvantages from this duplication usually outweigh benefits. When the personnel management system for the Party runs in parallel with that of government, civil servants are subject to dual subordination which often brings conflicts between needs and requirements from these two management entities and prevents civil servants from being appropriately assigned or developed (Poon *et al.*, 2009; World Bank, 2016)

1.3. Imperatives

Imperative 1. Ensure that merit drives the entire HRM process.

a. Reform hiring and promotion of civil servants, ensuring competition, publicity, and transparency.

b. Strengthen the foundation for performance management (PM) by clarifying roles and responsibilities, particularly those of agency heads.

Imperative 2. Enhance the foundation for transitioning to a position-based system.

a. Make more serious efforts at conducting job analysis and creating job descriptions.

b. Use more specific criteria for recruitment.

Imperative 3. Implement the wage reforms as stipulated in Resolution 30c.

a. Create room for increasing salary by successfully implementing downsizing as planned, ensuring that downsizing does not hurt the policy capacity of the public service.

b. Devise effective incentives and rewards for high performance.

Imperative 4. Evolve design and delivery of training.

a. Make training more demand-driven and performance-oriented.

b. Strengthen training for HR professionals.

c. Strengthen HRM training for line managers.

d. Utilize donor-funded training programs in a more systematic way.

Imperative 5: Review the roles of and relationship between the Party and Government in managing civil service.

a. Minimize overlaps and duplications that make timely and effective talent management difficult.

b. Clarify the demarcation line between relevant authorities in personnel administration and political appointment.

Despite the seriousness of HR issues in Vietnamese government as listed in the previous section, fortunately, there is much room left for improvement as well. Then what must be done to improve the current situation? The following imperatives can be the first steps toward progress in AHRD of government sector.

In general, it should be ensured that merit drives the entire HRM processes. The importance of merit-driven HR processes is especially highlighted in SEDP 2016-2020, which states that competition, publicity, and transparency rather than seniority should be ensured in the process of hiring and promotion of civil servants. The first step of this reform should start from "perfecting laws on recruitment, arrangement and task assignment suitable to qualifications, capabilities and strengths of recruited civil servants and public employees" as stated in PAR 2011-2020. To fully adopt merit-based principles in the HRM process, using competitive exams in both promotion and appointment of top and mid-level should be considered rather than guaranteeing lifelong employment with automatic promotion based on seniority. In addition, laws on promotion and appointment should be based on performance management as well. To be more specific, the foundation for PM should be strengthened by clarifying roles and responsibilities, particularly those of agency heads, in order to make them accountable for their performances by either rewarding or giving penalties. Performance information yielded in the process of PM should facilitate these processes; therefore, laws should be further perfected and revised to employ performance-based evaluation and rewarding and commendation of public employees and civil servants.

In this context, the foundation for transitioning to a position-based system should be enhanced because such a system can actually produce a synergy effect in promoting merit-based principles when implemented with the first imperative. For example, one of the many benefits of a position-based system is the ability to recruit and promote the right person to the right job based on job requirements (Poon *et al.*, 2009); thus, by conducting job analysis and creating job descriptions, every process of HRM can make use of the respective qualification information to find officials with the appropriate competencies. In brief, there should be more serious efforts at job analysis and job descriptions and utilization of the resulting information for setting specific criteria for HR processes as stated in both SEDP 2016-2020 and PAR 2011-2020 to firmly establish a strong position and merit-based HRM system.

When discussing some problematic HRM issues in the government sector, low salary and incentives have been mentioned as a place for reform. Recently, the Vietnamese government took a step to solve this problem by raising the minimum wage by 5% for the public sector for the first time in three years. Although this increase in the wage itself is valuable, there is still a long path left for wage reform in that salaries between the public and private sectors are still far from comparable: private sector salaries have increased by 10% to 15% every year from 2013 to 2015 ("Vietnam Raises Minimum Wage," 2016). Therefore, in order to address many problems related to low salary, appropriate wage reforms as stipulated in Resolution 30c[2] should be implemented. During the reform process, government should create room for increasing salaries by successfully implementing downsizing as planned and devise effective incentives and rewards for high performance (Can, 2013; Poon *et al.*, 2009). Although salaries and non-salary allowances should be substantially reformed to ensure the quality of life of the public workforce after cutting down overstaffing, downsizing should not hurt the policy capacity of the public service. Regarding the incentive system, as PAR 2011-2020 states, the laws

2 Under Resolution 30c/NQ-CP, the government resolves to perfect salary and wage policies during the state administration period of 2011-2020. By 2020, salaries will be substantially reformed to ensure above-average quality of life

concerning rewards and commendations should be revised to link performance to compensation while developing credible methods of performance evaluation at the same time (Commission on Growth and Development, 2008).

The fourth imperative suggests evolving design and delivery of training. Unlike the current training that emphasizes meeting general requirements (ADB, 2014), the new training should be more demand-driven and performance-oriented. Demand-driven and performance-oriented qualities can be found in various reform efforts, which SEDP explains as "high ethical qualifications, competency, sense of responsibility, and professionalism" and PAR as "good ethical qualities, firm political stuff, high professional capability and professionalism, and devotedly serving the people." Moreover, this new training system should strengthen HRM training for both HR professionals and line managers. Training of those professionals and line managers is required for full implementation of the first three imperatives in that they are the ones who are responsible to carry out those solutions. Without appropriate knowledge and skills in HRM, it is almost impossible to design and implement related policies.

Lastly, concerning the training problem, utilizing donor-funded training programs in a more systematic way can be a useful solution as well. Ohno (2014) criticized current donor-funded training programs for not improving the quality of public service and stimulating the brain drain, explaining that steps should be taken to reform the related funded programs to raise the average quality of the workforce.

Imperatives concerning differentiating the roles between the Party and government are rather more easily said than done; however, it is still worth mentioning the problem because the current dual system often hinders effective implementation of HRM. Therefore, it is necessary for the government to review the roles of and relationship between the Party and Government in managing civil services. Many overlaps and duplications resulting from confusion in the dual system make timely talent management difficult (Acuna-Alfaro & Tran, 2016; Poon *et al.*, 2009; World Bank, 2016); thus, minimizing these unnecessary tasks can contribute to raising the quality of the government. However, without reforming the current system in which workers receive and follow orders from two different subjects, it will be difficult to minimize duplication of processes and tasks. The reform process should begin with clarifying the demarcation line between relevant authorities in personnel administration and political appointment. This issue can be addressed by first differentiating the two different roles of the Party and government: while the Party is responsible for "leadership," government is for "execution" (Poon *et al.*, 2009). Then there should be separate laws or secondary legislation passed to confer public workforces at least some degree of political independence. Only when these preconditions are set can demarcation lines be drawn between the Party and government's central HR department.

2. SOEs

2.1. Situation

In 2009, Vo (9) stated that "SOEs lag behind Multinational Corporations (MNCs), the latter offering higher wages and more sophisticated human resource management (HRM) policies (including performance-based pay schemes and better training) and thereby attracting younger and more talented employees out of the domestic SOEs into other MNCs." Years later, the same problems are still common, implying the related problems have not been solved and still exist in the SOE sector. To be more specific, SEDP 2016-2020, which was drafted after the evaluation of the implementation of SEDP 2011-2015, still emphasizes the need to promote "restructuring and improving management quality and efficiency of SOEs, especially public sector economic groups and corporations." Had the previous efforts been successful in this area, there would have been no need for SEDP 2016-2020 to include redundant goals from 2011-2015. Lan (2016) explains that there are still no specific policies to overcome the continuing shortage of high-quality human resources and the brain drain[3]. Moreover, when analyzing the current situation of SOEs, SEDP 2016-2020 discusses shortages of high-quality human resources by mentioning difficulties in recruiting "skilled employees for technical and management positions" and having brain drain to MNCs." Considering the issues suggested in the various documents, it can be inferred that inefficiencies in many Vietnamese SOEs mainly result from longstanding HR problems.

2.2. Issues

Issue 1. A slow transformation in HRM systems

a. Transformation in the recruitment and selection practices has been weak.
b. Performance management is not working in a way that contributes to long-term organizational goals.
c. There are constraints in designing and implementing remuneration practices.
d. There has been no significant progress in improving training and development systems.

3 In the 2012 World Economic Forum's Financial Development Index, Vietnam scored 3.1 out of 7 in the brain drain category under the business environment pillar, ranking 51 out of 62 countries.

Issue 2. Low HRM capacity

a. HR is not seen as a strategic business partner.

b. HR managers have limited capacity.

Issue 3. Merit plays a limited role in the appointment process of high-level positions

a. Political considerations heavily influence the appointment and selection process.

Before listing all the HR problems in SOEs, it is worth mentioning a significant change in the operation of SOEs. As in many centrally planned economies, the personnel function of SOEs was performed by the administrative department (Cox, 2014). While the government was responsible for most of the inherent management activities of SOEs, the administrative departments performed limited roles such as keeping personnel records. However, after implementation of Doi Moi in 1986, administrative departments were given more strategic personnel responsibilities including recruitment and selection, performance appraisals, compensation and benefits, and so on (Cox, 2014). Even though this change in management responsibilities was expected to bring more modern HRM practices to SOEs and create a more active atmosphere, HRM transformation has been slow, and lack of HRM capacity as well as organizational inertia, including the politicized nature of HRM processes, still prevents an effective transformation to strategic human resource management systems in SOEs (Cox, 2014).

To elaborate further, four problems contribute to a slow transformation in HRM systems in SOEs. Transformation in the recruitment and selection practices has been weak, and there has been no significant progress in improving training and development systems. Concerning recruitment and selection, SOEs focus on internal promotions and personal recommendations in both processes; nepotism, favoritism, and Confucian values still play big roles in these processes (Cox, 2014; Pham, 2011; Vo, 2009). Furthermore, despite previous efforts to improve organizational efficiency by introducing changes in training and development (T&D) programs, not many significant achievements have been noticed mainly due to limited resources (Vo, 2009). Moreover, performance management is not working in a way that contributes to long-term organizational goals. Current PM systems are largely used to justify short-range goals, pay increases, or promotions rather than to identify long-term goals such as career development (Vo, 2009). In addition, organizational culture that is not aligned with PM ideas often deters the effective transformation of current systems. For example, the prevalence of nepotism and Confucian values as well as problems embedded in the appraisal system such as prejudice, favoritism, insufficient knowledge of the employees' performance, ignored outcomes, wasted time, and deteriorating relationships among workers obstructs implementation of systematic PM in SOEs (Cox, 2014; Quang & Dung, 1998, cited in Pham, 2011). Underdevelopment of PM systems also places constraints on appropriately designing and implementing remuneration practices in that an effective PM system that accurately measures workers' performance is a precondition for fair rewards. Remuneration should be based on merit instead of tenure, seniority, or personal relationships in order to motivate the workforce to be responsible for their tasks as in the private sector. However, a superficial performance culture provides favorable conditions for SOE officials that let them enjoy positive incentives like monetary rewards and promotions in case of performance improvement while freeing them from accountability when they make mistakes or incur losses as the state bears the losses from negative consequences (Phong, 2012).

Low HRM capacity of SOEs also hinders effective implementation of strategic HRM practices. Until recently, SOEs have not considered HR as a strategic business partner and thus have not focused on related management strategies for business success. For example, a majority of SOEs only changed their personnel functions to "HR" without considering differences in management methods or administrative roles in talent management or HR development (Cox, 2014; Nankervis *et al.*, 2016). Accordingly, the strategic function of HRM has been neglected, leading to weak links between organizational goals and managerial/personal goals. In other words, while individual-level goals should be linked to those at the organizational level for better performance of SOEs, goals at different levels do not show correlations and often result in goal ambiguity or multiplicities.

These unclear goals partially contribute to another problematic factor: limited capacity of HR managers. Without clearly understanding the contribution of individual achievements on overall organizational objectives, managers as well as general staffs are more prone to take wrong directions in their work. Yet, these are not the only contributors to HR managers' limited capacities. At the macro level, considerable legacies from the centrally planned economic system still persist and frustrate HR managers in that there are still red-tape and governmental bodies that constantly exert influence in addition to complicated legislative duplications that encourage managers to only take safe actions guided by regulations (Cox, 2014). On the other hand, at the micro level, most HR professionals transferred from personnel departments have limited experience in HR functions, by which most professionals become narrow-sighted to a particular area and have trouble cooperating with others from different functions. Further on, support functions to improve capacities of HR managers like HR information management, knowledge management, career development and rewards systems are rather uncommon in reality

(Nankervis *et al.*, 2016).

Finally, a politically influenced appointment process for high-level positions may cause some problematic HR situations. Although there have been some efforts to reform the Civil Service with the introduction of new laws, meritocracy is still not upheld in the appointment and selection process of SOEs, and political influence still takes a larger share in HRM processes. In Vietnam, the Party Organizational Committee (phong to chuc) system, which assists or "intervenes" in many appointment and management practices of HR, is also established in SOEs (Warner, 2013). With appointment process for high-level positions heavily influenced by political considerations, SOEs have less incentive to actively adopt and implement more advanced HR practices. A comparison between SOEs and foreign enterprises (FOEs) in Vietnam is illustrative in this regard. Figure 1-7 shows a graphical illustration of comparison between enterprises in these two sectors across a series of dimensions of HRM performance. It is no wonder that SOEs are losing their talents to private firms, especially FOEs.

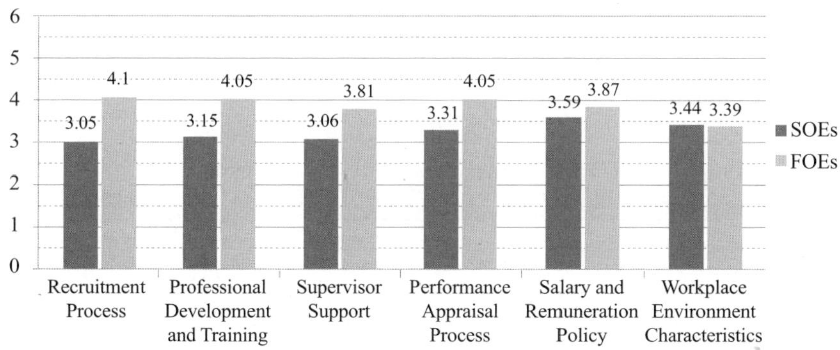

Source: Adapted from Nguyen et al. (2015)

Figure 1-6 Comparison between SOEs and FOEs in terms of HRM[4]

4 Refer to Appendix 3 for the full set of questions.

2.3. Imperatives

In order to solve the HR problems listed in the previous section, the following five imperatives must be considered for reform.

Imperative 1: Modernize HRM subsystems.

a. Make recruitment and selection practices more open, merit-based and transparent.

b. Design and implement performance management in a manner that contributes to employee development.

c. Give more discretion in the design and implementation of their own reward systems, while lessening the control over salary management.

d. Make more investment in updating training courses and methods and in developing managerial staff.

Imperative 2: Enhance HRM capacity.

a. Hire and develop HR professionals to be strategic business partners.

b. Enhance the visibility and capacity of the HR unit.

Imperative 3: Establish a management training institution for SOEs.

Imperative 4: Include an HRM capacity dimension in the efficiency assessment of SOEs.

Imperative 5: Make sure that merit plays a greater role in the process of filling top-level positions.

a. Make the appointment and selection process more open and merit-based.

b. Strengthen the performance management of top-level managers.

First, HRM subsystems should be modernized in order to stimulate the transformation of HRM systems. Considering current weaknesses in recruitment and selection practices, practices should be more open, merit-based and transparent. By using the word "open," this solution includes not only Vietnamese, but talented foreigners as well. In the past, SOEs have faced many restrictions on employing foreigners, especially in higher positions (Budiman *et al.*, 2009). However, talented foreigners can become great assets by providing useful skills in underdeveloped areas like finance and marketing or by contributing to training and development programs. In fact, there should be more investment in updating training courses and methods to develop managerial staff. A related goal is included in SEDP 2016-2020: "concentrate on training, improving quality of management staff."

In addition, designing and implementing performance management in a manner that contributes to employee development must be done in order to not only stabilize true performance culture, but also improve the remuneration process. In designing the PM system, a forced-ranking system can be considered to maximize the effectiveness of the system in the initial stage of PM (Budiman *et al.*, 2009). A forced-ranking system sets the proportion of workers for low and high rankings and evaluates the workers by comparing them to each other. If the system operates as planned, workers can get incentives according to the ranking they receive. Such a system helps workers understand that performance matters (Budiman *et al.*, 2009). When the performance evaluation is conducted in a clear manner and yields results that workers can agree to, remuneration becomes fairer and easier to determine because it is based on performance information. However, challenges still remain. If SOEs are not given more discretion in the design and implementation of their own reward systems and State control over salary management is not lessened, it will not be possible to improve the remuneration system based on merits.

Second, there must be efforts to enhance the currently low HRM capacity. For this imperative to succeed, SOEs should first accept HR as a strategic business partner. Then, they should hire and develop HR professionals who can become strategic business partners and enhance the visibility and capacity of the HR unit at the same time. There have been some attempts by SOEs to align organizational objectives and individual performance goals (Vo, 2009), and SEDP 2016-2020 lays out plans to develop high-quality HR in the business administration sector and to implement independent assessment of SOEs under Decree No.61/2013/ND-CP[5] to motivate SOEs to improve their performances.

Moreover, in order to implement the first and second imperatives more effectively, SOEs may consider the following two options: (1) establish management training institutions for SOEs and (2) include the HRM capacity dimension in the efficiency assessment of SOEs. Establishing a training institution that specializes in business administration is a feasible option. Given the constraints that many SOEs have in the design and implementation of the training programs in management and the poor quality of existing management schools (ranked 61 out of 62 countries; World Economic Forum, 2012), establishing specialized training institutions would be instrumental in developing high-quality, skilled managers for various types of SOEs.

Considering the current concerns over the expansion of the public sector, training institutions in the form of Public-Private Partnerships (PPPs) can be considered as a preferable option. For example, the Vietnam Chamber of Commerce and Industry (VCCI) could cooperate with major private organizations in the business community to jointly provide in-demand trainings. On the other hand, as demonstrated in the case of Korea, a comprehensive SOE management evaluation with a well-designed incentive system could contribute to enhancing the efficiency of SOE management activities. When implemented

5 Decree 61/2013/ND-CP is provided in Appendix 4.

by a powerful, centralized authority across the board, such an evaluation scheme would be able to create competition among SOEs. Considering that SOEs are currently evaluated in terms of their financial performance per Decree No. 61/2013/ND-CP, adding a HRM dimension in the present evaluation scheme can be considered a reasonable option.

The last imperative concerns the political influence in the appointment process of high-level positions. In order to address this issue, SOEs must concentrate on making sure that merit plays a greater role in the process of filling top-level positions. More specifically, the appointment and selection process for top positions should also be open, merit-based, and independent of political forces so that the appointed/selected managers are capable of carrying out various activities in service of the commercial interests of their enterprises and related stakeholders rather than of their own self-interest. As in the case of low or mid-level managers, performance management of top managers should be strengthened in order to fully draw out their potential in enterprise management. In brief, as in the approach taken by SEDP 2016-2020, leaders should be appropriately assigned, and their management capabilities and business efficiency must be strengthened.

3. Science and Technology (S&T)/ Research and Development (R&D)

3.1. Situation

SEDP 2016-2020 states that "science and technology have not yet become dynamics for the improvement of labor productivity, competitiveness and promoting socio-economic development" to express Vietnam's concerns regarding slow technology renovation. It points out the limited capabilities of the S&T workforce and a lack of leading scientists as major reasons behind this situation. Indeed, Vietnam has a weak HR base for innovation. According to OECD (2014), "Vietnam ranks eleventh out of twelve East Asian countries in terms of S&T HR capacity," and has "one of the lowest numbers of R&D researchers relative to the size of its population."

The impact of this low HR capacity in S&T sector can be seen in the World Economic Forum's Global Competitiveness Index of 2015-2016. The 12th pillar of the Global Competitiveness Index (GCI) considers innovation and provides a score from 1-7 based on scores from seven sub-sectors. In 2015-2016, Vietnam's index score for innovation was 3.2, not even reaching the average score, and it ranked 73rd out of 140 countries. Table 1.2 presents the subcategories under this pillar and Vietnam's scores.

Table 1-2 Global Competitiveness Index (GCI) of Vietnam for 2015-2016

	Rank*	Score
12th pillar: Innovation 1-7 (7 = best)	73	3.2
Capacity for Innovation 1-7 (best)	81	3.8
Quality of Scientific Research Institutions 1-7 (best)	95	3.3
Company spending on R&D 1-7 (best)	57	3.3
University-Industry Collaboration in R&D 1-7 (best)	92	3.3
Government Procurement of Advanced Technology Products 1-7 (best)	28	3.9
Availability of Scientists and Engineers 1-7 (best)	75	3.9
PCT patent application applications/million pop.	91	0.2

Source: Adapted from World Economic Forum (2015)

** Out of 140 countries*

The same result holds true for the report by OECD (2014), which mentions that brain drain among S&T researchers is actually a more serious problem in Vietnam than in other growing countries like Malaysia, Thailand, China, or Indonesia. All these countries ranked higher in aspects of the GCI innovation pillar.

The main consequence of this low HR capacity is limited progress in S&T innovation. The weak HR situation constrains innovation and competitiveness in the business sector, where periodical technology updates are required. In the end, this weak HR base for innovation will serve as a significant threat to the vision of an intellectual economy.

3.2. Issues

Issue 1. Inadequate quality and quantity of faculty in universities

a. Lack of staff with Master's and PhD degrees

b. Faculty numbers do not match rapidly increasing tertiary enrollments

c. Poor teaching, research, and entrepreneurial skills

d. No effective system of incentives and accountability in place for faculty

Issue 2. Inappropriate quality and quantity of S&T managers at all levels (central, provincial, local, GRI)

a. Limited knowledge and skills for the making and implementation of STI policies

Issue 3. S&T programs fail to meet the changing demand and economic needs

a. Courses not aligned with the market needs, out of date or too theoretical

Issue 4. S&T workforce development relies too much on the public sector.

a. Insufficient private delivery of higher education

b. Limited use of partnerships for S&T workforce development

Issue 5. Demand-side constraints cause shortage in the supply of high-quality S&T human resources

a. Not enough students are enrolled in S&T graduate programs

Most of the problems contributing to the weak HR base for innovation involve one key HR issue: quality and quantity of workers. While the current workers at almost all levels show low quality (Anh, 2015), many programs intended to improve their quality contain inherent problems as well. Moreover, limited resources on the demand side of the S&T/R&D workforce impede recruitment of talents and effective training. The OECD (2014) identifies a series of HR problems in the Vietnamese innovation system, some of which have particular importance in terms of AHRD. The problems can be further clustered into the following five issues.

To begin with, many university faculties are inadequate in quality and quantity. In terms of quality, most faculty members only hold Bachelor's degrees, resulting in poor teaching, research, and entrepreneurial skills among them. According to the OECD (2014), only 16% of researchers in universities and 3% in colleges in Vietnam hold a doctorate degree. Therefore, the skills supplied from such faculties are often of low quality because they are out of date, too theoretical, or incapable of meeting the labor market demands (OECD, 2014). With these conditions, it is not hard to predict the weak performance of public-sector research. In fact, Vietnam scores 3.3 out of 7 in quality of scientific research institutions under the GCI innovation pillar. Public-sector research is quite far from satisfying criteria of excellence and relevance, and in most cases, does not contribute to social and economic development (OECD, 2014). The quality problem is also rooted in the limited resources and ineffective system of incentives and accountabilities for staff (OECD, 2014). Because faculty members in public institutions are considered civil servants, they are paid low salaries, given limited opportunities for advancement, and appointed and promoted based on political affiliations rather than their achievements. This situation makes the public sector unattractive to high-quality researchers, especially when the private sector competes with the public and provides much more attractive career incentives. This leads to another big problem, which is that faculty numbers are not matching the rapidly increasing tertiary enrollments in Vietnam.

The next issue concerns the quality and quantity of S&T managers at all levels including central, provincial, local, and GRI. Limited knowledge and skills for the formulation and implementation of Science, Technology, and Innovation (STI) policies are of greater concern for those at the managerial level. Vietnam has a National Innovation System (NIS) which includes over 3200 managers working at various agencies at different levels who are responsible for formulating policies and procedures, implementing S&T programs, and supervising staffs (OECD, 2014). However, these managers have rather weak capacities. To elaborate, according to the Creative Productivity Index produced by The Economist Intelligence Unit & Asian Development Bank (2014), Vietnam ranked 16 out of 24 countries in its economy's relative economy's relative performance[6], even ranking lower than Lao PDR (9th), People's Republic of China (11th), and Thailand (15th). This medium level of creative productivity can be ascribed to those S&T managers who should have pursued efficiency in fostering innovation by balancing input and output well. Without quality S&T/R&D managers spurring innovation, it will be hard to overcome the middle-income trap. To make the situation worse, although the World Bank (2014: 3) suggested that "a sound basis for policy design requires systematic evidence on the performance of the innovation system and its constituent parts through statistics, qualitative analysis and feedback," Vietnam

6 According to The Economist Intelligence Unit & Asian Development Bank (2014: 4) report, the GCI concerns with "how proficient economies are at turning innovation 'inputs' such as skills or infrastructure into innovation 'outputs' such as patents or scientific publications."

has an underdeveloped system for policy making related to R&D, innovation, and other relevant information. Managers' limited knowledge and skills for STI/R&D management in addition to a non-systematic information base all limit making and implementing STI policies (OECD, 2014).

The third and fourth problems both concern the limited capacity of the public sector to develop high-quality S&T officials. First and foremost, many S&T programs fail to meet the changing demand and economic needs. Courses or programs provided by incompetent instructors are not aligned with market needs, outdated, or too theory-focused. Many business firms reported that scientists educated in Vietnamese universities lack practical knowledge, hindering them from effectively contributing to technology development (OECD, 2014). Vietnam has taken this issue seriously and included "revamping syllabus, teaching and learning methods for all grades and levels" as a goal to achieve in SEDP 2016-2020.

Although it has the same underlying problem, the fourth problem focuses on a different aspect by pointing out the over-reliance of S&T development on the public sector. Because the public sector has limited S&T/R&D HR capacity to promote innovation, the private sector is expected to play a bigger role in raising workers' S&T/R&D skills. However, in reality, there is an insufficient private delivery of higher education partially due to limited use of partnerships for S&T/R&D workforce development. Although there have been many efforts in the past to engage the private sector (OECD, 2014), Vietnam is still far behind other East Asian countries in private higher education because solutions to attract private sectors for investments in S&T research, innovation, and application have been ineffective (SEDP 2016-2020). Moreover, Foreign Direct Investments (FDI) do not play effective roles in that most of them are in low to medium technology industries, where only a few high-quality technology transfers or investments can occur (Commission on Growth and Development, 2008).

Finally, demand-side constraints cause shortages in the supply of high-quality S&T human resources (OECD, 2014). Compared to the past, young students are studying in many different fields, and the share of S&T graduates is declining. Therefore, Vietnam has a "HRST pipeline that is shrinking at the beginning and at the end, which is often found in most advanced countries, and is suffering from this trend more than most other Asian catch-up countries" (OECD, 2014: 200-201). This shortage of students enrolling in S&T graduate programs is aggravated by demand-side constraints in the labor market. In order to motivate students to enroll in hard science programs, business firms need to compensate them with salaries and rewards. However, many small and medium-sized enterprises (SMEs) in Vietnam do not have the necessary resources to offer a satisfactory level of compensation to human resources, requiring the public sector to support them in promoting higher level education.

3.3. Imperatives

Imperative 1: Improve the quality and quantity of faculty in universities.

a. Increase investment in and support for faculty

b. Design and implement performance management to motivate faculty and hold them accountable for performance.

Imperative 2: Enhance the quality and quantity of S&T managers.

a. Implement the governmental goal to double the number of managers by 2020.

b. Develop and provide education or training programs in S&T management.

Imperative 3: Ensure that S&T curriculum properly meets changing demand and economic needs.

a. Create mechanisms for tertiary education to incorporate industries' and other employers' inputs into course design, while giving universities more autonomy in the design and implementation of curricula.

Imperative 4: Facilitate the private sector's contribution to the development of S&T/ R&D workforce.

a. Provide incentives for more private entities to provide education at the tertiary level.
b. Utilize FDIs as a vehicle for S&T workforce development.

Imperative 5: Provide more favorable conditions for S&T personnel.

a. Consider public subsidies for higher enrollment of postgraduates in strategically important S&T areas.
b. Launch a selective postgraduate fellowship program for study abroad.
c. Scout potential returnees and give them powerful incentives to return.

Although resolving the previously suggested problems does not solely guarantee the improvement of HR capacity in the S&T/R&D sector, it is clear that only limited or even no further progress can be made if the listed issues continue to be prevalent in the field. Thus, this report suggests imperatives after reviewing the major S&T/R&D related documents, of which report by OECD (2014) especially provides a series of important ideas to apply. The ideas can be boiled down to five major imperatives.

First, it is important to improve the quality and quantity of university faculties. The key to this improvement lies in investment and support in faculties. In other words, as stated in OECD (2014), the current faculty stock should be boosted for tertiary education through a mix of recruitment and benefit-related policies. Using the current stock maximally by improving their quality and allocating them appropriately can be an efficient solution until more students graduate with advanced degrees in the longer term. Inviting foreign experts is another feasible option, for they can provide both students and faculty members with specialized skills and knowledge. Moreover, faculty quality can be improved by providing either intrinsic or extrinsic motivation and holding them accountable for their performances. Certainly this process cannot be achieved without designing and implementing a stable performance management system. With effective PM, the quality of all research outputs and related activities can be evaluated and rewarded with monetary incentives or honors.

Second, quality and quantity are not only concerns in terms of university faculty. The quality and quantity of S&T managers must also be enhanced to build a strong base for innovation (Anh, 2015). For this imperative, the government must implement its goal to double the number of managers by 2020 within the Ministry of Science and Technology (MoST). The government has set a goal to increase the number of S&T managers by 20% in total and those with Master's degree by 479%; moreover, it is also trying to increase the number of S&T managers in other ministries by 25% and at provincial and local levels by 25% as well (OECD, 2014). Simply achieving this goal will at least partially alleviate the quantity-related concerns regarding S&T managers.

However, different approaches should be taken to address the quality problems, and development and provision of education or training programs in S&T management can be a good start. Providing managers with opportunities to participate in fellowship programs like short-term training programs, needs-tailored support programs, and separate high-level management programs should bring them up to date in terms of S&T management practices (OECD, 2014). In fact, leading East Asian countries like South Korea and Singapore experienced the benefits of specialized S&T management programs in the process of economic growth and industrialization, and Vietnam's S&T management programs are loosely based on Korea's experiences (OECD, 2014). Therefore, some existing management programs could be fine-tuned to employ various materials related to more sophisticated S&T management practices such as planning and managing of research projects and system analysis and synthesis.

While the first two imperatives considered university faculties and S&T managers as important subjects, the third imperative focuses on potential S&T experts and suggests methods to raise their quality. To build a strong base for innovation, it is important to ensure that S&T curriculum properly meets changing demands and economic needs. To be more specific, mechanisms for tertiary education to incorporate the inputs of industry and other employers into course design should be created, while giving universities more autonomy in the design and implementation of curricula. In fact, there has been little interaction between tertiary institutions and employers, implying there is much room left to convey demand and economic needs in the curricula (OECD, 2014). By designing new mechanisms that promote interaction between institutions and employers, more practical inputs and changing trends can be incorporated into the curricula from the consultation process. Labor force and employer surveys, regular graduate tracer studies, and labor market and economic observatories could also produce valuable guidance for curriculum designers as they respond quickly to demands from markets (OECD, 2014). However, if universities are not given the autonomy to design and implement their own S&T curricula, this positive prospect becomes rather uncertain because flexibility is needed for the timely adoption of new trends and needs. Furthermore, diversifying and updating mechanisms such as student internships, part-time tertiary education, and in-service capability-building programs can improve skills needed for innovation.

Fourth, private sector contributions to the development of S&T/R&D workforce need to be facilitated. Limited approaches to workforce development often hamper creativeness. Therefore, while motivating public training institutions to respond to the demand for skills, incentives should be provided for private entities to provide tertiary education. Among many alternatives, PPPs can be best used for this. By increasing their training investments, private enterprises can enjoy the advantage of influencing universities' curriculum design, and private institutions can earn high rates of return with low cost (OECD, 2014). These private deliveries should be used especially in the fields of Science, Technology, Engineering, and Math (STEM), research and application, and HR training. Along with this effort, FDIs should be utilized as a vehicle for S&T/R&D workforce development. According to the World Bank (2016), the global knowledge frontier can be accessed through international linkages, and using selective FDI projects can be the best means to promote this kind of knowledge transfer.

In addition, favorable conditions should be provided directly to S&T personnel in order to maximize their positive effect. While a number of policies can be considered and implemented, this paper offers three useful methods to increase the number of S&T experts based on the OECD (2014) report: 1) consider public subsidies for higher enrollment of postgraduates in strategically important S&T areas (p.163), 2) launch a selective postgraduate fellowship program for study abroad (p.163), 3) scout potential returnees and give them powerful incentives to return (p.163-164). Labor markets are unable or unwilling to provide adequate rewards to postgraduates, so public subsidies become very important in the initial stage of graduate studies. Considering this situation, in order to develop strategically important S&T areas[7] as a national agenda, public subsidies in form of scholarships for enrollment in either domestic or foreign universities and advanced study abroad should be provided to postgraduates. Moreover, launching a selective program for 2-3 years abroad to talented graduate students will support them in returning to important S&T areas. However, while it is important to raise a new generation of experts, it is equally important to scout potential returnees, "turning a brain drain into a brain gain"(World Bank, 2013: 36) in order to strengthen the national S&T/R&D capacity. Conditional scholarships that require return to and work in Vietnam and powerful incentives like higher compensation and high-level positions can be considered, yet these can only be short-term solutions. In the long term, careers in Vietnam itself should sound attractive to potential returnees, and this can be achieved in several ways, such as establishing a sound working environment and investing a large amount of public money in the S&T/R&D field or reducing red tape and making S&T/R&D institutions and universities independent of political influence. The returnees can be expected to improve access to global networks and provide better training and education for the next generation (World Bank, 2013).

Figure 1-8 below shows all 15 imperatives suggested in this research. They are categorized according to the management time frames: left-hand alignment indicates more immediate action needed, while a longer length represents the need for long-term effort. As the figure illustrates, none of these imperatives can be fulfilled in the short term, but they do require immediate action and a long-term perspective. A summary of these imperatives organized according to their respective issues can be found in Figure 1-9.

7 Refer to Appendices 5 and 6 for a full list of strategically important S&T areas.

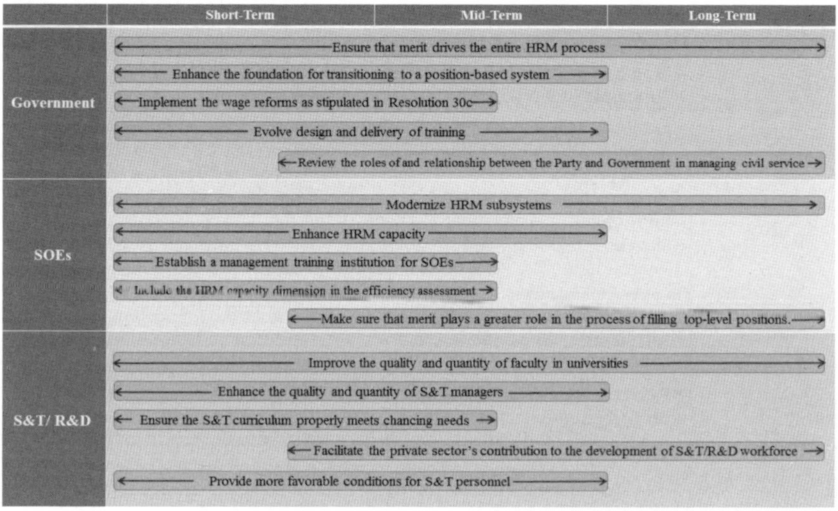

Figure 1-7 Imperatives at a glance

	Issues	Imperatives
Government	1. Limited progress in promoting the principle of meritocracy • Seniority rather than merit still plays a greater role in every stage of the HRM process. • Progress in implementing performance management has been slow due to lack of capacity for and interest in it.	1. Ensure that merit drives the entire HRM process • Reform hiring and promotion of civil servants, ensuring competition, publicity and transparency. • Strengthen the foundation for performance management by clarifying roles and responsibilities, particularly those of agency heads.
	2. Slow progress in strengthening elements of a position-based system • Reforms were enacted but not properly implemented.	2. Enhance the foundation for transitioning to a position-based system • Make more serious efforts to conduct job analysis and create job descriptions
	3. No significant improvement in salary and incentives • Wages are still too low and can only cover about one-third of basic needs. • Overstaffing remains unsolved, making salary reform slow.	3. Implement the wage reforms as stipulated in Resolution 30c • Create room for increasing salary by successfully implementing downsizing as planned, ensuring that downsizing does not hurt the policy capacity of the public service. • Devise effective incentives and rewards for high performance
	4. Upgrading training has been slow • Training and retraining methods have much room for improvement in terms of scope and quality. • Donor-funded training programs are not managed in a systematic way.	4. Evolve design and delivery of training • Make training more demand-driven and performance-oriented. • Strengthen training for HR professionals. • Strengthen HRM training for line managers. • Utilize donor-funded training programs in a more systematic way.
	5. Dual subordination system constrains effective talent management • Duplication between party and government rules makes developing technically competent human resources more challenging.	5. Review the roles of and relationship between the Party and Government in managing civil service • Minimize overlaps and duplications that make timely and effective talent management difficult. • Clarify the demarcation line between relevant authorities in personnel administration and political appointment.

	Issues	Imperatives
SOEs	1. Slow Transformation in HRM systems • Transformation in the recruitment and selection practices has been weak. • Performance management is not working in a way that contributes to long-term organizational goals. • There are constraints in designing and implementing remuneration practices. • There has been no significant progress in improving training and development systems.	1. Modernize HRM subsystems • Make recruitment and selection practices more open, merit-based and transparent. • Design and implement performance management in a manner that contributes to employee development. • Give more discretion in the design and implementation of their own reward systems, while lessening the control over salary management. • Make more investment in updating training courses and methods and in developing managerial staff.
	2. Low HRM capacity • HR is not seen as a strategic business partner. • HR managers have limited capacity.	2. Enhance HRM capacity • Hire and develop HR professionals to be strategic business partners. • Enhance the visibility and capacity of the HR unit. 3. Establish a management training institution for SOEs 4. Include the HRM capacity dimension in the efficiency assessment of SOEs
	3. Merit plays a limited role in the appointment process of high-level positions • Political considerations heavily influence the appointment and selection process.	5. Make sure that merit plays a greater role in the process of filling top-level positions • Make the appointment and selection process more open and merit-based. • Strengthen the performance management of top-level managers.
S&T/R&D	1. Inadequate quality and quantity of faculty in universities • There is a lack of staff with Master's and PhD degrees. • Faculty numbers do not match rapidly increasing tertiary enrollments. • Teaching, research and entrepreneurial skills are poor. • An effective system of incentives and accountability is not in place for faculty.	1. Improve the quality and quantity of faculty in universities • Increase investment in and support for faculty. • Design and implement performance management to motivate faculty and hold them accountable for performance.

	Issues	Imperatives
	2. Inappropriate quality and quantity of S&T managers at all levels • Knowledge and skills for the making and implementation of STI policies are limited.	2. Enhance the quality and quantity of S&T managers • Be sure to implement the governmental goal to double the number of managers by 2020. • Develop and provide education or training programs in S&T management.
	3. S&T programs fail to meet the changing demand and economic needs • Courses are not aligned with market needs, out of date or too theoretical.	3. Ensure that S&T curriculum properly meets changing demand and economic needs • Create mechanisms for tertiary education to incorporate industries' and other employers' inputs into course design, while giving university more autonomy in the design and implementation of curricula.
	4. S&T/R&D workforce development relies too much on the public sector • Private delivery of higher education is insufficient. • Use of partnerships for R&D/S&T workforce development is limited.	4. Facilitate the private sector's contribution to the development of S&T/R&D workforce • Provide incentives for more private entities to provide education at the tertiary level. • Utilize FDIs as a vehicle for S&T workforce development.
	5. Demand-side constraints cause shortages in the supply of high-quality S&T human resources • Not enough students are enrolled in S&T graduate programs.	5. Provide more favorable conditions for S&T personnel • Consider public subsidies for higher enrollment of postgraduates in strategically important S&T areas. • Launch a selective postgraduate fellowship program for study abroad. • Scout potential returnees and give them powerful incentives to return.

Figure 1-8 Summary of Issues and Imperatives

CHAPTER TWO:

ADVANCED HUMAN RESOURCE DEVELOPMENT FOR THE GOVERNMENT OF VIETNAM

Sung Min Park

Professor, Graduate School of Governance, Sungkyunkwan University (SKKU)

Ⅰ. Introduction

Ⅱ. HUMAN RESOURCE DEVELOPMENT IN VIETNAM

Ⅲ. Specifications of the AHRD Agencies

Ⅳ. Specifications of AHRD Programs

Ⅴ. Specifications of the AHRD System

Ⅳ. Lessons from Korea's Experience and Policy Recommendations

CHAPTER TWO:

ADVANCED HUMAN RESOURCE DEVELOPMENT FOR THE GOVERNMENT OF VIETNAM

I. Introduction

Reform initiatives in Vietnam's public sector have delivered remarkable economic growth over the last 20 years. The demands and challenges for sustainable development require the government of Vietnam to carry out various initiatives to strengthen the public sector's developmental orientation and to advance strategic policy plans appropriate for national industrialization and modernization by 2020 and beyond. To confront incessant social, economic, political, and environmental challenges, the country needs high-quality and competent human resources equipped with competitive political and managerial power to run public organizations of the public sector organizations. Vietnam has been implementing a wide-ranging public administration reform agenda for more than a decade, but modernization of the public sector in Vietnam means that greater efforts need to be undertaken inhuman resource development (HRD), hence human resources are the priority in organizations, so in order to survive and flourish, there is no better way than managing that HR force effectively (Nguyen, 2011).

The Vietnamese government affirmed one of three objectives for rapid and sustainable national development through human capital development until 2020. The objectives emphasized the following: (1) rapidly develop human resources, especially highly skilled employees; (2) focus on reforming national education basically and comprehensively, and (3)closely combine human resource development with science, technology and application.[8]

As a critical and integral component in achieving the vision of national development and modernization of the Vietnamese government, a well-entrenched and strategic public human resource development program needs to be in place. Focusing mainly on the forerunners of the government (i.e., middle managerial positions or higher.), mere training and development programs as a routine HRD activity may fail to provide and sustain the required knowledge, skill, and ability (KSA) to perform organizational tasks. Drawing from applicable theoretical and practical experiences of public HRD in Korea, the Vietnam public sector may employ advanced human resource development (AHRD). The AHRD philosophy is a visionary and strategic HRD that the organization can adapt and take advantage of opportunities, realizing the objectives while providing the best opportunities for individual development. As a strategic HRD policy, it includes HRD activities that reinforce public officials' competencies through a variety of human resource management and development (HRM/D) system and training programs for public officials with middle managerial positions or higher.

This report details a contextual and environmental (i.e., external and internal conditions) scanning of the Vietnam public sector that may influence AHRD planning, implementation, and evaluation. Drawing mainly from Korea's hands-on experience and know-how in leadership development through advanced HRD approaches, this report maps out the implementation and adoption of AHRD as a suggestion and recommendation for a strategic civil service HRD system in Vietnam.

---

8 Government Resolution 30c/2011/NQ-CP, passed November 08, 2011 at the XIth National Party Congress

II. HUMAN RESOURCE DEVELOPMENT IN VIETNAM

1. Overview of HRD Agencies and Institutions in Vietnam

The HRM/D roles, duties, and responsibilities of various agencies and institutions are defined and enshrined in the constitution, laws, and other related regulations (e.g., labour law, education law, etc.). For government employees (including those who are working in the leading party system), the governing laws include the Law on Public Officials and Civil Servants.

1.1. Ministry of Education and Training

The Ministry of Education and Training (MOET) is a line ministry of the government and the key agent in charge of the policy formulation and implementation of national general education in Vietnam. It maintains local authorities including the Department of Education and Training (DoET) and Bureau of Education and Training that belong to the same level as local People's Committees in terms of organization and personnel.MOET is responsible for education and training at the national level and is divided into 19 departments and several related units. It includes every level of education including pre-school, general education, professional education, tertiary education, and continuing education. The particular responsibilities of MOET are:

1. Set policy and promulgation of regulations affecting curriculum;
2. Research, writing and publishing of textbooks;
3. Manage enrollment and students;

4. Monitor academic assessment procedures and quality assurance;
5. Maintain infrastructure and facilities;
6. Select staff and personnel for educators;
7. Develop future education plans; and
8. Suggest and initially draft proposed legislation related to education matters such as establishment and construction of universities, policies on study abroad and the building of an educated elite, scholarship, and so forth.

Regarding the function assignments and decentralization of the public service delivery agencies related to education, MOET is responsible for the professional performance and regulation of educational institutions under it, but not for ownership or finance, except for the major public universities (e.g., Hanoi National University and Ho Chi Minh City National University (VNU),which fall directly under the Prime Minister's Office. The ownership and administrative/financial responsibility for the bulk of educational institutions, including all school-level general education, falls under the purview of Provinces or Districts, which have substantial autonomy on many budgetary decisions in accordance with the constitution. Some institutions are also controlled by other central ministries, although these are mainly at the higher education levels (senior secondary and colleges).

In light of public administration reform (PAR), MOET has a number of missions, being accountable for ((a) building programs for informatics and foreign languages training and (b) building and giving guidance on the content and training methods for courses on economic management for cadres and civil servants and public servants (CCSs) of ministries, industry, and local government in cooperation with the Ministry of Planning and Investment

(MOPI). It is also in charge of building up high-quality HR for the Public Service in the future through organising CCSs to study abroad through a number of projects such as Scheme 322[9]through which civil servants and public servants identified as potential leaders, managers or professional experts in the public sector received scholarships for postgraduate education overseas.

1.2. Ministry of Labour, Invalids and Social Affairs

The Ministry of Labour, Invalids and Social Affairs (MOLISA) is a specialized agency of the government responsible for the administration and governance of employment, vocational training, labour wages and remuneration, social insurance (e.g., compulsory and voluntary social insurance, unemployment insurance), occupational safety, social protection, protection and care of children, gender equality, and combating social evils. MOLISA employees are referred to as field workers and administer public services under the jurisdiction of the Ministry.The duties and authorities of MOLISA are specified as below:

1. Submit to the Government draft laws and regulations in accordance with given authority.
2. Direct, provide guidance, monitor and cooperate with stakeholders in proposing and implementing related laws, regulations, strategies, plans, and programs.
3. Provide guidelines and monitor the implementation of policies on employment and un-employment insurance, Vietnamese workers working overseas under employment contracts, employment and salary/wages,

9 Now under review as part of the source for initiative of a 911 Scheme. See more at Vietnamese Overseas Scholarship Program (VSOP), www.vsop.org.

compulsory social insurance and voluntary social insurance, industrial safety and occupational health, people with special contribution, social protection, child protection and care, social evil prevention and control, and gender equality.

4. Manage activities of IT application in the area of labor and social affairs and people with special contribution as specified by law.
5. Manage specialized medical activities in the areas of labour and social affairs and people with special contribution as specified by law.
6. Govern public services within the given authorities of the Ministry as specified by laws; issuing standards and norms, processes, procedures, guidelines, and economic-technical standards applied to activities of public service provision under the authorities of the Ministry and sector.
7. Carry out activities of internal coordination and collaboration, international cooperation and integration in the areas of labor and social affairs and people with special contribution as specified by law.

2. SWOT Analysis of the Current Government System in Vietnam

Table 2.1 summarizes the results of SWOT analysis of the HRD environment in Vietnam that serves as a foundation in sustaining HRD in the Public Service in general and AHRD in particular.

Table 2-1 SWOT Analysis

Strengths	Opportunities
• Outstanding human resources throughout the country • Majority at the golden age for working • Centralized and nation-driven management and effort to promote HRD • Studious habits and good learning capability • Strong will for the public service reform	• Internet accessibility provides a great source of information for knowledge, skills, and job opportunity • Many FDI investors and business and international organizations working in Vietnam
• Better orientation toward development of the system of universities and qualifications needs to be in place • Poorly specified output-benchmark for each and all level of education and training • Insufficient attention is given to working skills (including soft skills)compared to ideology; skills that are badly needed for modern working environments include working with mass-media, crisis management, self-management and navigation, and working under pressure are open for discussion in the current system	• Extreme approach to HR techniques, especially those imported from the business sector and abroad • Brain drain • Unpredictable world economic circumstances • Low incentives from HR policy perspectives such as talent management, salary • Disorganized HRD systems in the public sector • Lack of professional HR experts • Signs of negative organization culture remain in all types of organizations in all sectors
Weaknesses	**Threats**

III. Specifications of the AHRD Agencies

1. HRD and AHRD Authorities

1.1. Decentralization of HRD and AHRD

Decision No. 44-QD/TW (November 14, 1992) of the Politburo of the Communist Party of Vietnam explicitly stated that the Party has direct and uniform leadership over human resource management and development of the whole political system. Important regulations and decisions reflected in various documents of the Party ordered and provided guidelines for the decentralization of cadre management (see Decision No. 67-QD/TW dated July 4, 2007) and authority to introduce candidates for the Politburo (see Decision no.68-QD/TW dated July 4, 2007).

1.2. Central Committee for Organization

The Central Committee for Organization (CCO) is the advisory body of the Central Committee, directly and regularly advising the Politburo and the Secretariat of the Communist Party of Vietnam on guidelines and major policies in the fields of organization, staff, party members, internal political protection of the political system, managing personnel and officials of the Party, the Fatherland Front, and mass political and social organizations. The CCO is also a specialized agency of professional organizations and cadres, party members that protecting internal politics of the Central Committee.

1.3. Ministry of Home Affairs

The Ministry of Home Affairs (MOHA), previously the Government Committee on Organization and Personnel (GCOP), is responsible for two important areas of state management, namely, organization and personnel. The transformation of its status from a Committee to a line Ministry is considered desirable given the state of organization and personnel compared to increasing challenges to public administration reform (PAR). Its functions, authority and structure are indicated in Decree No. 45/2003/ND-CP 2003 and are updated and changed as needed. Generally, MOHA is the central agency responsible policy-making, management of civil servants, and training of public servants. These services (or functions) are provided by the CCO for Party members. MOHA has two-fold responsibilities: (1) policy making, providing guidance, and monitoring the policy implementation process; and(2) designing a set of training programs for each and all grades of civil servants and public servants.

1.4. Provincial Department of Home Affairs

The Provincial Department of Home Affairs(DOHA) is the functional organ of the People's Committee but also is under the monitoring of MOHA—in vertical relationship. The Head is responsible to the Chairman of the People's Committee on the matters of human resource management. The recruitment, promotion and dismissal of the Department's head are decided by the People's Committee Chairman/woman with the consultation with the MOHA Minister. The structure of the Department often consists of three units: (1) The Organization and Staffing Unit is responsible for HR matters; (2) The Local

Government Construction Unit is responsible for issues such as maintenance of borders and election; and (3) The General Administration Unit responsible for services to maintain and support organizational operation such as logistics, information service and other administrative procedures. Consistently, DOHA of the People's Committees is responsible for (1) identifying and analyzing local training needs; (2) producing training strategies and plans; (3) determining targeted trainees and matching courses; assess training results; making feedback to related training institutions to ensure competence-based training; arrange resources for training (especially in terms of budgets); and (4) integrating training with overall organization development.

1.5. Department of Organization and Human Resource Management

Correspondingly, there is a Department (or Committee) of Personnel/ Human Resource and Organization (DoPO) in the line ministries and each government organization. The ministerial DoPO is responsible for organization and personnel of the administrative bodies and member PSDAs(Professional Services Development Assistance Scheme)except those under administrative and personnel block-grant schemes.

2. Agencies Providing AHRD Services (Training Institutions)

The cadres and civil servant training (CCT) agencies in Vietnam include Ho Chi Minh National Academy of Politics (HCMA), the National Academy of Public Administration (NAPA), provincial schools of politics, ministerial training schools, and district training centers. These agencies are shown in Figure 2-1 Table 2-2 summarizes the responsibilities of CCT. Detailed information about AHRD agencies is provided in Appendix 3.

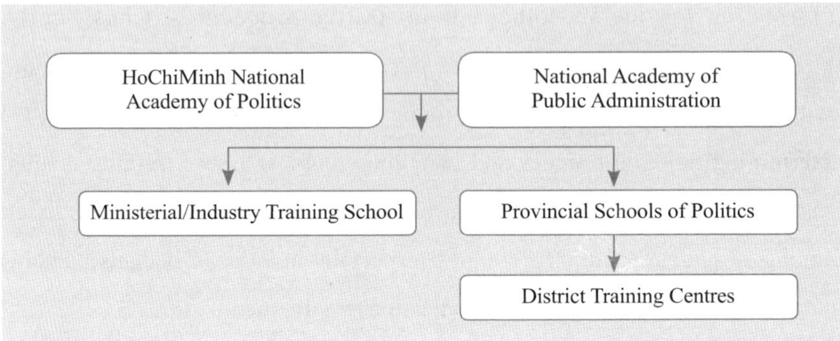

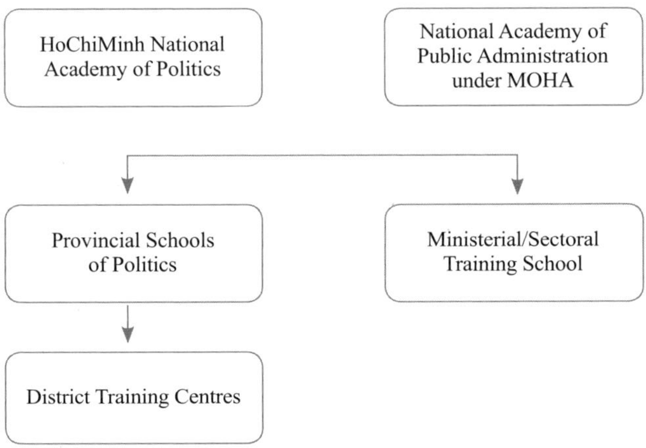

Figure 2-1 Cadres and Civil Servant Training (CCT) Agencies in Vietnam

Table 2-2 Responsibility of Cadres and Civil Servants Training

	Ho Chi Minh National Academy of Politics	National Academy of Public Administration (NAPA)	Ministry's School for Civil Servant Training	Provincial School of Politics	District Center for Civil Servant Training
Programs			*		
Experts		*	*		
Principal Experts		*	*		
Senior Experts		*	*		
Advanced theoretical training	*				
Professional training[10]		*	*	*	*
Position-based training	*	*	*	*	
Commune CCSs				*	*
PhD	*	*	*		
MA	*	*	*		
BA	*	*	*	in coordination with NAPA)	

10 Profession training provides professional knowledge and skills, such as training in secretarial work, accounting, and lower-general administration.

3. Issues in the AHRD Agencies

It is obvious that the agencies in charge or involved with AHRD are mainly at the Central Party and Government level, while the lower-level agencies provide the foundation for the AHR or the potential AHR to lead AHRD. Improving Specifying, clear-cut roles among stakeholders in managing AHR are one of the strengths of AHRD agencies. Accordingly, there are efforts to re-structure the system of training institutions and redefine the rights and responsibilities of training institutions (with Decree No. 18). There are also more investments in these institutions in terms of bidding for research projects or missions, administrative, and personnel block grant. However, the institutional framework for AHRD is still insufficient and there is no clear-cut delegation in CCS management between the Party and the Government agencies, between Government levels, or between sectors and functional bodies. Theoretically, this mechanism works smoothly because "Party members played an important role at all levels of the government apparatus; the higher echelons of government were usually party members, particularly at ministerial level". However, there is a risk of over-intervention of the Party in the Government's business.

A significant amount of the state budget is allocated each year for training (in accordance with the requirement of at least 40 hours of training a year for each civil servant). While this shows a positive signal of increasing awareness of the significance of CCTs, it also brings into question its efficiency. Cost and benefit analysis is more likely than the trainees to be the concern of the government and training institutions. Self-financing is popular in the private sector but is neglected in the government. The "socialization" of education and CCSs training in general and AHRD in particular is still in its infancy.

Training almost always means free training, with most tuition fees coming either from the State budget or from multilateral or bilateral project budgets. The contribution of beneficiaries is regulated, but is rather a formality.

In that sense, the enhancement of socialization in training not only helps to reduce the overload for current institutions but also could bring competition into the system, which ensures increased efficiency and effectiveness. However, socialization in CCTr can be further improved.

IV. Specifications of AHRD Programs

1. Training for Civil Servants and Public Servants (CCT)

1.1. Significance of CCT

A strong commitment to CCT can be explained partly because of the priority given to political education. The role of CCT in PAR is to

1. increase CCSs' dedication to serving the people;
2. increase CCSs' knowledge, skills and expertise to not only help trainees to solve day-to-day basic problems but also involve them in creating incentives for the CS as a whole;
3. cultivate the uniform pattern of though;
4. Strengthen the loyalty to the Party;
5. induce a positive and effective working style;
6. advance CCSs' careers and facilitate personal development;

7. promote formal qualifications to the CS.

1.2. Types of CCT

Types of CCT can be classified into education, pre-service training (PST), short-term training courses, training for potential leaders, and coaching and mentoring. Basically, education includes bachelor, master, and doctoral programs; pre-service training is classified as the general program which is compulsory for all potential CCSs and probationary candidates; and short-term training courses are for updating training and professional enhancement. Upgrading training is expected to establish the link between training and career, taking into account job requirements for CCSs to get promotions. Training for potential leaders is an initiative that aims to establish a cohort of leading competent experts in all fields of state management who will get involved in making important policies. Lastly, coaching and mentoring is a low-cost and effective method of learning which helps increase effective communication.

2. The Development of Training Systems and Programs

In a nutshell, Vietnam has gone through a number of stages of training for officials along with changes and transitions of the economy and public administration. Given the shortcomings of the process of designing training programs and the programs themselves, the training for officials in general and AHR in particular have had a number of positive results. See Appendix 4 for and overview of the development of training systems and programs for Vietnam.

Firstly, programs have become more open and flexible for the line ministries and local authorities to adapt to the realistic needs of the industry and localities. The requirement for lecturers to obey the key viewpoints, content, and structure as stated in the program or curriculum has also become less strict. Secondly, establish a better link between training programs with working positions. Thirdly, given that there are a number of points open to discussion, the coherence between training programs has improved. Fourthly, practical ability or skill developments have taken stronger focus in recent training programs. Finally, training program are better and more up-to-date, taking into account the features of today's world and recent advances in leadership and management science.

3. Training Program for Director Generals (DG) and Deputy DGs

In Decision no. 685/QD-BNV (July 3, 2014), the Ministry of Home Affairs announced a training program for ministerial department-level director general (DG) and deputy director general (DDG) positions and their equivalents. This program aims at building up and improving knowledge, skills, and behavior through 120 hours of training over the course of 3 weeks. The program consists of three parts:

1. Generic knowledge such as "the outcomes of the socio-economic development of Vietnam in the course of industrialization, modernization and international integration;"
2. Management and advisory skills such as "Strategic thinking," "Policy advisory and making policy proposals," and "Mobilizing staff;" and
3. Fieldtrip and writing Policy Proposal.

There is also a tailored training program for high-ranking experts, many of whom hold leadership and management positions including high-ranking ones. In Decision no. 1107/QD-BNV (October 8, 2013), the Ministry of Home Affairs announced a training program for high-ranking experts. This training program is divided into three parts administered over the course of 6 weeks:

1. Generic knowledge: 14 modules again are divided in to Advanced knowledge such as "Public administration in development"; "Strategy formulation and management in the public sector"; that added by 4 guest-talks talks on practice of the industry/locality.
2. Skills: such as "Motivation skills", "Project management", Empowerment skills".
3. Fieldtrip and writing Policy proposal.

4. Training Programs for Potential National Strategic Leadership

4.1. Purpose of the Training Program

The Politburo assigned the Head of the Organization Steering Committee as Head of the Steering Committee and the Chairman of the Reviewing Board for training contents and curriculum.[11] Leaders from the Central Organization Committee, Ho Chi Minh National Academy of Politics, the Propaganda

11 Based on the proposal by the Academy, the Central Organization Committee submitted to the Politburo their Statement No. 120-TTr / BTCTW (May 9, 2012) on the opening of strategic senior leader training programs. At the meeting on June 1, 2012, the Political Bureau gave an opinion on the Proposal by the Central Organization Committee and the Standing Committee Secretary, on behalf of the Politburo, signed Notice No. 98-TB/TW on June 29, 2012.This was the Announcement of the Politburo Conclusion on the opening of training courses to senior strategic leaders, in which the Politburo basically agreed on the purpose, requirements and contents of the training courses, the course participants, training methods, implementation schedule, and assignment and coordination as proposed by the Central Organization Committee.

Central Committee, the Ministry of Internal Affairs and the Office of the Party Central Committee were appointed as members in the Steering Committee. The basic purpose of the training program is to supply the theoretical knowledge, practical experience and some basic skills to strengthen socio-economic awareness, revolutionary stance; developing vision and strategic thinking, leadership and management capacity building; training and retraining of revolutionary morality, manners, public service responsibilities of senior leaders of the Party and State under the requirements of national industrialization and modernization, the country development and the international integration.

4.2. General Introduction of the Program

- **Participants of Training Programs**

The participants are identified as those cadres in the strategic planning sources of key officials for provinces and cities directly under the central government and central agencies; alternate members of the Central Executive Committee (XI); strategic members of the Central Executive Committee XII; strategic leaders and officials of ministries, branches and mass organizations at the central level and in the provinces and cities directly under the Central Government, from 2015 to 2020. Specifically, at the central level: strategic leaders for the positions of Ministers, Heads of the Party Central organizations, Heads of the central socio-economic organizations, the strategic leaders for the positions of Deputy Ministers, Department Vice Heads (with the Heads as Members of the Politburo or Party Secretariat); at provincial levels: the strategic leaders for the positions of Secretary of provincial and municipal party committees (in Hanoi and Ho Chi Minh cities including the planning positions of Secretary and Deputy Secretary, Chairman of the People's Council or the

Municipal Committee).

• Training Schedule and Methods

The training follows an active learner-centered teaching method full time for four months at Ho Chi Minh National Academy of Politics. Primarily, methods of teaching include presentation, team projects, case studies, guided discussions, self-study, and practical research. The materials are updated, realistic, and divided into two categories: required and optional.

• Process and Structure of Developing Training

After obtaining the direction of the Politburo on opening the training courses and the participants, the Academy has developed the program content. It is comprised of six modules, including the study visit and five basic modules. See Appendix 5 for the process and structure of the training program.

• Teaching Planning

Based on the training program contents, the Academy has agreed with the Central Organization Committee onthe time of courses. With the numbers of each course enrollment determined by the Central Organization Committee, the Academy has built schedules for lectures, outdoor activities and in-home study visits for the whole course. These have been sent to the Steering Committee, the Class Organization Board, the lecturers, the students and related units. At the end of the course, the Academy has actively coordinated with the donors to build up study abroad training programs for selected participants. The participants in the programs are from ministries, departments and central agencies and various central and local agencies; the heads of the delegations are normally Deputy Ministers or higher. Because of this fact, the abroad working trip of the delegations has to receive the consent of the Permanent Secretary of the Party Central Committee and the Prime Minister.

• Lecturers

Lecturers are leaders, senior managers, experts, scientists or researchers with teaching experience inside and outside the Academy. For important topics, the invited lecturers are senior leaders of the Party and the State, key leaders of ministries, sectors and provinces and professional instructors with experience in specialized fields. Lecturers who will present complementary thematic reports are normally officials of ministries, departments, provinces or the leading experts with thorough understanding of the guidelines and policies of the Party, the State and practice in the reporting field.

• Extracurricular Activities and Study Visit

These activities are done with the motive of "learning through action" and "knowledge comes with practice". The objective of these activities is to help the learners add practical knowledge to the theoretical modules and have opportunities to compare with their own experience and local situation and to capture more of the economic models and challenges from which to draw lessons learned to apply creatively in leadership and management in the working fields of each student. They include extracurricular activities, study visits, and practical research works with monitoring and evaluation by the Central Organizing Committee.

• Foreign Experts and Study Visits Abroad

Recognizing the meaning and significance of strategic senior officials' training courses, the Director of the Academy has directed the Department of International

Cooperation and the Subcommittee of International Thematic to establish relations with foreign partners to support experts and funding for the class. After an active working process, the collaborative projects with the International Cooperation Agency of Japan (JICA) and the International Cooperation Agency of Korea (KOICA) were completed and approved over the course of four years from 2013 to 2016. The Academy is the acting agency and the Director of the Academy is the project Director. The overall objective of the project is to introduce the policy development experience of Japan and Korea to senior officials in Strategic Leaders classes. Appendix 6 summarizes some issues and important lessons on foreign experts and study visits.

• Course and Learning Outcome Assessment

In order to improve the quality and contents of lectures and class management, the Board of Directors meets monthly with the class monitors to listen to comments and feedback about the class organization and classroom management. Before the end of each course, the Academy will collect the opinion of each student for each content, lecture programs and research trips in the country and abroad. Based on the feedback of the students, the Academy will adjust the program suitable for subsequent courses. In the study program, after the finish of each module, the students are required to write an essay. The Director of the Academy established the Council for Essay Evaluation, including experts, scientists and officials with high prestige inside and outside the Academy who have directly participated in the lectures and research.

To ensure that essay evaluation and thesis assessment are conducted seriously, properly and objectively, the Director of the Academy has issued a Regulation on the writing and assessment of the essays and thesis. Each essay is evaluated by two members in the Council separately. For thesis evaluation, for each course, the Director of the Academy establishes 4 Councils, each with

5 members who are specialists inside and outside the Academy. At the end of the course, each participant is given a certificate for attending the Strategic Leaders Training program.

4.3. Overall Assessment of Training Programs

• **Strengths**

The development and administration of training programs were consistently directed and monitored by the Politburo, the Party Central Committee's Secretariat and the Steering Committee of the classroom. At the same time, there is a smooth and synchronized coordination between the Central Organizing Committee, Central Office, Ministry of Finance, and other relevant authorities with the Academy.

Students participated enthusiastically with good attitudes and excellent discipline. The lecturers and reporters are professional experts and scientists with great prestige and practical experience. Especially noteworthy was the participation of many comrades who are senior leaders of the Party, the State, the National Assembly, Government and central unions.

• **Weaknesses**

Some themes of the reports on teachers' evaluation include presentation, not spending much time for discussion and opinion exchange between the teachers and students and that teaching plans are frequently adjusted due to schedule issues. The grading of essays, practical research reports and graduate theses is still too high compared with the actual quality. Professional background and positions of students in each classroom have been uneven.

• **Challenges**

The invitation of lecturers and reporters is difficult as some senior officials are too busy with work and business trips and cannot give lectures. Some participants are senior officials of the central and local agencies, thus sometimes they have to stop classes for them to attend Central Committee meetings or the National Assembly or to resolve unexpected work at their offices. There are also issues for the foreign experts such as language barriers and translation problems which make the quality of the lectures not fully reflective of the experts' ideas, uneven quality of the teaching material translation and the change in schedule of the experts. The Academy sometimes has not evaluated the full capacity of the foreign experts and this has to be done by the donors. Lastly, students are not open to listening, discussing and debating with international experts.

• **Opportunities**

The construction of training programs with entirely new contents and methodology has created opportunities to upgrade the capacity of the Academy's lectures, making contribution to the overall renovation of the training programs of the Academy. The fact that the participants are strategic officials at the central and local authorities is a good opportunity to promote cooperation with the Academy's central agencies and localities.

The training of senior cadres for the Party has elevated and affirmed the position and prestige of the Academy.

The invitation of foreign experts and organization of abroad study trips for strategic leaders have contributed to understanding and cooperation, advertising the country and Vietnamese people, learning experience from other countries, changing awareness and the vision and maintaining and broadening cooperation for training and scientific research.

5. Issues in the AHRD Program

In 1997, NAPA set up the Committee of Curriculum Design which is affiliated by the President of NAPA. In 2013, the Office of 1677 (after the name of the document issuing the mission) on designing and redesigning training and education programs and curricula that was also set up at HCMA. This is to say that the awareness about the significance of training for officials has been well translated into realistic action. In addition, more research programs, both internal and coordinated with international stake-holders, have been conducted, providing a better foundation for designing and delivering training programs. However, we have constantly observed that, firstly, Learning Needs Analysis (LNA) is weak, being among the key reasons for training failures. Hence, what has been trained is often a matter of what the trainers know rather than what participants need.

Secondly, to a large extent, overlapping and duplication of training content both within and between training institutions is noticeable. Still, programs and lectures over-emphasize theoretical perspectives, hindering the gaining of new skills needed for performance. Again, this reflects the failure in analyzing training needs and understanding the nature of learning as well as the learners.

Thirdly, training relying mainly on lecturing though group-work/discussion has been tried. There is likely a one-way communication flow in which the trainers transfer knowledge and trainees receive it. With the overload of trainees in a classroom, discussion is difficult, if any occurs at all. With the exception of workshops and conferences (especially those provided by donors), the number of attendees is often over 50 and even reaches 150 in a classroom. The ethos of CCTr objectives and training methods should encourage opposite and different ideas.

Lastly, training evaluation strongly emphasizes quantitative aspects, so the overwhelming impression is that the outcomes of training are likely to be heavily quantitative measures. Too often reports on CCTr focus on the numbers of participants. Analysis of the characteristics of each group, special needs in the input and feedback during and after the process are often neglected and the information about these issues is often similar to previous reports. One reason is that under pressure to produce visible results to impress budget determiners, donors and authorities, the easiest way is to impress by proliferation of courses and trainees.

V. Specifications of the AHRD System

1. Evolution of HRD and AHRD System in Vietnam

Cadres and civil servants are managed by a dual system that involves the Government of Vietnam (GOV) and the Communist Party of Vietnam (CPV). Public service has been set up and tempered in the crucible of wars against colonization and reconstruction; the role and involvement of the CPV is incompatible with the establishment and development of public service. The CPV plays a key role in the holistic human resource management such as the delegation of cadre and civil servant management. This assignment is conceived in various CPV documents and reconfirmed in various GOV policies.

The very first regulation that directly targets cadre and civil servants' management was the Regulation on Civil Servants in 1950. This law regulated the rights and responsibilities of civil servants as well as the organization and management of the civil servants' grades (ngach).

In light of "đổi mới", the GOV highlights the increasing importance of professional and competent cadres and civil servants. Besides the Law of Labour, various policies have been made and the quality of regulation has gradually improved. Ordinance 25/CP passed in 1993 defines the titles and criteria for cadre and civil servants 'grades as well as a new salary system and was seen as an important turning point for the institution. The directions and guidance made by the Politburo and the Secretariat General include, among others:

- Resolution 03-NQ/TW of the Central Executive Committee VIII, dated June 18, 1997 on "Strategy of human resource for the period of accelerated industrialization and modernization of the country";
- Conclusion 37-KL/TW dated February 2, 2009 of the Party Central Executive Committee X on "Continue to promote the strategy of human resources in the period of accelerated industrialization and modernization of the country"; and
- Resolution no. 12-NQ/TW dated January 16 of the Party Central Executive Committee XIon "Some urgent issues in Party building today".

Among the essential policy solutions adopted by the GOV through Public Administration Reform (PAR) was the Ordinance on Cadres and Civil Servants 1998. This ordinance provides a general guideline on the setting up of agency-based cadre and civil servant management considering the peculiarities of an organization. One of the most important changes is for commune officials to be regarded as cadre and civil servants. This development allows the commune to be "more appreciated by the government and the society in general" while giving them "more confidence and pride when serving people". More importantly, it shows the change in institutions, shifting towards a more systematic and effective HRM policy.

Within the framework of the 2001-2010 PAR Master Program, an action plan (i.e., Action Plan 4)[12]focuses on the improvement of the quality of cadre and civil servants. The plan identifies and addresses the shortcomings of the workforce through various initiatives which can be categorized as (1) improving the legal framework on cadre and civil servants' management; and (2) reviewing and improving current civil servants' management. The latter could possibly be achieved by introducing and/or enhancing the management approach, such as effective reward system, salary reform, block-grant initiative and IT application and computerization.

The 2011-2020 HRD Strategy for Vietnam suggests various strategic reforms and directions for HRD. It emphasizes the need for good physical health, comprehensive development of intelligence, determination, competence and morality, self-learning capacity, self-learning, initiative, self-reliance, creativity and being able to adapt and quickly respond to the needs of work and life. Consistently, the 2011-2020 PAR Master Program reiterates professionalism, responsiveness, dynamism, transparency and efficient public service of the GOV. The program indicated that one of the leading objectives

12 The Action Plan proposes four focal points to improve, covering (1) institutional framework of cadres and civil servants' management; (2) the salary system; (3) CCT; and (4) working ethics and commitment.

is to establish a system capable of building competent and morally upright civil and public servants. Specifically, the 2011-2020 PAR Master Program identified the following concrete tasks:

1. By 2020, the civil servants and public servants are adequate in terms of quality and quantity to perform government tasks;
2. Development of a competent human resource who has high moral quality, political courage, professional competence, professionalism through appropriate training and education techniques;
3. Issuing, addition and adjustment of regulations on working position, professional technical criteria for all positions, including management and leadership;
4. Designing an appropriate staffing structure linked well with the position-based system;
5. Improvement of legal framework for recruitment, appointment, task assignment, assessment; organizing up-grade examinations in accordance with competitive principle; competitive examination for leadership and management position at director and equivalent levels, provincial director and equivalent level downwards; and
6. Renewal of the content and programs of civil servant training (CCT); practicing a wide range of training types including mentoring for those on probation, grade-based training, management and leadership training; compulsory annual training before appointment. Accordingly, the Master Program indicates a Project on "A Strategy of cadres and civil servant education and training in the period of 2011-2020".

2. Key Features of the AHRD System in Vietnam

2.1. Dual System

The unique political feature of Vietnam manifests a parallel interaction and relationship between the ruling Communist Party of Vietnam and the leading force of the government—the Government of Vietnam. The agenda for AHRD will go through a mandatory process of Party caucus setting the directions and guidelines; while the government, as in many other regimes, enacts laws and regulations. The government leaders and advanced human resource (AHR) officers—both Party members and civil or public servants—implement the reform initiatives. Hence, they are obliged to abide by two sets of equivalent orders to fulfill their party and government functions.

2.2. Cultural and Legal Values

The combination of traditional cultural values and legal foundations has been demonstrated in cadres and civil servants' management. In some cases, regulations and analysis of cadres and civil servants' management directly adopt cultural values. In others, those values are interpreted as the legal foundations. For instance, the Confucian culture has left its own mark on the way the civil servants have been trained and managed, placing a great premium on interpersonal trust. It is not a surprise to see that the Yin and Yang philosophy—a profoundly Confucian value—has been adopted indirectly in public service life. The two dependent opposites of Yin (representing dark, cold and secret) and Yang (representing bright, sun and heat) are merely translated in the quest for balance and continual change in the public service. The aspiration for balance is reflected in the quest for both Duc (or Nhan)(morality and benevolence) and Tai (or Tri) (competence and talent).

In these ways, traditional values interact and inform modern values (i.e., the Do's and Don'ts—things that cadres and civil servants are allowed to do and not to do) specified in Ordinance 1998. Maintaining the current system is closely linked to preserving past values. Official documents and speeches of the elites often quote the experience of predecessors and ancestors. Public service development is characterized by various uniform and constantly reformed principles. HR managers believe that transformation is certain. This allows them to promote a tolerant and optimistic working-style and management method, especially in the case of dealing with failures and solving problems and conflicts.

2.3. New HRM and HRD Techniques

The HR system of the public service in Vietnam has learned selectively a number of HRM and HRD techniques that originally developed in the business sector, international agencies or in the West. For example, part of the performance management process now is to allow some public service delivery agencies (e.g., National Publishing House) to employ a performance-related pay (PRP) system. A careful study and application of a position-based system in managing staff and open and competitive examinations for leadership positions are now also being pilot tested.

3. Systems and Methods of AHRD

AHRD is a visionary and strategic management program of training and development interventions (such as planning, rotation) of the human resource to ensure that organisations can adapt and take advantage of opportunities, realizing the objectives while providing the best opportunities for individual development. The key practical systems and methods for AHRD in Vietnam are planning for the source of potential officials, training and rotation.

3.1. AHR Planning

The basic principles of workforce planning[13] must follow the spirit of openness and dynamism. Openness is in terms of quantity—one person can be selected as a resource for a number of positions. Each position should be planned for at least 2 to 3 comrades, and each official can be expected to undertake 2 to 3 positions. Planning should not be limited within each industry, local and unit, it should be reviewed regularly—annual planning supplements and adjustments are needed, putting into the planning new factors and taking out of the planning those who do not meet the requirements of the new situation. Dynamism refers to the annual review of those who are in the pool considering their circumstances (removing those who are no longer eligible), updating their eligibilities and other factors that may affect their qualification to enter public service.

---

13 There are two major policy documents of the Communist Party of Vietnam that clearly emphasize workforce planning, focusing mainly on future leaders and managers. The first is Resolution No. 42-NQ/TW dated November 30, 2004 of the Party on Planning the source for future leaders and managers in the period of accelerated industrialization and modernization of the country. The second is Conclusion no. 24-KL/TW dated June 5, 2012 of the Politburo XI on Continuing to promote the planning and rotation of leaders and managers 2020 and the following years.

3.2. AHR Recruitment and Appointment

3.2.1. Selection of AHR

Selection (including planning and appointment) is one of the important stages of the process of advanced human resource development (AHRD) in Vietnam. This group is specifically focused at the departmental level and equivalent and above. In order to contribute to staff strategy in the time of promoting industrialization and modernization of the country and Vietnam's development strategy to 2035, it is extremely important to overcome weaknesses in the process of public servant selection and appointment, as well as propose new solutions to this issue. In this study, we would like to describe and assess the status of the plan and appointment of advanced leaders in Vietnam today and propose some new solutions to this issue.

There are two major policy documents of the Communist Party of Vietnam that clearly emphasized workforce planning—focusing mainly on future leaders and managers. The first is Resolution No. 42-NQ/TW dated November 30, 2004 of the Party on planning the source for future leaders.

A. Basis of the Selection of Advanced Human Resources

<u>Actual Status, Policy, Legal System, and Proposed Policy Directions</u>

The 3rd Central Resolution of the 8th Central Executive Committee of the Communist Party of Vietnam states the policy on building staff and public servants with quality and capacity is the key factor to determine the quality of the machinery of the state: "Leaders must be comprehensively trained and fostered in knowledge firstly about political line, state management, socio-economic management; as arranged and transferred for the needs and interests of the country, they can be rotated from central to local, from local to central and from province to province. The mechanism of selecting, electing and transferring key leading positions at all levels must be reviewed thoroughly and propose necessary reforms in accordance with the policy". See Appendix 1 for detailed discussion.

3.3. AHR Training

Conventional methods of accumulating knowledge substantially rely on training. According to Torrington and Tan (1994), training is "the process of improving a person's knowledge and skills. It may involve changing his attitude so that he can do his job more effectively". However, what is more important is the way training produces an impact on trainees.

Training as a process consists of Learning Needs Analysis (LNA), training service provision, training evaluation and post-training action, which refers to following up plans to transfer training to performance. LNA is related to the identification of organizational needs, occupational needs and individual needs in order to guide and inform training interventions. This factor was argued to be missing in failed training intervention. The detailed analysis on training is discussed in the AHRD program.

3.4. AHR Rotation

It is necessary to refer to Resolution No. 11-NQ / TW, dated January 25, 2002 of the Politburo on Rotation of leaders and managers at all levels. This resolution was continued in Conclusion no. 24-KL/TW, dated June 5, 2012 of the Politburo XI on Continuing to promote the planning and rotation of leaders, managers 2020 and the following years.

The purposes and requirements of official rotation are to fulfill political tasks and facilitate young officials' comprehensive training and fostering in planning and in reality. By circulating and assigning officials in tough regions and fields, talented individuals can be found in order to be trained, challenged and prepared to become official staff in the long term.

- **Objects:** Leaders, managers in ministries, departments, branches and other state and local agencies who are required to be circulated for training and fostering before being appointed in leading positions according to official planning.
- **Schedule of Official Rotation:** Based on the planning, business demands, capabilities and strengths of the officials, the competent authorities shall prepare schedules and measures of official rotation at their own managing level. Before making decisions, competent leaders' representatives must have meetings with the officials to inform them of the purposes and requirements of rotation, listen to the officials' suggestions and discuss with the organizations or units they will leave and join.
- **Responsibility of Implementation:** Executive committees, party organizations, agencies, units and individuals are under obligation to implement decisions of official appointment and rotation from competent levels. Welfare must be ensured for circulated officials and their stability of work and life must be soon facilitated.

3.4.1. Outcomes of Official Rotation

The Politburo's Resolution no. 11-NQ/TW was able to meet the requirements of reality, seriously implemented by localities and branches and have significant initial outcomes. Official rotation has both helped potential officials to practice and grow and facilitated in-place officials' development. The initial outcomes of the rotation of leaders and managers have enhanced the evaluation, planning, training and fostering of officials, partly helping to overcome stagnation, partiality and close-mindedness. The detailed outcomes of the rotation are summarized in Appendix 2.

4. Overall Assessment of AHRD System

4.1. Strengths

Since PARCP 2001-2010 and 2010-2020 were promulgated, the public service has observed noticeable change and improvement. Among many efforts, the strengths and success of AHRD can be described as follows:

- **a.** More and better policy solutions (that are more proactive, updated, feasible, coherent and economical) on AHRD.
- **b.** More proactive AHRD planning, including efforts to systemize the job descriptions, and now drafting job description for management and leadership positions (better foundation for TNAs).
- **c.** Ambitious but careful rotation programs.
- **d.** Better decentralization and devolution of AHRD (CCO, HCMA, NAPA, provincial training school), enhancing the role and capacity of training schools of line ministry, agency & provincial schools; Decree No. 18/2010/ND-CP on training for cadres & civil servants.
- **e.** A good blend of systematic methods of training and learning.

f. Defining training as a compulsory condition for appointment and promotion.

These are all placed on the foundation of a number of improvements in the Public Service and Public administration reform, such as:

g. An acknowledgement of the difference between civil servants and public servants by law.

h. Recruitment & promotion: competitive examination for division management level (Announcement No. 202-TB/TW on Piloting the reform in selecting Provincial Director-level & Division level managers).

i. A gradual transition from career-based (with job security) toward a combination with position-based.

Attracting and retaining talent, such as the case of Quang Ninh, Da Nang.

j. More position-based and need-based tailored trainings

4.2. Weaknesses

A number of points need more attention and improvement in terms of AHRD, including:

• **AHR Planning.** A more long-term strategy, plans and efforts to identify, nurture and develop AHR.

More effective and efficient solutions need to be in place to attract the talents from the other sectors foreigners to become leaders, such as provision of scholarship for student in and abroad.

The development and implementation of staff planning in some localities and units are primarily based on staff assessment, not derived from mission requirements and practical capabilities of staff. Planning has not been mounted with staff training and use, leading to many formal and unfeasible projects. The quality of staff planning has been low and uneven, and most of the planning schemes have no foresight. The staff planning structure has not been balanced, there have been less young and female staff, and staff qualifications and trainings in many places have not been appropriate and have failed to meet mission requirements. In general, staff planning in the past has had no connection between subordinates and superiors, between local and central government, between sectors and fields of work, etc. Before the 11th Party Congress, positions in the Central Executive Committee, the Politburo, the Secretariat and key leadership positions of the Party and the State were not planned; before in preparation for the XII Congress of the Party, we have planned for positions in the Central Executive Committee, the Politburo, the Secretariat and the titles of key leaders of the Party and State basically more detailed and specific.

- **AHR Training.** More innovative solutions for training provision.

The link between training needs analysis (TNAs) and training and usage of outputs is weak. In addition, training for AHR or potentials should be made in a more strategic way, containing many types of capacity building. The decentralization and coordination among agencies and institution in providing training activities of all types should be improved. Mobilization of resources and a sense of competitiveness should be provided in training.

- **Performance and Career Management.** PMS appears to be synchronized and one-sided, lacking adequate prominence in key areas.

Benchmarking tools have been used in some areas of administrative service such as business license granting and birth and death registration. Various measures have been established that indicate clearly the requirements to be met in terms of deadlines, standards, transparency and responsiveness to ensure the improvement of policies and services provided. However, this appears to be internal benchmarking rather than cross-sector learning or competition.

Current criteria for assessment are under fierce scrutiny. They are imbalanced or one-sided in that past achievements, attendance records, loyalty to the system, viewpoint and personality are overemphasized rather than performance or outputs and outcomes that are measurable, giving too much weight to status and emotions. In some periods, personnel appraisals gave priority to the social/family condition and the working process, while in other periods, they are biased towards academic degrees and qualifications and seniority. As an impact of culture on the Public Service, seniority overweighs merit; the system views that knowledge and expertise are equivalent to seniority.

Regarding rotation, besides the results obtained, the implementation of Resolution No. 11 of the Politburo also has some drawbacks. Several committee levels and Party organizations did not create consistent awareness and did not have high determination to implement, resulting in slow and uneven implementation; the rotation and training of officials in some locals were not based on assessing, planning and training officials. The rotation of leading and managing officials was generally inadequate, self-contained and did not promote strength of the force, so there was an excess or lack of officials in some localities. The policy of rotation and arrangement some leading official positions who are not local people was aimed at improving the partial, stagnating, self-contained, poorly implemented situation because there had been no specific regulations yet. The selection of rotating locations and positions in some cases were still unreasonable, even to the wrong industry and profession, which not only did not meet the training requirements but also limited the contribution of rotating officials. The managing, monitoring, concerning, and facilitating officials rotated by agencies, especially by the former and latter places had not been regulated specifically, leading to inadequacy and inaccuracy in assessing, arranging and using the officials after rotation. Here are additional weaknesses:

1. Coordination and collaboration among AHRD agencies;

2. Brain-drain; and

3. More investment in building learning organization for that the AHR and the potential AHR are motivated and committed.

4.3. Threats

In designing and delivering a sound AHRD system, a number of threats may arrive that the policy process practitioners should bear in mind, including:

- The impact of the dual system and the risk of duplicate controlling systems.
- Lack of policy coherence and consistency.
- Lack of resources for harmonizing conflicting values and methods.
- The national education cannot change overnight.
- The distance, and even worse, the prejudgment, between the public and private sector.
- The mismatch between software and hardware, meaning the mindset and the practical system and methods to develop and use of AHR.

4.4. Opportunities

The AHRD system can have many more opportunities thanks to the development of the society itself, the public service and the system of AHRD efforts. The integration and participation of Vietnam into many international and regional treaties bring in opportunities for AHR and potential leaders to take part in searching for solutions. A new Party's and State's term of leadership starts now, showing the way and providing a foundation for both 8policy and practice to improve the quality of leaders and managers.

The development of ICT and active participation of the mass-media into social and community life also bring about better chances for AHR and the potential to make use of it and to create dialogue with the community. The social mobility of high-quality human resources presents the opportunity to change the "blood" of the mindset and working style.

Support from international development agencies (such as KOICA) and international counter-parts (such as Yonsei University) is important. Last but not least, more direct and open policy dialogue with business has been conducted so AHR and potential leaders can practice fundamental skills in leadership at the policy level such as listening and responding to the needs of the business.

IV. Lessons from Korea's Experience and Policy Recommendations

1. Recommended AHRD Reform Paths

1.1. Building a Comprehensive AHRD Agency

a. *Strategic Process and Activities for an Improved AHRD Agency*

The Central Training Institution (now National Human Resource Development Institute [NHI]) for Public Officials greatly contributes to the reinforcement of public officials' competencies and national competitiveness. Training institutions for public officials must continuously reform the organizational culture, structure, and programs in accordance with both internal and external environmental factors under a systematic frame, enhance appropriate leadership competencies and values and endlessly innovate leading public officials. The important dimensions are (see Figure 2-2):

- Environment: The wide internal and external environment that directly affects the organization's functionality
- Leadership: The ability to exercise influence on the organization to achieve goals and vision
- Culture: The shared lifestyle or values that affect the organization members' convictions and behavior
- Structures: The determination of the power structure, such as deciding the way of working, adjusting, controlling, or decision making
- Process: The overall activities throughout the organization, including the delegation of authority, conflict control, and decision making

• People: The target of human resource development

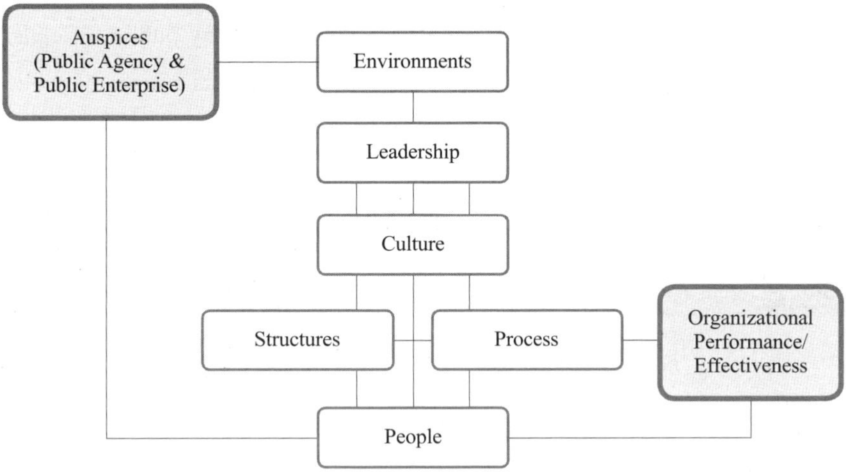

Figure 2-2 AHRD Agency Model

b. The Korean Case

The Korean Government established and operates the National Human Resources Development Institute(NHI) and Local Government Officials Development Institute (LOGODI) in order to strengthen the capability of central government and provincial government officials. These excellent educational institutions have been contributing to the enhancement of the Korean economy and producing outstanding public officials for over 50 years and highlight how important it is for HRD institutions to have organized systems and formal authorities to train public officials for the enhancement of national competitiveness.

(1) National HRD Institute

NHI has a long-standing history and tradition. It has reformed the institution consistent to changes of the generation, conduct a variety of programs, and largely contribute to achieve national development led by public officials. Table 2-3 presents the diverse activities pursued by NHI in its training of public officials for the past 60 years.

Table 2-3 Development of Korean Officials' Training System and Program

Regime	Background	Goal of Training Program	System of Officials' Training
Introduction period of training (1949~1960)	• National crisis after liberation and war		• National Officials Training Institute was founded in 1949 • Introduction of American-style administrative management training • Legal/institutional system is poor
Period of training expansion (1962~1972)	• Nation-leading economic development • Economic development 5-year plan was enacted (1962) • Trained civil servants necessary for social/economic development	• Understand political ideology and democracy • Understand urgent problems of underdeveloped countries' economic development • Develop overall understanding of national administration • Acquire administrative management techniques • Establish a sound national view • Establish a national identity	• Founded a government training agency (Ministry of Government Administrative Management Bureau) • Founded Central Officials Training Institute (1961)

Takeoff stage of training (1972~1981)	• Eradicated poverty in rural areas and cities • Implemented Saemaeul campaign • Necessity of practical training emerged.	• Strengthen the Saemaeul campaign strengthen and widen • Increase Saemaeul campaign spirit and ideology training • Improve civil servant's ability in order to strengthen national development.	• Enactment of Act on the Education and Training of Public Officials (1973) • Reinforced 5-year cycle of compulsory education • Implemented on-site education • Newly founded the research development division (1974)
Takeoff stage of training (1981~1993)	• Olympic hosting ability	• Strengthen ideological training in overcoming crisis/chaos • Strengthen moral and ethical training for public office • Strengthen educational capacity on economy • Emphasize liability of public officials in preparation for 88 Olympics	• Civil servant training development 5-year plan (1982) • Subdivided into spirit, duty, and professional education
Civilian government (1993~1998)	• Globalization • Democratization • Decentralization (local government system	• Enhance foreign language education • Transfer authority to local training institutions	• Converted from basic education into professional education system • Delegated plan-approving rights to each chief of central administrative agency with training • Expanded into 46 Officials Training Institutes
Nationalist government (1998~2003)	• IMF crisis • Advent of knowledge information age (development of ICT technology)	• Overcome the economic crisis • Harmonize democracy and market economy • Strengthen performance management & goal management training	• Restructuring of Central Officials Training Institute (1999) • Strengthened computerization, informatization, and cyber education • Newly founded selective professional curriculum.

NHI's current vision and missions have grown from this historical

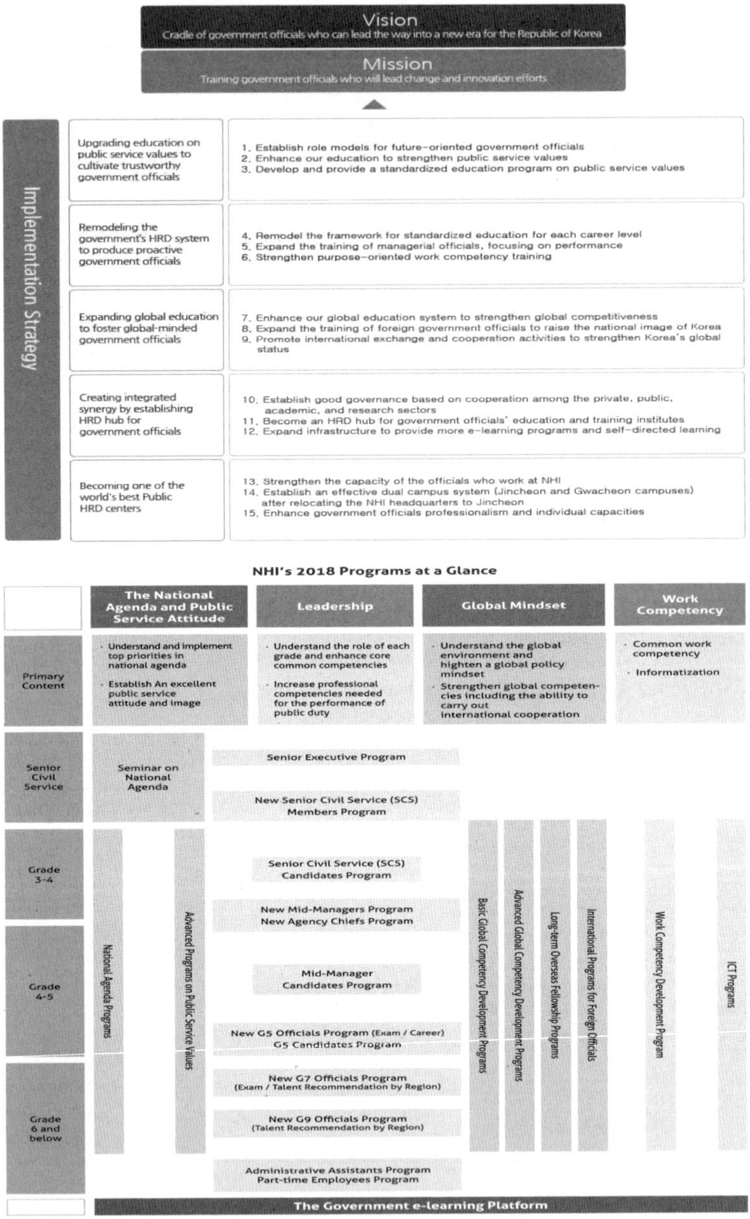

Figure 2-3 Operational Framework of the National HRD Institute

development. Figure 2-3 shows the current framework by which it operates.

(2) Local Government Officials Development Institute (LOGODI)

LOGODI has worked since 1965 to train high-potential individuals for regional growth. LOGODI has taken the lead of the Saemaeul Movement of each region and focused on training local public officials so that the central government contributes all over the region. The Saemaeul Movement is hailed as a miracle that led to the hyper-growth of Korea. It has definitely been the biggest contributor to the many economic breakthroughs.

Lately, LOGODI has been educating servants and/or officials about government's major policies and carrying out both advanced and intermediate level leadership training programs. Through exchange among developing countries, LOGODI has been sharing its experiences and methods of training local public officials. It has been training public officials through a systematic organization so that foremost strategies of the Government such as the Agricultural Community Development Promotion Policy can be transmitted and enacted in each district. LOGODI not only enhanced the capability of the public officials, but also contributed to local implementation issues and economic growth of the country.

C. Recommended Integrated HRD Agency

For a government employee training organization to do its job, it is crucial that the organization have power. In Korea, the NHI and LOGODI have been enthusiastic government employee professional training organizations. There is high government support as well as autonomy and authority in planning and in carrying out programs. Furthermore, the government gave them full support, recognizing the importance of government employee training. Korea is currently working hard to develop employees' capabilities through these two organizations. In addition, these organizations are ever changing based on the environment and changes in government policies. They are constantly introducing relevant and effective training programs to enhance employees' competencies. Thus, at the organizational level, the organization has to be constantly upgraded. The head of the organization should also be consulted for leadership and thinking about training programs. A government employee training organization should be more sensitive to the environment and country policies than any other organization. Korea, in this respect, has a very good systematic organization system. Seeing the changes that the NHI has made

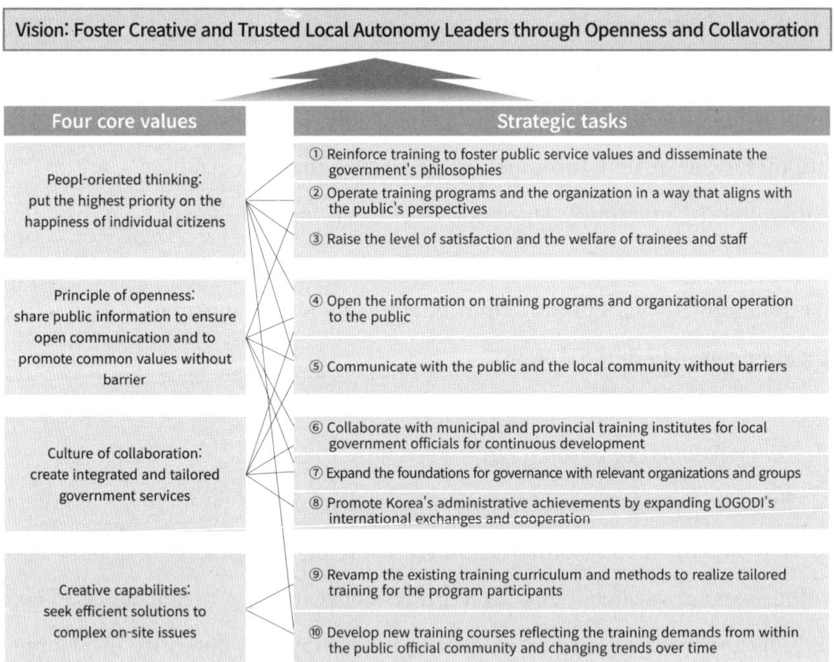

Figure 2-4 Operational Framework of the LOGODI

in its training programs and goals based on the trends of the day, Vietnamese government employee training organizations should also put their efforts to make fast adaptations to the new trends. In addition, the government should never end their support for these organizations to always reform and change. Their authority and status should be increased.

Practically, we recommend the Government of Vietnam to:

1) Establish a central HR educational institution and promote managerial communications within the departments. Central HR educational institutions must identify various training approaches and focus (i.e., competency-based). Tailored HRD interventions should be based on the needs of the organizations.
2) Setup a distinct and separate civil service education institution for central (e.g., NHI in Korea) and local (e.g., LOGODI in Korea) public officials. The existence of the central educational institution which plays a key role in the education of public officials is very important. However, considering the operational efficiency and characteristics of education, it is also necessary to consider a method to separate the education of public officials into central and local as the system in Korea does. Such systematic and reliable educational institutions improve efficiency in educating public officials as well as the quality of education, enabling more professional, continuous and systematic education of public officials.
3) Privatize managerial functions/authorities and institutionalize international collaborations and interactions. It would helpful public officers with high positions to contribute to their organizations' transformation and creation if they could work with a more flexible and reformative educational system through private institutions or

internationally advanced educational training.

4) Develop leadership and management. Public officers with high positions have significant responsibility to manage major decisions of each organization, establish the direction for the future of the organization, and facilitate organizational effectiveness through appropriate leadership toward the members of the organization. Therefore, public officers with high positions should understand the overall organizational task as well as possess a higher level of professionalism and revolutionary competencies for the improvement of the organization. It is essential for them to receive leadership education and enhance their administrative competencies.

1.2. Building a Comprehensive AHRD Program

a. Strategic Processes and Activities for an Improved AHRD Programs

The AHRD model of this study is expected to add apre-test phase, modifying the traditional HRD model with four phases. This is because, despite the abundant experience, know-how and knowledge of South Korea, there may be difficulties in designing a model in accordance with the culture, context, and characteristics of Vietnam. A pre-test will help circumvent errors which may be made by holistic and large-scale approaches on the national level. Accordingly, in order to minimize false steps in implementing national leading HRD, we will receive feedback from some of the civil servants by conducting a pilot-test. Using the results, it will be possible to establish an effective HRD strategy which prevents time and pecuniary costs arising from processes of designing policies and programs as well as implementation, evaluations, and feedback. Figure 2-5 shows the model for the process of establishing a comprehensive AHRD program.

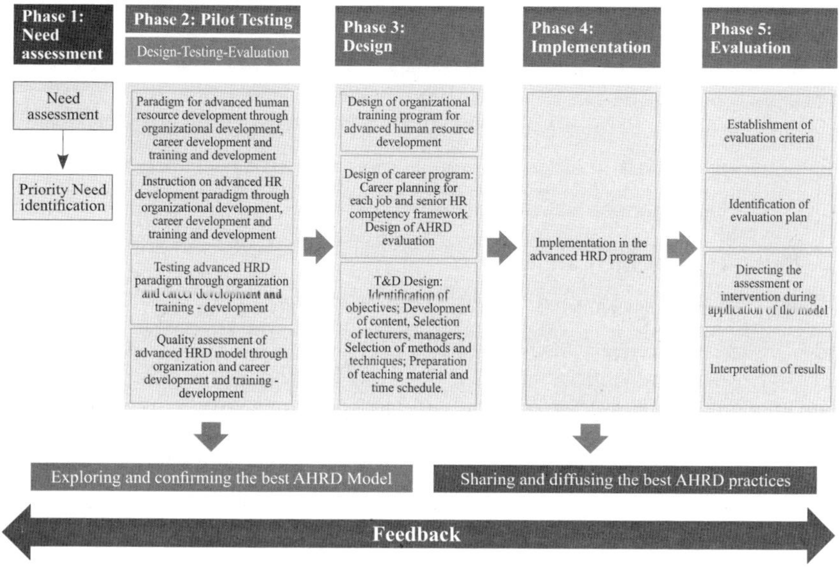

Figure 2-5 A Process Model for AHRD Programs

Phase 1: Assessment of the Need for AHRD

The first stage in the process of defining the AHRD model in practice is aimed at creating theoretical models as an empirical basis for that model. In this step, AHRD needs will be evaluated as the basis for the corresponding theoretical models. There are two steps: (1) Review the development needs of AHR and (2) Select and identify priority needs for the development of AHRD.

Phase 2: Pilot Testing

At the end of the needs assessment, we move to phase2, in which we will conduct pilot tests to minimize possible lapses and receive feedback from some of the public officers.

Phase 3: Designing AHRD Content

On the basis of the pilot test in Phase 2, we will proceed to construct in detail the training program for developing knowledge, skills, and abilities of high ranking officials in order to establish more effective HRD programs.

Phase 4: Implementation

This is the stage of large scale application (no longer in the experimental group) of the AHR training and development process. During the implementation process, assessment and feedback tools will be used as a basis for managing, directing and adjusting the process. This adjustment will bring about the optimal efficiency of the AHRD training and development process.

Phase 5: Evaluation: Summarizing Results of AHRD

This stage uses the criteria for evaluating training and development output. The evaluation results are the basis for feedback and adjustment of the elements to improve the AHRD T&D process.

Training evaluation is a system for measuring whether trainees have achieved learning outcomes due to training interventions. We will evaluate the effectiveness of HRD programs and policies. Advanced HRD programs may reinforce the competencies of the government employees of Vietnam.

In terms of the administrative environment, the management of human resources and the developmental system, the educational institution, and so on as mentioned above, this study aims to propose strategies for Vietnam called 3i for the future.

Korean Case

Developing, implementing, and evaluating training programs is a process that not only increases the quality of the program itself but also is necessary for the development of the capabilities of government officials. This report mentions two examples (i.e., NHI and LOGODI) among the various training programs that have been implemented in Korea's government.

(1) Public Service Values Training

NHI founded a training program for public officials to re-establish their view of public office, the nation, and ethics in order to develop transparent workings and fight corruption. The cultivation program encourages public officials to self-examine their public career according to public service values and establish a clean image. Furthermore, a specific action plan is to be set up to enhance the employees' public value orientation through this process. Specific information about the training program is as follows.

- Purpose: To possess a committed and serving mind, strengthen their capability to practice public service values by recovering humanity and morality, and moreover, to induce the spread of desirable view of the nation, public office, and ethics throughout the community.
- Primary Educational Contents
- **Understand Public Service Values.** Understand and acquire basic knowledge of three key public service values (view of the nation, public office, and ethics)
- **Enhance Practical Competency.** Enhance self-esteem and practical competency (behavioral change) through participation learning.
- Training Programs
- New Generation of Hope and the Roles of Public Officials (view of public office)
- Public Service Ethics (view of ethics)

• Public and Historical Consciousness (view of the nation)
• Spirit of the Constitution and Public Service Values (view of the nation)
• Introspection on Proper Public Service Values
• Seek to practice Public Service Values (internalization)

(2) Training Program for High Ranking Officials

The training program for high-ranking officials lasts 43 weeks, composed of an intensive training course (22 weeks) and a deep case study and utilization course (21 weeks). This training program is formed not only to input information but also to use the information to extract actual results. The intensive training course consists of 4 learning contents: public service values, public leadership, professionalism, and global capacity. The trainees are also required to complete the following courses: training of public value instructors, interview committee, mentoring/coaching, and policy consulting. On the basis of the first half of the training contents, the second half of the program focuses on lectures about public service values and participation in interviews such as the civil service examination more to deepen and deliver the learned contents.

These systematic training systems are known to establish proper public service values, leadership qualities in high-ranking officials, professionalism, and global capacity, ultimately contributing to the enhancement of national competitiveness. In addition, the Korean Government operates leadership programs and training programs for high officials as shown in Figure 2-6

Category	(22 Weeks) Intensive Training		(21 Weeks) Research Utilization
Training Manners (Methods)	Structure Training (Phased, Systematic)		Unstructured Training (Self-directed Learning)
Contents	**Introduction**	**Main Programs**	**Training Outcomes**
Public Values	Self-Examination	• Public value instructors training	• Public service values lecture/propagate
Public Leadership	Leadership analysis	• Mentoring/Coaching • Interview Committee training	• Mentor/Coach activities • Interview Committee activities
Work Profession	Launch research plan	• Policy consultants training • Information/SW Mind	• Perform government designated research
Global	Global capacity	• Global mind • Languages	• Attend international conferences/seminars

Figure 2-6 Training Program for High Ranking Officials

b. Recommended Interactive HRD Programs

1) Adopt diverse leadership and talent development programs that put emphasis on public values and global perspectives; design and implement HRD programs that are highly valuable and acceptable (e.g., HRD interventions must specifically address the gap between organizational goals and mission with the civil servant's knowledge, skills, and abilities.

First of all, diversifying the educational programs is essential in terms of the position, the job, the theme, and educational means. For public officers with low positions, the general level of education on the job would be central, whereas public officers with higher positions should receive education on leadership to lead the institutional members to establish the vision and strategies together and attain the institutional goal as a whole. Especially, the development of more professional programs would be needed for public officers with high positions since they are require more professional abilities, leadership, management skills, and so on than general officers.

Furthermore, the diversification of educational strategies is necessary. More creative and more effective educational strategies such as problem-based learning, flipped class, and e-learning would enhance the efficiency of the education.

2) Activate training and development interventions based on rank and position and/or competency-based approaches.

For example, the program for the cultivation of the value of public officers could be different based on the rank of the government employees even though this education is for all employees. High-rank officials should be educated about what sense of duty they should have in designing and implementing policies. On the other hand, lower-rank government employees would be taught about the attitude of a public official in serving the public. In addition, various educational program methods should be implemented to increase professionalism in employees of different positions.

3) Implement diversification of HRD programs and improvement of program efficiency through active introduction of field trips to advanced fields of practice targeting high-ranking officials and human resources

managers

It is necessary to examine other HRD programs by supporting short-term and long-term field trips to advanced countries with well-prepared administrative and human resources systems targeting high-ranking officials and human resources managers. Such field trips will help the participants to find and appropriately modify programs and systems that are realistic to Vietnam as well as acquire various know-how and useful tips. In addition, such field trips enable the participants to broaden their vision beyond the programs that are currently operated in Vietnam, discover various programs and consider efficient operation methods. Such visits to advanced countries can be utilized as excellent opportunities to establish networks with the countries they visit, diagnose the current status of Vietnam after returning to Vietnam and receive official and non-official advice. Meanwhile, the Senior Civil Services System needs to train elite, professional public officials with a cosmopolitan outlook. In regard to international training, the institution should design an appropriate problem-solving type of education and training system for its public officials. Such training programs should be supported with long-term funding (Choi & Park, 2013)

4) Professional efforts are needed to develop and implement an educational training program.

Korea employs numerous internal and external professionals to develop and implement a single educational program. In addition, strict evaluation is imposed upon these educational programs to assess their effectiveness. This process produces great educational programs and high satisfaction from government employees.

5) Evaluation of the performance and reward for educational program needs to be established.

It is important to plan and form next-level programs by evaluating what has been accomplished and the extent the educational goals have been achieved through the previous educational programs. Also, educational training needs to produce educational effects that could be translated into actual job operation as it requires many individuals' time and money invested. Therefore, the programs with high effectiveness should be more encouraged through performance evaluations. It would be essential to put efforts such as offering incentives to the administrators of the educational institution so that it could come up with creative and effective educational programs.

This study examines the problems in each phase of human resource management depending on development process of the ARD constructed earlier, and sets up the strategic AHRD process model (at the system, agency and programs). This study establishes the model as follows in order to create the AHRD program which can strengthen KSAs of high ranking officials of Vietnam government officials

1.3. Building a Comprehensive AHRD System

a) Strategic Processes and Activities for an Improved AHRD System

In order to establish the AHRD model in enhancing the competencies of Vietnam's public officials, the Party and the Government may consider the following processes. First, carry out an in-depth, wide-ranging, and objective analysis of all factors—both internal and external—that are critical in fostering high-quality advanced human resource. Second, understand the vast human resource issues and adopt HRM approaches cognizant of the political, cultural, and socio-economic conditions of the country. For example, it should be examined whether fairness and openness are guaranteed in the process of recruitment and selection of human resources and whether educational training is rightly offered or the current program proceeds properly and achieves the intended outcomes. In addition, a careful and objective assessment should be conducted of the performance outcomes of highly educated employees in the public service as well as an analysis of the validity of the evaluation and the reward mechanisms used to effectively motivate employees.

The key principle of the HRM/D approach the civil service system of Vietnam should adopt is "highly competent leaders and managers for competent governance". In this case, the Vietnamese civil service must establish a strategic reform agenda integrating a comprehensive AHRD perspective. The advanced and tactical HRD system is an effective reform effort that is fit to address the current and future challenges of the country. Establishing an AHRD system must ingrain a basic value that is, "the right training and development for the right person and the right competencies for the right job". The overall HRM/D system does not operate in isolation; it interacts and must work in harmony with various organizational values and consider environmental trends and issues. In Vietnam, critical developments may affect the HRM/D reform strategies and approach, including world economic development that encourages an open-market, ASEAN integration, changing workforce demographics, challenges to trust in the government, budget cuts, demands for efficiency and productivity, emerging workplace reforming and reengineering initiatives and centralization and decentralization.

As it moves towards being a competitive country and transitions from middle to high income, the Government of Vietnam has to engage an advanced HRD system. Lessons from the reform efforts of various countries can give

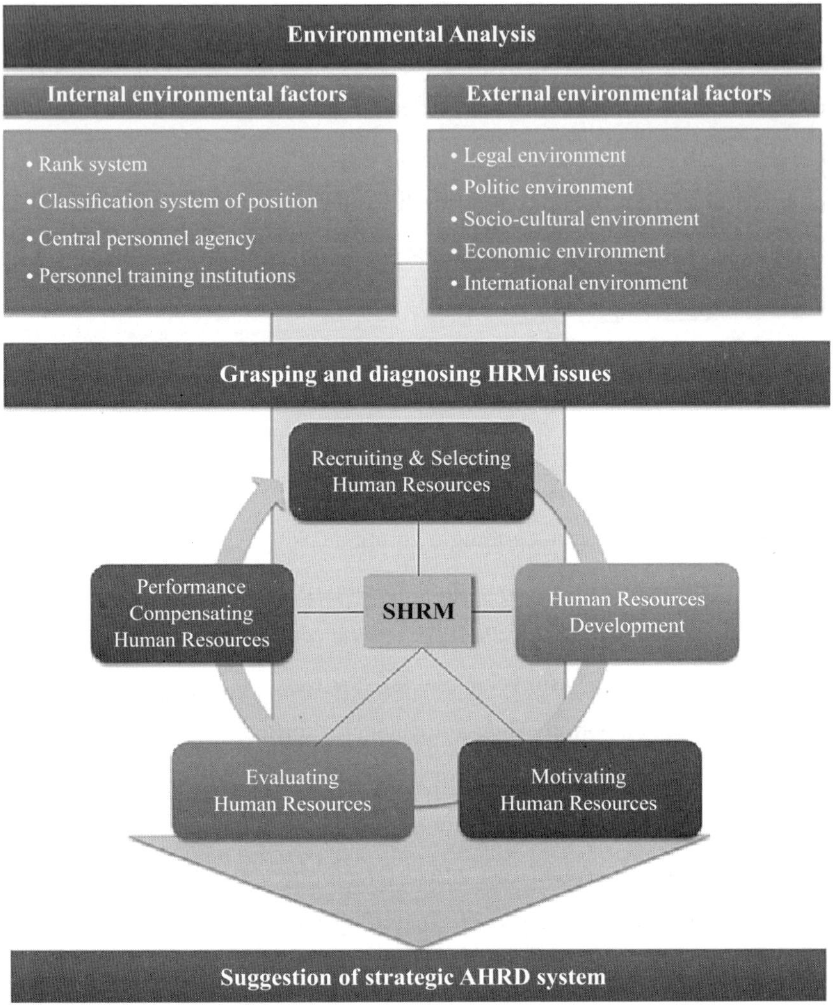

Figure 2-7 AHRD System Model: Strategic and Analytical Processes

numerous insights, specifically the strategic reforms and initiatives of the Korean civil service (see detailed discussion below). Nonetheless, adopting practices from different contexts may require an effort to harmonize them with the present political and governmental circumstances of Vietnam. Figure 2-10 shows the AHRD System Model.

b) Korean Case

(1) Open Competitive Employment (Civil Service Examination) and Open Position System from Private Sector

Korea has implemented a procedure in which an open competitive examination is taken by unappointed people when employing new government employees. This is a huge help to provide a fair and equal opportunity to all and for the government to employ outstanding employees. The employment examination for Korean government employees is composed of the Public Administration Examination intended for 5th rank and the Civil Service Examination for 7th and 9th rank employees.

The Open Position system is a procedure in which people are chosen through open competitive employment. This ensures that the employees are the best fit for jobs which require a high level of professionalism and policy-making capability. Korea is increasing its share of open competitive employment because of the fast-changing administrative environment that includes an increased variety and professionalism of administration as well as professionalization and more highly educated manpower. Currently, Korea implements open competitive employment through the following principles; (1) securing outstanding individuals with professionalism; (2) combating stagnation of government organizations; (3) contributing to performance-based administration; (4) rectifying the apathetic attitudes of government officials.

Table 2-4 The Process of Open Competitive Employment

Establishment of a Plan	The establishment of plans regarding test schedules and number of applicants
Announcement and Application Period	Announcements made through Internet and newspapers Acceptance of applications
Setting Exam Questions	Selection of exam organizers and venue for setting and verifying exam questions
Examination Period	Selection and announcement of testing centers Proctor training Administering the test according to the manual
Grading	Electronic grading for multiple choice questions Before setting the final score, written test scores are revealed and open to objections and evaluation
Announcement of successful applicants	Acceptance decided by consideration of the test control committee; Announcement on the website Personal SMS services provided
Administration of Prospective Employees	Registration of prospective employees among the final successful applicants 5th rank government employees: Basic training and trial period under the MPM 7th and 9th rank government employees: Designation of government departments of prospective employees and management of employees by each government department

After the adoption of the open position system, several public offices are now experiencing change and competition. Considering that government departments are also seeking to employ performance-oriented management, it shows that this policy is taking on a major role in changing the public management paradigm in Korea.

(2) The Senior Civil Service System

The Senior Civil Service system was adopted to initiate changes to the senior government officials that have a fundamental role in major government policy decisions and management. In the whole governmental perspective, these government officials are to be deployed in various work assignments considering their competencies, knowledge, skills, and abilities. The underlying strategy of the approach is to increase competition and openness to encourage high performance and ownership.

Since 2006, the Korean Senior Civil Service has gone through several developmental stages. Among the major characteristics are as follows:

• **Comprised of head officials and higher ranks**

Approximately 1500 Korean employees comprise the senior civil service. Some senior officials of local autonomous entities are also part of the senior civil service.

• **Senior civil officials are managed by the human resource department based on their performance rather than position or status**

The 1~3 ranks of senior civil officials have been abolished. Human resource management is done based on the employee's duty and position so that human resource management can now choose a person fit for the job without being affected by rank. Salaries are based on work and performance rather than rank or seniority for senior civil officials.

• **Increase the openness of senior civil officials and increase competition.**

An open recruitment system in which senior civil officials have to compete with private and civil servants of other government departments has been introduced and managed. About 30% of SCS positions are filled by open recruitment, which attracts civilians as well as public officials at agencies across government. Those senior officials who fall short of required performance or capabilities may be dismissed from their authority by the Appointment Screening Committee of the MPM.

• **Systematically manage the performance of senior civil servants and develop their abilities**

A performance report in which a performance contract is made including performance goals and evaluation that has been discussed with their superiors. It is used to evaluate the extent to which their goals have been reached. In order to be a senior civil service official, candidate training has to be fulfilled. Furthermore, candidate training is managed in a realistic manner in which the chiefs of departments are educated based on real-life examples of the fundamental abilities that a senior civil service official should have before becoming one.

• **Keeping the foundation of the career civil service system as well as widening the responsibilities of senior civil officials.**

The rules of performance-oriented management in the human resource management of senior civil officials and political neutrality are guaranteed. Furthermore, retirement age and status have been kept in place. However, senior civil officials that lack performance and ability will be subject to strong human resource management based on objective and fair judgment.

Various developments were achieved after the implementation of the SCS training program in Korea, including:

1) Change in organization culture: The negative appraisal due to the guarantee of positions that employees are lazy and apathetic attitudes is no longer in place. The negative impression has changed.

2) Spread of performance-oriented culture in bureaucratic society:

Performance contracts are made according to position performance contracts.

3) The realization of individual and tailored training: Efforts have been made to improve deficient abilities and talents and offer personalized training programs.

4) Realization of strong human resource management: Penalties are given to the position when performance and capabilities do not meet a certain standard.

c) Recommended Institutionalized HRM/D Systems

It is highly recommended that the Government of Vietnam and the Party consider HRM/D system transformation. As HRM and HRD are very intimately associated, taking appropriate HRD strategies requires the preparation of well-organized HRM system. Our fundamental recommendations are outlined and discussed below.

First, transformation of HRM system through the following approaches:

1) Introduce a formal and systematic government employee examination.

Most Korean employees are employed through an open examination system managed by the government's human resource management department. Such an examination system is likely to minimize Vietnam's long problem of the patronage system in personnel practice. In addition, the examination is a free opportunity for all that will allow many competent young Vietnamese citizens to become government employees. As a result, outstanding individuals can be employed as government officials.

2) Design a Hybrid Recruitment System and open recruitment through competitive civil service examination.

High-rank officials requires a lot of professionalism and capabilities in the Vietnamese public service. The examination should be widely used only for general positions, while positions that require a high level of professionalism should bring outstanding individuals from outside sources. The recruitment process should ensure free, fair, and equal employment opportunity.

This study suggests a method to introduce both a civil service examination system and a special recruitment system. It is necessary to build the public service workforce through an open recruitment system which brings outside experts with expertise and a civil service examination system which recruits and develops young and potential talents into administrative experts through the HRD program. Especially, the civil service examination system should be operated separately from the examination system for recruiting managers and the general examination for recruiting entry-level personnel. The capacity and expertise of public officials should be secured through such a system and should recruited people should be developed into excellent talents through the HRD.

3) Induce HRD performance improvement in each government organization through the development of a HRM/HRD innovation index.

It is necessary to develop an innovation index which can measure how much effort each government organization is making in the HRM and HRD fields. The level of innovation by each organization should be determined through this innovation index, and a strategy for innovation in insufficient fields should be established. It is also necessary to measure needs for innovation in the HRM and HRD of the whole public sector by dividing the innovation index into 3 parts including institutional innovation (short-term), human innovation (mid-term) and cultural innovation (long-term) and to re-consider the role of HRD for innovating the public sector.

Meanwhile, coupled with the strengthening of merit-based system, education will increase professionalism in public service. First of all, educational programs are necessary to resolve problems resulting from insufficient prior training. These programs must be co-managed by universities, private enterprises, and research agencies. A sufficient budget must also be set aside for educational equipment and facilities, bringing in internationally-renowned experts, and designing programs emphasizing real-world applications. These measures force trainees to engage in active problem solving by making them incorporate everything they have learned from lectures and previous experiences (Choi & Park, 2013).

4) Set up an effective and customized HRM/HRD system for high ranking officers.

High-rank officials choose important policies of a country and also have the responsibility to take care of a public organization. As a result, how these people are chosen, trained, and paid are all significant issues. Korea has the SCS system that is just for high-rank officers. It is expected that competition in view of performance will be active in a bureaucratic government setting and will be more prominent when personalized management system is well planned for and persistent for the high ranking officials

5) Prepare the educational system through an explicit job description.

Going into a new job or taking on new tasks requires understanding and competency. Education background prepares a candidate/employee to easily adapt as needed for the performance of the job. The practicality of the education system and taking into account the needed competencies are crucial.

6) Create a position for the development of the country and the individual.

Vietnamese human capital that was supposed to work for the government is often attracted to work in the private sector both domestic and abroad. Maintaining a high quality of employees for public positions can be regarded as a type of competition. It is important to determine the relevant national competencies that may encourage employees to stay in the government. Public institutions need continuous quality education to promote the development of the individual as well as the institution.

7) Conduct performance management and reform the performance evaluation system.

It is necessary to offer appropriate rewards for those who attain high performance and complete suitable training programs. A special management education should be implemented for those who are lacking in performance or who have been underachievers so that they can see the causes of their low achievement and find motivation to enhance their work ability and to carry out their jobs. In particular, it is recommended to implement distinct, customized education programs for those who are in high performance and low performance.

8) Offer appropriate rewards.

The current payment policy of the government in Vietnam highlights equality, but it is necessary to adopt a differential reward system according to the degree of one's performance to compete with domestic and international corporations. Providing appropriately high rewards for those who highly achieve affects their motivation. Therefore, adopting a clear evaluation of performance and a reward system in accordance would be expedient.

The central educational institution for the public officers needs to be realigned. The central educational institution needs to construct programs and activities that will enhance the effectiveness of the education and training of professionals in public service. Specifically, the central educational institution for public officers should have the ability to manage the education of the public officers for the central and local governments as well as the nationwide public officers. Thus, the institution itself needs to increase its ability to provide to the extent it can provide education for the administrators of HR professionals in each institution and customized consulting for each institution.

Moreover, the institution needs to be professionally, systematically, and competitively realigned so that it can consider not only simple theoretical education but also job education, psychological education, ethical education, and retirement education that would be utilized throughout a public officer's career, from entering the job and to retirement; it should play a role to consider strategies to constantly develop and improve public officers.

Third, law/policy for the HRD of public officers should be systemized. Specifically, it is necessary to realign the central educational institution for the public officers and to have more systemized and detailed laws and policies to emphasize the importance of the HRD in each governmental institution. In the case of Korea, the law and policy for the public officers have been modified several times. Reconstructing the related policy and law in accordance with time passage and changes would be an important precedent to make new HRD programs that will enhance the professionalism and competence of public officers.

In Vietnam, in order to step up and implement staff planning and rotation in the coming years, the committees and Party organizations should implement the following:

1) Promote staff planning and rotation along with the synchronized innovation in other steps in staff organization; first reform the employee's performance evaluation system. Build standards and assessment criteria for staff positions according to working efficiency and credibility of officials, Party members and the people. Select mechanisms through annual contests and examinations for staff from equivalent or lower departments under the motto "Do the job until it is done".
2) Innovate staff training toward selecting graduates with honors at prestigious universities and appointing them to the localities (the places with difficulties and on demand) to foster and train, thereby planning selectively long-term staff resources.
3) Innovate contents, methods and forms of training and retraining in staff planning according to staff positions, combining theory and practical skills to handle problems arising from practical work; increase knowledge about thinking and strategic vision. Develop and implement a system of collective leadership and management; key officials must go through the key positions in the lower ranks to get staff training and challenges.
4) Strictly implement the three stage structure in planning committees, leadership and management at all levels. Competent authorities only approve and validate the committee-level human resource plans when they meet these requirements.
5) Promote rotation to train staff and implement the arrangement of leading and managerial positions for staff who are not local people at the provincial and district levels. Develop and implement regulations for

a rotation plan and the process of transferring and arranging a number of leadership positions and management at the provincial level, district level for staff who are not local people.

Table 2-5 The Vietnam AHRD Recommendations: From a Strategic Perspective

	Short-term	Mid-term	Long-term
Agency	• Establish a central HR educational institution and promote managerial communication within the departments.	• Setup a distinct and separate civil service education institution for central (e.g., NHI in Korea) and local (e.g., LOGOTI in Korea) public officials.	• Privatize managerial functions/authorities and institutionalize international collaborations and interactions.
Program	• Adopt diverse leadership and talent development programs that emphasize public value and global perspectives; design and implement HRD programs that are highly valuable and acceptable (e.g., HRD interventions must specifically address the gap between civil servants' KSA and the organizational goals and mission).	• Activate training and development interventions based on rank and position and/or competency-based approaches.	• Diversify HRD programs and improvement of program efficiency through active introduction of field trips to advanced fields of practice for high-ranking officials and human resources managers.
System	• Introduce a formal and systematic government employee examination. • Design a Hybrid Recruitment System: open recruitment through competitive civil service examination.	• Induce HRD performance improvement by each government organization through the development of a HRM/HRD innovation index	• Set up an effective and customized HRM/HRD system for high ranking officers.

2. Vietnam 2030: Towards Prosperity, Creativity, Equality and Democracy

2.1. Changing and Challenging Context and Higher Expectation

The Party and the Government must exert efforts to initiate necessary reforms—state, political, and public management—to achieve the country's vision for 2030 toward prosperity, creativity, equity and democracy. Building advanced human resources is an important component for Vietnam to advance toward this vision. Improving AHRD in Vietnam will take place in an ad-hoc situation and context which can be characterized as having "wicked challenges". AHRD seems to exist within diverse stakeholders and multiple variables.

External challenges of the public service include:

- Globalization and the pressure to improve competitive advantages while coordinating and collaborating;
- Technology advancement and breakthroughs, especially ICT;
- Economic reform and the quest for restructuring;
- Changes in public mindset and lifestyle and changing expectations from society affecting public satisfaction and public trust;
- The tendency to rethink the role of the state in the course of development;
- Changes in social human resources and social mobility;
- The improved capacity and emerging role of the private sector;
- Pressure to prove the legitimacy of the leading political party in the context of democracy;
- The threats of the "middle income trap".

Internal challenges of the public service may include;

- The "publicness" of public service;
- The complexity of public service activities;
- The complicated criteria to measure the public service;
- The diversity of the social labor and workforce within the public service;
- The need to improve the effectiveness and efficiency of the public service as part of publicly stated commitment and objectives;
- Public administration reform (PAR) efforts and obstacles.

Challenges coming from the civil servants and public servants themselves may include their internal drive for job and career development,[14] backward knowledge and inadequate skills, conflicts due to generation gaps between millennials or young and baby boomer civil and public servants, and stress syndromes resulting from modern working life.

2.2. Competency-based Framework and AHRD

The development of high-quality human resources including AHR has been stated as one of the three strategic breakthroughs of the national strategy for transformation. The national socio-economic model for that HRD becomes the key pillar for improving national competitive advantages and sustainable development.

The Communist Party of Vietnamese determined to invest in HRD, pointing out that HRM/D must establish an available source or pool of leaders

14 According to official figures from reports on public administration reform 2011-2015, the total number of cadres and civil servants from district-level up as of December 2013 was 312,401; that of commune-level was 227,253; and that of public servants in June 2014 was 1,995,414.

and managers ready to deploy to all levels of government (i.e., central to local levels). These leaders and managers must possess the required moral qualities and organizational competence to effectively carry out the work of industrialization and modernization, sustaining national independence and the transformation towards socialism. At this turning point for Vietnam, in March 2016, a group of researchers from the World Bank and the Ministry of Planning and Investment proposed the *Vision of Vietnam 2030: Towards Prosperity, Creativity, Equality and Democracy*.

The HRD approach should move towards a competency-based framework—identifying core competencies for leaders and managers and for AHR in particular. Historically, the criteria for competence of DG and DDG level leaders and managers have been stated in a number of regulations such as Decision no. 83/2004/QDD-BNV of Minister of Ministry of Home Affairs on the position-based competence required for local Department Director and the equivalents of the People's Committees of the provinces and central-owned cities.

A group of researchers from Hanoi National University on human resources for public administration proposed a framework of competence which contains 14 leadership and management skills and personal characteristics (each then goes with a set of particular indicators) as follows:

a. Practicing public service ethics;

b. Understanding the locality;

c. Professional skills;

d. Monitoring and management skills;

e. Human resource management skills;

f. Self-managing.

According to Nguyen Su, leaders in the public sector must have three qualities to lead successfully: (1) "Tri" (Knowledge), (2) "Bỉ" (Love and Caring) and (3) "Dũng" (Courage). The ongoing draft of the decree on a competence framework for leadership and management positions including that of Vice Minister, Director General, Deputy Director General proposes a leadership competence framework including moral qualities such as patriotism, pursuing public ethics "Cần, kiệm, liêm, chính, chí, công, vô tư" competence that calls for core competence, experience, knowledge and education qualifications.

In a nutshell, advanced human resources need to possess (or acquire) moral qualities for public good, including integrity, honesty, responsibility and accountability, courage, commitment, continuous searching for development and self-respect as well as leadership and managerial competence which may include listening and prompt response and setting and sharing vision.

CHAPTER THREE:

ADVANCED HUMAN RESOURCE DEVELOPMENT IN STATE-OWNED ENTERPRISES

Ilhyun Jo
Professor, Department of Educational Technology, Ewha Womans University

Ⅰ. Introduction

Ⅱ. Status of AHRD Systems for SOEs in Vietnam

Ⅲ. Case Studies on AHRD in Vietnamese SOEs

Ⅳ. Lessons from the Korean Experience

Ⅴ. Policy Recommendations and Imperatives

CHAPTER THREE:

ADVANCED HUMAN RESOURCE DEVELOPMENT IN STATE-OWNED ENTERPRISES

I. Introduction

Vietnam has been running efficient free markets in parallel with socialist values by promoting economic and social development plans. These policies are suggested in three key documents: *the Vietnam 2035 Report, Socio-Economic Development Strategy in Vietnam 2011-2020*, and *Socio-Economic Development Plan in Vietnam 2011-2015*. These plans established two noticeable targets in common. The first is to develop the quality of human resources and enhance Vietnam's competitiveness for the future. The second is to improve state rationality and modernity by overcoming inefficiencies in the state sector including state-owned enterprises(SOEs).

To achieve these challenging tasks, the roles of the Party, government, and SOEs have become ever more crucial. Restructuring of SOEs seems to be an especially important structural reform to achieve these goals (Sjoholm, 2006). Although equitization is mainly suggested to improve SOEs' effectiveness, it might not always be the best solution because of two characteristics of SOEs: the willingness to retain competitiveness in response to the market mechanism and to utilize the results of market mechanism as resources for preserving socialistic values beyond the private interests of capitalists and shareholders at the same time.

This dual nature of the SOEs has produced the ills of state monopoly capitalism, producing unfair competition and corruption in the public sector by interfering in the market mechanism (Chia, 2013). The scarce resources wasted in the country (e.g., land, finance, human resources, etc.), the deliberate avoidance of market competition with foreign direct investment (FDI) or private enterprises, and the resulting diminished productivity (e.g., capital productivity, employment, contribution to the national economy, etc.) due to the overlapping of these problems are raising concerns about the operating system of public enterprises in Vietnam. To handle the current situation and create a more rational, industrialized and modernized economy, SOEs in Vietnam should undertake structural reforms beyond the external structure in order to suggest their own development models and grow as the main agent of production that supplies financial and human resources.

With natural resources, human resources have been an important asset for which Vietnam has had to achieve significant developments within a short time (Quang, T., & Dung, H. K., 1998). Human capital is one of the core resources for the production of goods and services. However, not only are humans involved in the process of production like financial capital and land, they also secure, utilize and control the other two impersonal resources: natural and financial. In other words, humans are resources themselves, but at the same time they are meta-resources (Dalkir, 2011). As mentioned above, considering the unique situation Vietnamese SOEs are facing that is caused by its structural duality and the consequent contradictions, the strategic value of Human Resources Development(HRD) practices is emphasized. The problem is that both the quality and quantity of human resources as a strategic leverage for SOEs to lead Vietnam into economic and social development are not up to scratch. Human resources of SOEs in the country are lacking in many aspects compared with foreign state-owned companies, private companies and even government agencies. Senior executive managers, or AHR (Advanced Human Resources) who are in the position of solving management problems and cultivating the human resources in general of the future generation have low management competencies compared with younger workers who are highly literate and have strong self-developing motivations.

Managers who are trained well can drive innovation within the organizations, and this could have a vertical trickle-down effect to inspire the development of workers and provoke a horizontal ripple effect to expand innovation to other organizations (Ruiz, P., Ruiz, C., & Martínez, R., 2011). The history of Korea's economic development and equitization of SOEs, where highly motivated elite managers played the role of flagships in the fleet of low-performing, low-motivated workers from rural areas, clearly indicates that AHRs are strategic targets for the Majungmul Effect.[15] For this reason, advanced-level managers in SOEs were set as main targets which can guide the innovation.

Improving advanced-level managers' competencies is an efficient way to improve organization's competitiveness since their needed skills and attitudes are more generic across the different functional characteristics of diverse industries. Investment of limited HRD resources in the development of function-independent skill sets of general management should yield greater impact than investing in the development of thousands of different job-task skills across the SOEs in Vietnam. Moreover, the developed AHRs can lead

15 Majungmul is a pure Korean compound word, Majung (meet) and Mul (water). It means —priming water‖ in English. Priming water is the —first water‖ needed when trying to use a pump which has not been used for a long time. That is, when the handle is pumped to try to draw water, there is no pressure or seal. It is necessary to prime the pump by pouring water back down so that an abundant supply may then begin to flow.

organizational innovation of scale as change agents after training. In terms of training methods, AHRD requires multiple training methods. Multiple training methods imply the need for field problems, examples and experiences, evaluation and feedback, generalization and a modularization-centered approach of training contents beyond the theory-centered and fragmented lectures currently in place. In sum, for the development of AHRs in Vietnam's SOEs, we need to focus on depth and quality instead of width and quantity of interventions.

Development of AHRs requires multi-dimensional, sustainable, and long-term approaches. Korea's experience indicates that three infrastructures should be established in this challenging pursuit: Institutionalization, Contents, and Expertise.

Institutionalization includes establishment of a professional government institute that is dedicated to the design, development, and implementation of interventions (training and non-training) for AHRs from SOEs across a spectrum of industries and sizes. Legal and financial support for the institute should also be a critical part of institutionalization.

Contents involve the development or acquisition of effective and quality interventions to meet the needs of AHRs (Rothwell, W.J., Hohne, C.K., & King, S.B., 2000). Development means creation of new custom-designed contents from scratch, which has both strengths and weaknesses. Strengths include ecological validity and flexibility to the specific context and needs of Vietnamese SOEs. Weaknesses include cost in time and money and risk of inconsistent quality. Acquisition is the process of selecting and adapting readily available contents to suit Vietnam's contextual specificity. This option saves time and money, and risks involved are minimal. When tested quality contents are available at low or no purchasing cost, especially for context-free domains and where not much development expertise is accumulated internally, acquisition could be an appropriate option (Dick & Carey, 1996). Interventions are twofold: training and non-training (e.g., selection, performance management and assessment processes). Traditional HRD relies more on training, which is effective for knowledge and skill development. Attitudes and motivation, however, are better developed by non-training interventions such as incentive systems, assessment and evaluation, and equipping appropriate tools to the workers. Mixture of the two types of interventions is recommended in real-world situations (Swanson, R.A. & Holton, E.F., 2009).

Expertise includes trained professionals and accumulated knowledge capital within and around them. HRD is a highly knowledge-intensive profession. A competent HRD professional is not born but created through years of academic training and practical experience. Needs analysis, instructional design, material development, delivery of instruction, and measurement and evaluation are few examples on the long list of the expertise needed for HRD professionals. Some expertise is embedded in individual HRD practitioner as his/her knowledge, skills and abilities. Some expertise, however, is materialized in the forms of models, tools, and methods, and thus is readily available to HRD practitioners. Without expertise, investment in the institutionalization and contents is not realized to the benefits of trainees.

Challenging tasks for HRD to drive state-led socio-economic development needs to establish practicable and specific plans for various tasks such as the range of tasks, expected goals, procedures, related systems, etc. It also requires a simulation of the expected problems and solutions during these tasks. The Republic of Korea had a similar problem of ineffective AHRD systems in SOEs in the 1970s and 1980s. However, strategic and systematic development and implementation of training and non-training interventions for the AHRs in SOEs helped Korea to make improvements in organizational effectiveness and competitiveness. As a result, Korea's SOEs, such as KT (Korea Telecom), Nonghyup (National Agricultural Cooperative Federation), and Korea Coal Corporation (KOCOAL)have grown into competent and productive contributors to the national economic development of Korea.

Doing a case study on the experience of success and failure of other countries that had similar socio-economic contexts can be more useful than just learning from theories. For this reason, the study aims to explain Korea's strategies for AHRD plans and suggest implications from the lessons of Korea that will be very useful and effective to improve the effectiveness of AHRD programs for the managers of SOEs in Vietnam, which can increase the competitiveness of SOEs in Vietnam and the country for the future.

II. Status of AHRD Systems for SOEs in Vietnam

1. Issues of SOEs in Vietnam

SOEs in Vietnam have played an important role in the country's fast economic growth. However, there is a growing need to restructure SOEs to increase their efficiency and sustainability. HR departments in Vietnamese organizations should be focused more on improving regulations concerning rewards and punishments to motivate employees as well as to attract appropriate people (Nguyen, T. N. D., Mylett, T., & Teo, S., 2013). Reasons for the inefficiency and un-profitability of SOEs are many, but poor management mechanisms are considered the major cause. Since employees and managers in SOEs are not seriously appraised by enterprise results, and thus are not motivated to work for the better results, there has been no impetus to use advanced business management strategies such as marketing and human resources management. Rampant nepotism, cronyism, and lack of market-oriented mindsets aggravate the problems (Mogaka, D. O., 2011). Managers with developed competencies in effectively motivating and efficiently managing employees could be vital factor in SOEs with rigid incentive systems and a deficiency of meritocracy.

In order to survive the harsh tests of the market and ensure sustainable growth, Vietnamese firms need to pay more attention to training for their employees. Training has the potential to promote the development of employees with the knowledge and skills necessary to facilitate the implementation of different strategies and to respond to changes in the ever growing competitive environment (Thang, N. N., & Quang, T., 2011). Although human resources are intangible, managing them is especially important because doing so is closely related to organizational efficiency and outcomes. However, SOEs in Vietnam seem to have poor management systems particularly in human resources distribution, strategic inspection, assessment and training. Evaluation of training programs is practically neglected by the human resources department because training evaluation is not considered a task of the department (Quang, T., & Dung, H. K., 1998). In addition, SOEs in Vietnam lack strategic management mechanisms for human resources in planning, compensation, training and performance appraisal. This is mainly due to the fact that SOEs are usually dependent on decisions regarding human resources made by the State. Lack of structured and standardized curricula and training programs, underutilization of a systems approach to training and development methods, prevalence of de-centralized training functions and lack of dedicated AHRD training institutions are additional sources of the less-than-ideal situation of SOEs.

2. General HR in Vietnam's SOEs

2.2. Laws and Policies for HR in SOEs

The main emphases in HRD in the period of 2011-2020 are (Vietnam Government, 2011b):

1. to develop proficient management, experts, enterprise managers, skilled laborers, and leading staff in research and development;
2. to carry out high-quality human resources training programs and projects. In the socio-economic development plans for the 2011-2015 period, Vietnam focused on specific policy areas of HRD like (Vietnam Government, 2011a):
   i) renovate education and training systems;
   ii) improve the quality of human resources and pay attention to leadership, management, business governance, research and development;
   iii) improve the quality of education, particularly at the tertiary level;
   iv) focus on the quality rather than expansion of training, attaching importance to vocational training aimed at training 1 million rural laborers a year;
   v) adjust the policies on pre-school education and education in mountainous areas; and

vi) provide educational opportunities for more people in the industry;

3. to closely connect enterprises and facilities using laborers, training institutions and the State to develop human resources to meet society's demands.

The above strategic AHRD policy directions have been further elaborated in specific policy measures in the five-year socio-economic development plans (SEDPs) for the period of 2011-2015 and 2016-2020. The SEDP for the period of 2016-2020 which was recently adopted by the National Assembly in April, 2016 put the policy priority on AHR quality improvement and accelerate research and development capacity. In detail, these policies are meant to renovate quality assessment in education and training systems and to improve life skills, reduce workload in pre-tertiary education and encourage self-study and creativity. Great emphasis is also given to developing a knowledge economy with a high-quality workforce in research and development and improving vocational training to meet the requirements for economic development and integration. It is clear that "to improve the quality of human resources in leadership, management, business governance" has received a lot of attention from the Vietnamese government, specifically for the period of 2011-2015.

Since the economic reform started in 1986, there have been laws and policies to improve human resources in Vietnam. Vietnamese legal frameworks for human resources are mainly focused on technical-vocational education and training (TVET). Although AHRD is not always about TVET, since the concept of TVET has been broadened to the advancement of highly skilled workers in diverse sectors and it is mainly about having the quality human resources, it is a crucial part of human resources development in Vietnam (Kim, J. I., Kim, D.,

Nam, I. C., Kim, M. J., & Lee, H., 2011).

Educational Law 2005 and the Vocational Training Act are the main legal frameworks in which to develop human resources. With these laws, there are a number of regulations for the development of curriculum frameworks, statutes of TVET schools and regulations for exams at schools. The Decree on State Supervision of Vocational Training, which was approved in 2009, restates that the Ministry of Labour and Social Affairs (MOLISA) operates vocational training programs. Similarly, the Ministry of Education and Training (MOET) has established regulations on TVET. To recap, institutions for TVET (e.g., vocational training centers, job guidance centers, colleges, etc.) must follow frameworks issued by MOLISA and MOET.

The government has recently established Decree No. 69/2008/ND-CP to promote TVET development. It puts more emphasis on the responsibility of the government to arrange for land for the educational institutions and reduce taxes for the schools. The decree also states the importance of implementing educational programs in line with social demands. For example, the government agreed to establish a National Steering Board for human resource training in response to social demands for workforce development.

External factors as stated above put strong pressures on SOEs for internal reform. In order to survive and develop further in the context of changing domestic and international environments as well as the gradual removal of monopolist positions and privileges provided by the government, SOEs are now required to improve their business efficiency, enhance labor productivity, accelerate their business core-value and upgrade their international competitiveness. They now have to develop an effective competition strategy, put emphasis on technology innovation, develop a new product strategy, and more importantly, reform their business governance.

According to GSO's survey on labor and employment, on average, only 1% of total employment in Vietnam is in manager positions (General Statistics Office, 2015). Other occupations requiring highly educated and skilled labor, like technical employment and clerks, represent a low share of employment in Vietnam. In other words, labor in Vietnam currently works mainly in areas which do not require higher educational and technical skills (see Figure 3-1).

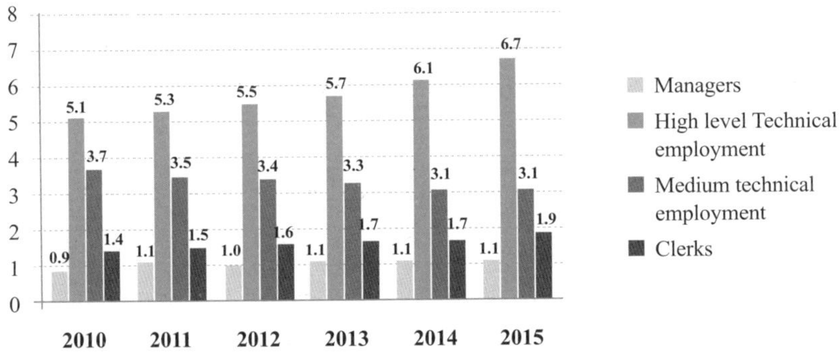

Figure 3-1 Shares of key employment groups by occupations (%)

In terms of training, programs to help managers develop appropriate management skills are scarce. The government introduced a VND119.4 billion program to train employees in small and middle sized enterprises (including SOEs) for the 2004-2010 period (Decision No. 143/2004/QD-TTg, 2003). This was a big help for SOEs to increase their competitiveness, but there is still a gap between the current frameworks for AHRD programs and the ideal ones.

3. SOE-General Suggestions and Future Directions

3.1. Integration of HRD and HRM Initiatives

Putting human resources management systems in line with training programs is essential for Vietnam. Commonly, SOEs are having a problem of low motivation for development and growth. To tackle this issue, an idea of meritocracy, which is a system in which rewards and positions are based on employees' ability and performance rather than tenure and socio-economic background, should be established. There are several ways to achieve this. First, a reward system considering the final results of training programs can be established. Second, AHR practitioners should be able to use HRD metrics (e.g., when making a decision like performance evaluation, compensation and promotion, etc.). For example, a rule that candidates for managerial positions should take certain training programs for leadership skills can be put in place.

Legal frameworks and policies are important factors in improving human resources development. Therefore, The Government of Vietnam needs to establish frameworks which could be the ground for establishing and operating a training institute. For example, the government should set up an organization in charge of training (including AHRD programs) for human resources. If each department has limited ideas and resources for AHRD, professional AHRD organizations can help them to concentrate on R&D.

3.2. Development of AHRD Professionals

To execute strategic AHRD, AHR practitioners must take on a proactive role. Being proactive means that AHR problems are anticipated and corrective action begins before the problem occurs, as compared to being reactive, which means responding to an already-existing problem. To construct systems for fostering AHRD practitioners, we suggest a competency model which consists of core competency and sub-activity to perform AHRD. This model is composed of two different types of competency which are "General" competency (i.e., the basic expertise of AHRD practitioners) and "Specific" competency (needed in the context of SOEs). Each competency is composed of related mental or behavioral activities.

3.3. Modification and Implementation of Proven Standardized Programs

The main targets for the AHRD are advanced-level managers who need special training programs related to their jobs and duties. Training programs by position can be defined as 'training programs for each level to improve adequate competency of employee for the position' (Chung, T. S. & Ju, I. J., 2000). The Management Training Program (MTP), originally developed in the U.S. in the 1950s and later adapted to the context of Japan, was introduced to Korea in 1967. MTP is a packaged and modularized training program designed by the application of ISD (Instructional Systems Design) process. This package is composed of development modules for 20 essential management competencies such as accounting, financial management, leadership, innovation and an integrated perspective on organizational decision making. Each module contains a learner manual, instructor manual, and supporting materials such as audio-visual media and worksheets.

MTP itself is a system. All training programs are structured and the results are measurable. The training environment is a pragmatically designed approach designed for small groups of people, normally nine to twelve per group. Maximum time is spent on interactive simulations designed to emulate the real world as near as possible. Also it can be run consistently without arbitrary variations from instructor characteristics. As a generic training program for managers, MTP is designed not only to teach managers about specialized knowledge and skills for managing a specific organization, but also mutual interchange of their opinions and experiences. Packages of standardized contents and materials which are divided by modules could be modified to the specific needs and contexts of Vietnamese SOEs and recombined on focusing the main issues of organizations.

3.4. Moving Target and Co-Evolutionary Approaches

Korean benchmark SOEs are on their own way for evolution. They have made strategic mistakes and tactical errors in their decades-long growth. Comparison and contrast of the AHRD practices of the SOEs in both Korea and Vietnam can be useful for both countries. Future collaborations for the co-evolution of AHRD systems of both countries should be most productive.

III. Case Studies on AHRD in Vietnamese SOEs

Clark (1940) claimed that the main focus of an economy's activity moves from the primary, through secondary and lastly to the tertiary sector as an economy develops. The primary sector of the economy is concerned with the extraction of raw materials. This includes farming, fishery, and mining. The secondary sector produces finished goods through activities like manufacturing, processing and construction. The tertiary sector provides services and activities include both production and exchange. Financial services, service, industry, and retail sales are considered examples of tertiary industries. SOEs in Vietnam comprise thousands of organizational entities representing all industrial segments. For the present study, we need to focus on a few SOEs that represent major types and levels of industries. This industry-representative sample has been carefully and collaboratively selected by Ho Chi Minh National Academy of Politics (HCMA) and Korean researchers.

In this study, we chose three representative SOEs from different industries (coal-mineral mining, IT and banking). The Vietnam National Coal and Mineral Industries group (VINACOMIN), which belongs to the coal-mineral mining industry associated with the primary sector, was chosen for the first analysis. As it provides essential services, VINACOMIN is less susceptible to equitization but also seems less sustainable as an economy develops. The coal-mining industry is fading in the Korean economy in terms of sales, profit, and employment volume. However, its 40 years of developmental history including the birth, growth, maturing, and systematic withdrawal, and the roles of the Korea Coal Corporation (KOCOAL) should provide priceless insights and lessons of a long-term life-cycle model for stage-relevant AHRD strategies of the now burgeoning Vietnamese mining industry.

Vietnam Posts and Telecommunications(VNPT), which belongs to the IT manufacturing and service industry associated with the secondary sector, was chosen for the second analysis. With its industrial characteristics (e.g., a need to catch up with the latest technology), VNPT is expected to implement a partial equitization process to increase its competitiveness. Korea Telecom (KT), one of the largest and most competitive high-tech companies in Korea today, should provide key success factors of AHRD for Vietnamese SOEs, especially for VNPT.

Finally, the Vietnam Bank for Agriculture and Rural Development (Agribank), which belongs to the banking industry related to the tertiary sector, was selected for the final analysis. Nonghyup was prime provider of financial and educational service to the war-torn rural Korean community and played an indispensable role in the success of the Semaul Undong, integrated local development programs which solved the absolute poverty problem within a very short time. The roles and responsibilities of Nonghyup in pre-industrialized Korea were not limited to the economic arena but extended to the social, rural, and even spiritual development of the nation. The unique history of Nonghyup makes it a living role model for the socio-economic development of Vietnam.

1. Coal and mining industry in Vietnam – VINACOMIN

1.1. Overview of Industry

Vietnam has great mineral potential, with more than 5,000 new deposits of 60 different types of minerals and natural resources (coal, bauxite, titanium, iron ore, chromite, oil and gas, copper, gold, phosphate rocks, rare earth, limestone, tungsten). Despite the broad endowment, current annual production is largely focused on only a few core commodities (coal and oil). Further exploration work and downstream industry development are required in order to improve its energy security and maximize the commercial exploitation of other minerals such as bauxite and rare earth.

To step up its mining technologies, especially in the domain of underground coal mining, Vietnam is focusing on the mechanization of pits, pit-propping and coal extraction in order to minimize resource loss, raise labor productivity and improve working conditions as well as industrial safety and hygiene. Replacing and discarding obsolete equipment and technologies are important. Thus, rational waste-discarding technologies are needed in areas where there are underground minerals to be extracted (Australian Trade and Investment Commission., 2015).

1.2. Overview of Organization

1.2.1. Roles

The Vietnam Coal Corporation (VINACOMIN) has been selected as a target for the analysis because it is a state-owned enterprise leading in coal mining in Vietnam and currently has big mining projects. The coal mining industry is an important economic sector in Vietnam and has over 170 years of history. Experiencing periods of up and down, Vietnam's coal industry has been thriving since VINACOMIN was established in 1995. VINACOMIN is one of 11 economic groups in Vietnam, is 100% state-owned and plays an important role in national strategies to ensure effective exploitation of mineral resources (Chuan, L. M., 2011a). VINACOMIN is the major coal producer in Vietnam, accounting for 95% of total coal production. It provides anthracite for the power sector and industries using coal nationwide and worldwide, invests in the development of power plants and in exploration and processing minerals, is involved in the chemical, engineering and construction materials industries, and offers trade support for the main industries of coal and minerals. The company operates within many different sectors such as coal exploitation, processing and selling, explosive and cement production, shipbuilding, automobile manufacturing, tourism, hotels, financing, services and power generation in thermal power plants.

VINACOMIN is pursuing innovation of structure and management in order to improve operational efficiency, choosing the strategy of developing diversified businesses based on coal operation under the motto "sustainable development of coal industry in Vietnam" (Chuan, L. M., 2011b).

1.2.2. Foundation

The Vietnam National Coal-Mineral Industries Group (formerly Vietnam National Coal Corporation) was established on October 10, 1994. Implementing an important task assigned by the State, right from the time it came into being, the Group set up a plan for "innovation of structure and management in order to improve operational efficiency", choosing the strategy of "developing diversified businesses based on coal operation" and the policy of "growing with customers and partners" (VINACOMIN, 2015a).

1.2.3. Demographics of employees

Ninety-five percent of the labor force in the Vietnamese coal mining industry is employed by VINACOMIN. The rest work in the steel corporation and local coal mines. Due to the development of the coal mining industry, the labor force in this industry has increased. (Nguyen, T. H. N., & Kretschmann, J., 2013). Figure 3-2 presents the labor force in the coal industry.

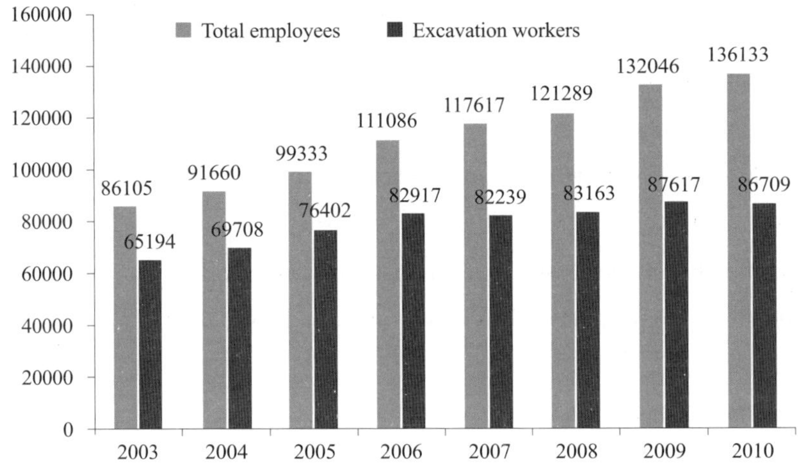

Figure 3-2 Total employees and excavation workers of the Vietnamese coal mining industry (Synchronized data from VINACOMIN from 2003 to 2010)

1.3. AHR features of VINACOMIN

1.3.1. VINACOMIN Business School (VBS)

With the mission "For the Success of the Learners, for the Development of the Enterprises", staff and employees of VBS determined to strive for unity and innovation in training of managers for the coal industry – Vietnam mineral in the renovation period and the international economic integration.

1.3.2. Issues of general AHR

HR issues of VINACOMIN are presented in Table 3.2 (VBS, 2014a):

Table 3-1 Issues related to AHR in VINACOMIN

Function	Training the enterprise manager according to the plan and strategy of VINACOMIN
	Carrying out scientific research in the field of economy-management and training
	Providing training, scientific research, management consulting and other services
	International cooperation in the field of training and scientific research on management
Task	Training the senior management according to the plan for the member companies that belong to VINACOMIN
	Training and updating knowledge to improve the qualifications, professional and leadership skills and work skills for the senior management and professional managers of the VINACOMIN member companies
	Training in foreign languages and information technology for the senior management and professional managers of the VINACOMIN member companies
	Training according to management subject for the senior management and professional managers of the member companies
	Training of administration management, economic management for professional managers, party managers, trade union, organizations of the VINACOMIN member companies.
	Implementing training services, conferences, seminars, scientific research, management consulting and other services according to customer needs.

1.3.3. AHR for advanced-level managers in VINACOMIN

VINACOMIN offers various training program for managers, including Office Management, Storage Management, Policy System, Financial Management and Cost Management etc. (VBS, 2014b)

2. ICT industry in Vietnam – VNPT

2.1. Overview of Industry

The government's strategy for the information and communications sector (ICT) is generally considered to have been well designed, with clear objectives to be achieved through relatively detailed policy instruments and focused projects. An important success factor of the ICT industry is market liberalization. At present, ICT markets are competitive, with multiple ISPs, software and hardware vendors and several mobile phone networks. The use of computers and telecommunication devices is widespread, popular and available at relatively low cost. Currently, telecommunication is the only decreasing item in Vietnam's monthly consumer price index. Several Vietnamese ICT companies have invested actively in neighboring countries as well as in Africa and Latin America (Anh, N. T. T., Duc, L. M., & Chieu, T. D., 2014).

All the telecom markets in the world now focus on value-added services. In the context of ARPU (Average Revenue Per Unit) reduction and low profit, a concession of 50% of the total revenues of mobile applications to content providers has highlighted the importance of mobile applications in attracting new subscribers and increasing operators' revenues. Some operators have organized mobile programming contests to boost the development of new applications with high quality. This is a first step taken by operators to adapt to the new circumstances (VNPT, 2016b).

2.2. Overview of Organization

2.2.1. Roles and Missions

With more than 90,000 employees, advanced telecommunications infrastructure, a service network that covers all 63 provinces and cities, as well as 67 years of experience, VNPT has always offered the market many modern postal. telecommunications and information technology products and services.

In the areas of telecommunications and information technology, VNPT provides a wide and comprehensive range of products and services, including voice, data, internet, other value-added services deploying an advanced network infrastructure and many IT solutions. By the end of 2012, VNPT was providing services to nearly 10 million landline subscribers, accounting for over 80% of Vietnam's landline market; more than 80 million mobile subscribers, accounting for over 61% of the mobile market; and nearly 3 million subscribers of the broadband Internet services MegaVNN and FiberVNN, equivalent to 64% of the total subscribers in this field. Customer trust will be the driving force that fuels VNPT to continue to offer new value-added products and services with quality at international standards, maintaining VNPT's position as a leading telecommunication/IT service provider in Vietnam.

2.3. AHR features of VNPT

VNPT officially launched an online learning system in 2011 (VNPT, 2016a). This e-learning system applied to the training and development of human resources contributes to the work of VNPT's computerized educational management. This online learning system can contribute to raising the professional qualifications of employees in VNPT (VNPT, 2011). Characteristics and issues of AHR in VNPT are as follows:

i. Lack of high-quality workers and leading experts in telecommunication. There is a paucity of experts in IT and telecom that makes it hard to cope with present challenges and to meet the requirements for future developments.

ii. Lack of young workers with professional qualifications, capability and qualities in the key areas, such as call center, telecommunications and satellites.

iii. Incomplete strategy of AHR development, with short-term, medium-term and long-term goals accompanied by a detailed plan of implementation and source of funding.

iv. Lack of uniformity in implementing the management functions of human resource development. Connection between recruitment, assessment, employment and training lacks coherence, compromising the ultimate goal of improving personnel's capacity and qualifications.

v. Assessment of labor is sometimes superficial and unreliable and thus discourages employees from developing to their full potential. Assessment is not based on scientific measures so as to properly measure the level of competency and fulfillment of assignments.

The training for human resources has several shortcomings. While training coverage is quite good, it sometimes does not come to the right workers since there is no comprehensive, long-term training program. The current training plan is often of a short-term nature and professionalism in training is not yet achieved.

3. Agriculture Banking Industry in Vietnam – Agribank

3.1. Overview of Industry

Vietnam's banking industry has grown tremendously from a mono-banking system to a huge network of banks and financial institutions. Over the past 24 years, the Vietnamese government has initiated many banking reforms to improve the efficiency and competitiveness of the banking system in the country, especially via the equitization of its state-owned banks. Nevertheless, the state remains the controlling stakeholder of these state-owned banks, holding at least 65% ownership in them.

The central bank's industrial and commercial lending department was converted to the Vietnam Industrial and Commercial Bank (formerly Incombank, now Vietinbank), its agricultural department to the Vietnam Bank for Agriculture and Rural Development (Agribank), its international trade department to the Bank for Foreign Trade of Vietnam (Vietcom bank), and its infrastructure department to the Bank for Investment and Development of Vietnam (BIDV). Currently, the SBV's role is narrowed to that of a central bank which includes the formulation of monetary policies, management of foreign exchange reserves, and licensing and supervision of credit institutions, a term that encompasses commercial banks, while its financial intermediation functions which include funds mobilization and allocation were shifted to commercial banks (APRACA, 2016).

The main activity driving the banking industry in Vietnam is commercial banking. There are currently 5 state-owned commercial banks, 33 joint stock commercial banks, 5 joint venture banks and 5 wholly foreign-owned banks. State-owned commercial banks are 100% or majority-owned by the government. Joint stock commercial banks have a more diversified shareholder structure which consists of public and private shareholders as well as other government-affiliated organizations. State-owned commercial banks hold a significant stake in the industry, with an estimate of 44.1% of total assets in the banking industry in Vietnam. Joint stock commercial banks followed closely behind, with 42.2% of the total assets in the banking system in the country. Nevertheless, charter capital for joint stock commercial banks is higher compared to state-owned commercial banks, with 43.8% of total charter capital in the industry compared to 30.8% of total charter capital for state-owned commercial banks (Tran, B. T., Ong, B., & Weldon, S., 2015).

3.2. Overview of Organization

3.2.1. Position of Agribank

Agribank is the agricultural department of the Vietnam Bank for Agriculture and Rural Development of the central bank's industrial and commercial lending departments. There are currently five state-owned commercial banks in Vietnam, four of which are the largest banks in Vietnam. These four banks include Agribank, CTG, BIDV and VCB; together they hold more than a third of the total combined assets in the industry. Agribank is the leading and largest commercial bank in Vietnam, with operating networks of around 2,400 branches and units nationwide and VND700 trillion in assets as of December 2013. The bank plays an important role in developing the agricultural and rural economy of Vietnam. As of the end March 2013, loans for agriculture and rural sectors totaled VND324 trillion, and Agribank provided nearly 70% of these loans (Tran, B. T., Ong, B., & Weldon, S., 2015).

3.2.2. History of Development

The Vietnam Bank for Agriculture and Rural Development (known as Agribank) was founded under Government Resolution No. 53/HDBT, dated March 26, 1988 on the establishment of universal banks providing financial services to not only the agricultural and rural sector but also a variety of economic fields. Agribank's operation is aimed at agricultural and rural development.

On November 14, 1990, Vietnam's Prime Minister signed Decision No. 400/CT, which gave birth to the Vietnam Bank for Agriculture (VBA). VBA is a multi-economic field business bank, with the focus on agricultural and rural development. On November 15, 1996, as authorized by the Prime Minister, the Governor of the State Bank of Vietnam signed Decision No. 280/QD-NHNN to change the name of the VBA to the Vietnam Bank for Agriculture and Rural Development, also called Agribank (APRACA, 2016).

Agribank is a state-owned commercial bank that operates under the Law on Credit Institutions and under the State Bank of Vietnam's supervision. With the new name, Agribank now carries out new functions apart from those of a commercial bank. Agribank provides medium- and long-term credit to build infrastructure for agriculture, forestry and fishery, which contribute to rural and agricultural development as well as industrialization and modernization processes (APRACA, 2016).

3.2.3. Demographics of employees

As of December 31, 2012, Agribank had 37,945 employees, 77% of which had bachelor and higher degrees. In 2012, Agribank recruited 1,772 new employees. Out of its total employees, 27% are under 30 years of age, 55% at ages from 31 to 50, and 18% aged from 51 to 60 (Agribank, 2012).

3.3. AHR Features of Agribank

HRD in agricultural industry and rural development has been one of the major tasks for AHRD in Vietnam. With more than 70% of unskilled people of working age in the rural areas, development may be unsustainable, preventing Vietnam's further economic development. The Party and State have launched a broad social program for agriculture and rural development. The core program is to develop human resources in rural areas and in the agricultural industry. Beginning now and until 2020, TVET must play a major role and train at least one million personnel per year to be semi-skilled or skilled workers who are able to work as professional farm, industrial and service workers. The program needs funding of around USD2 billion (Kim, J. I., Kim, D., Nam, I. C., Kim, M. J., & Lee, H., 2011).

Training programs specific to Agribank were designed based on the needs of employees and the labor use units. Training management methods have been renewed to attract more participants, with high average attendance of 81%. The Agribank Training School was established November20, 2010. In 2012, it organized 41 classes for 5,132 employees throughout the Agribank network. Topics included international payment, Internal Payment and Customer Accounting System(IPCAS), money laundering, credit card business, training for newly recruited staff, etc. Agribank's units (departments, representative offices and branches) also provided training for 113,048 employees. With the training activities, Agribank enhanced its staff qualifications for better contributions to the bank efficiency in the context of competition and integration (Agribank, 2012).

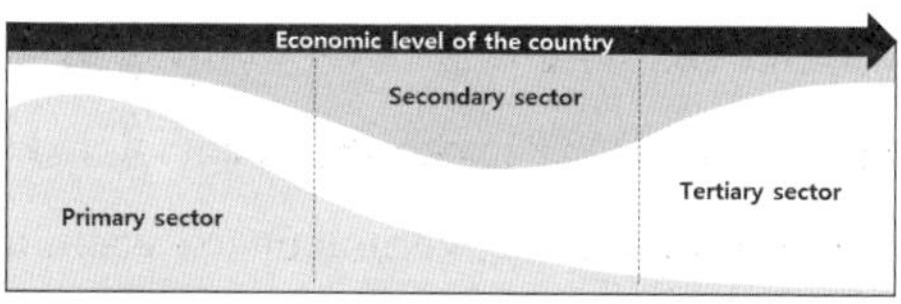

Selected SOE	VINACOMIN	VNPT	AGRIBANK
Industry	•Coal Mining industry	•ICT (manufacturing/service) industry	•Agriculture Banking industry
Status/Roles	•A state-owned enterprise leading in coal mining	•A state-owned enterprise operating in the area of telecommunication and post	•A state-owned bank for Agriculture and Rural Development
Features about HR	•High demand for know-how in efficient resource management •A huge shortage of skilled labor •Lack of safety standards	•Lack of high quality workers •Missing of a complete strategy of HRD •Lack of uniformity in the implementation of the management functions of HRD	•Weaknesses in management systems •No overall research about Asset and Liability Management (ALM) •On-demand training programs

Figure 3-3 Outline of Case Studies on AHRD in Vietnamese SOEs

IV. Lessons from the Korean Experience

In response to the need for economic development in Vietnam, this chapter shares the roles of government and experiences of AHRD development processes in Korea as it achieved dramatic economic development to solve the chronic problems of SOEs. From the ashes of years of war which brought social and economic disasters, Korea has grown into a leading nation remarkable for its high-tech industry. This was done because consistent and powerful AHRD was conducted nationally through central education institutions such as the Korea Productivity Center (KPC) and proven training systems such as the Management Training Program (MTP) with the financial and technical help of foreign donors. The vigorous 5-year government-led economic development plan required manpower and dedicated managers, and Korean AHRD successfully completed its mission to meet national priority needs. Although the conditions of Korea of that time are not perfectly matched with those of Vietnam today, as they share similar contexts, the Korean experience may be a visible and available model for Vietnam.

This chapter provides empirical suggestions for SOEs in three representative industries in Vietnam, paralleling them with three corporations in the same industries in Korea: Korea Coal Corporation (KOCOAL) in the coal industry, Korea Telecom (KT) in the IT industry and Nonghyup in the agriculture and banking industry. By analyzing the AHRD development procedures and AHRD systems through changes in Korea, implications can be drawn for SOEs in Vietnam.

1. Development of Economy and AHRD in Korea

1.1. Government-led economic development plan and AHRD

1.1.1. Government-led AHRD as a key driver behind economic growth in Korea

Figure 3-4 shows the growth rates of several countries between 1960 and 1980. Different speeds of human capital accumulation among countries are the main variable that could explain the differences in real economic growth rates. Government-led AHRD led to accumulation of human capital and contributed to economic development (Lucas, R. E., 1988).

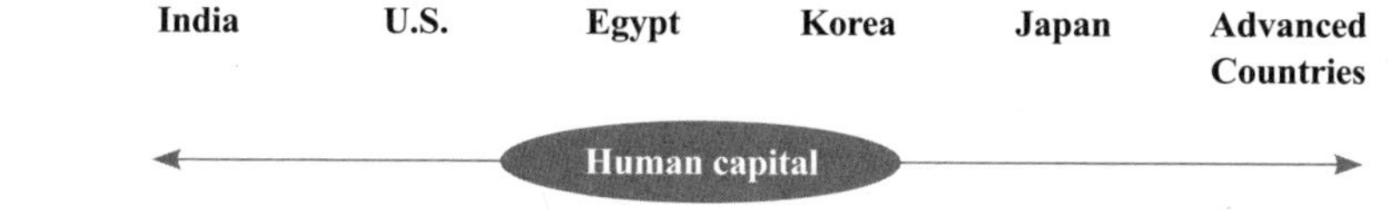

Figure 3-4 Real economic growth rates between 1960 and 1980

In particular, government-led education and vocational training policy are two main factors made Korea's successful catching-up economy (ILO, 2008).

1.1.2. Momentum for State-dominated AHRD

In 1962, the Korean government began promoting annual economic and business development plans. In 1967, vocational training law was established and full-fledged vocational training began in the country. This training was based on the awareness of the importance of developing human resources because it was anticipated that there would be increase of demand for manpower by expansion of industrial society and economic development. Furthermore, developing human resources, which needs long time, should be propelled parallel with industrial development. Existing unemployment prevention education and apprenticeship systems were insufficient for creating supply of workers, and institutional strategy was needed for active fostering of skilled manpower by employers (Appendix 1).

1.1.3. Legislation and performance agency

By legislating vocational training law and enlarging and regularizing vocational training, the Korean Ministry of Labor established a vocational training office and put vocational training departments and skill examination departments into its infrastructure to maintain systems for conducting vocational training plan. Afterward, as vocational training and active promoting of international cooperative projects expanded, training organization was enhanced several times (Appendix 1).

1.1.4. Contents of legislation

Vocational training was divided into in-plant vocational training and public vocational training. According to the Vocational Training Act in 1966, Vocational Training Management Corporation was founded and it implemented public vocational training. Public vocational training was in line with Science and Technology Human Resource policy in Korea in 1960s. This includes using facilities in state-owned enterprises or private enterprises for training, focusing on short-term skill training programs and moral education, making fundamental guidelines for technical education and providing certificates and licenses, and doing some research on methods for technical education. Based on this, policies to develop human resources in science and technology were made by using a variety of national institutes and facilities. Details are shown in Appendix1.

1.1.5. Training institution establishment

The Central Vocational Training Center as the centerpiece of vocation training institutions was founded to foster technicians, training instructors and a basic frame for vocational training institutions. It was formed through international cooperation between Korea and the Germany Busan Public Vocational Training Center and rural manpower was fostered through the Saemaeul Movement(SMU) in rural vocational training centers (Appendix 1)

Before Korea achieved independence as a fledging nation, it had accepted Western civilization through the influence of Japan. After Korea became independent as a fledgling nation in the mid-1950s, the intellectual basis for the detailed knowledge and productivity movement for economic modernization, corporate management and industry management had been adopted mainly from America and Japan. A group of intellectuals and entrepreneurs who was the main agents of productivity movement, observed high productivity of industries in developed countries such as U.S. and Japan. Lee(1980), who founded the Korea Productivity Center (KPC), focused productivity as the key factor to bring differences in outcomes of corporate management. Because he witnessed Japan had established Japan Productivity Center(JPC) in 1955 and the productivity movement which was enacted around JPC. KPC's basis of establishment was on Industry Development Law and it was launched as a special corporation. KPC was assigned the function of leading productivity improvement of the country.

1.2. Conversion to Meritocracy

SOEs in Korea have gone through a cultural conversion to meritocracy. Meritocracy is a political philosophy holding that power should be vested in individuals almost exclusively based on ability and talent. In March 2016, the Korean Ministry of Strategy and Finance provided proposal of recommendations to improve the ability and performance of employees in public enterprises or quasi-government organizations. Many of Public institutions in which competition within the organization is little and job stability is high have low possibility for management inefficiency, therefore they need to set up effective result management systems. The purpose of the Ministry's proposal was to improve organization productivity and establish a fair personnel system that supports the ability and performance improvement of employees in public institutions which have a performance-oriented culture.

First of all, the proposal provided standards for legitimacy of dismissals which are caused by lack of job performance, poor work performance and so forth. It is required to promote personnel and organizational performance improvement through providing opportunities for adaptation in managing poor performers, education rather than dismissal and relocation, etc. At first, the regulations of employment and collective agreement would be regulated. Objectivity of valuation basis, suitability of contents of evaluation, validity of evaluation methods and opening evaluation result for objective and fair assessment should be carry out. The employee can only be dismissed if, after providing education, training opportunity and relocation to suitable work, he or she does not improve or causes trouble at work.

2. Target Corporations in Korea

2.1. Coal and mining industry in Korea – KOCOAL

VINACOMIN is the leading coal and mineral mining industry in Vietnam. Coal and mineral mining is one of the important economic sectors of Vietnam. VINACOMIN is pursuing innovation of its structure and management practices in order to improve operational efficiency under the motto of "sustainable development of the coal industry in Vietnam". In addition, VINACOMIN is working for global cooperation and providing educational services for its members.

In terms of industry life cycle, coal and mining industry in Vietnam is in the growth stage. The situation VINACOMIN is facing is very similar to that of Korea in the 1970s. During this period, Korean employees went to Japan to learn new knowledge and skills in mining. Now the Korean coal and mineral mining industry is dying, so the people in the industry are searching for a way to adapt to this challenge. KOCOAL could be a good model for VINACOMIN in that they share common features.

2.1.1. Overview of industry

As shown in Figure 3-5 , Korean coal production has declined drastically in the last 25 years, with many coal mines closing. Coal production has declined 91% from its peak in the late 1980s. Currently, Korea produces only anthracite, importing all its bituminous requirements.

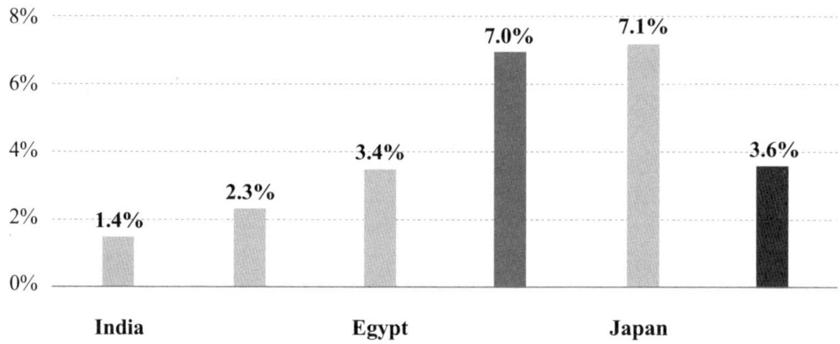

Figure 3-5 Korea's Coal Production (million tons)

Korea has five anthracite coal mines, three of which are operated by the state-owned Korea Coal Corporation (KOCOAL). KOCOAL is also examining production opportunities abroad and developing a mine in the Uvs province of Mongolia. This represents a significant decrease from the 347 mines in operation in 1988, a result of the government's policy of rationalizing domestic coal production. Production of coal in Korea is subsidized by the government, and the cost of production is higher than the cost of imports. Nevertheless, the government intends to stabilize supply and demand for anthracite coal, maintaining a minimum annual production volume, given that it is the nation's only natural energy resource. According to the Korean government's green growth policy and the G-20 initiative to abolish fossil fuel subsidies, the government has gradually reduced subsidies in the coal sector. They will come to an end in 2020. The main subsidy was for the production of coal and its use in the form of charcoal briquettes by low-income households. The subsidy covers briquette manufacturers, industrial accident insurance premiums, and school expenses for children of mine workers. Coal consumption in Korea increased by 55% between 2005 and 2012, driven primarily by growing demand from the electric power sector, which accounts for 62% of the country's coal consumption. Although the share of liquefied natural gas in power generation in Korea has increased rapidly, gas is a relatively expensive energy source for power generation. This gives coal a relative cost advantage over gas in the power generation sector. However, expected additions to the coal - fired power plant fleet are modest in the midterm and thus much of the growth in coal imports is expected to come from the industry sector, largely iron and steel production, which consumed approximately 12% of coal in 2010 (Global Methane Initiative, 2015).

2.1.2. Overview of Organization

2.1.2.1. Roles

The purpose of establishing KOCOAL was to advance quality of life and promote public welfare through the stable supply of coal by developing coal mines and managing coal production, process, sales, and accompanied business, on the basis of Article 1, Korea Coal Corporation Law (KOCOAL, 2016a). Since its foundation in 1950, KOCOAL has been contributing to the development of the nation and the advancement of quality of life through the stable supply of coal resources. To complete its mission, KOCOAL produced 180 million tons of coal until 2009, which is a remarkable achievement for the nation's sole government-owned coal corporation (KOCOAL, 2016d). The history of KOCOAL is provided in Appendix 2.

2.1.3. AHR features of KOCOAL

2.1.3.1. Establishment of Training Center

After the liberation of Korea from Japan, the domestic coal industry faced a severe labor shortage. Improving equipment and labor was crucial. For this reason, KOCOAL established a Skill-Training Center in 1957. Skilled laborers from this training center became leaders in developing private coal mines after the 1960s.

• History of AHR systems

1. Period 1: 1957 ~ 1994

In this period, training programs for mine workers were implemented. At first, employees in managerial positions were chosen and the training modules covered working on ground consolidation and health and safety regulations. However, as the number of training programs grew, more employees were able to be educated. The specific training programs by period are as follows:

- 1959: Training programs for the new employees were established and implemented.
- 1960: Programs to cover health and safety regulations were implemented.
- April 1964: Management Training Program (MTP) program was implemented, with 280 managers participating in the first program.

- May 1967: With the enactment of the Vocational Training Act, Korea's vocational training policy was formally introduced. With this system, the company was able to train employees and have a skilled workforce for the future.
- July 1967: Development of a KOCOAL Training Center began by obtaining authorization from the Ministry of Labor.
- 1969: Multiple programs for each level of employees including managers were initiated.

2. Period 2: 2013~2014

The institution downscaled organizations of the head office and mining station through organizational diagnosis with TF, the center for efficient operating manpower. Personnel expenses and debts were reduced and excess manpower was trimmed, promoting layoffs and field-centered manpower distribution. In this process, manpower was downsized in the core field of growing industry sector.

Abolishing the disparity with college graduates in recruiting and promoting new employees with a high school diploma, KOCOAL tried to break down the diploma-centered customs of personnel management system. Also the company adopted an evaluation system for level of difficulty to set reasonable goals. However, the standard for rating the degree of work difficulty was somewhat subjective, so sharing of evaluating methods among colleagues is needed. Result of organizational and personnel evaluation pursue to reflect appropriately for wages and personnel matters, whereas the systematic approach in management programs for low performers and additional compensation system besides official wages for high performers.

3. Period 3: 2015~2016

HR issues of KOCOAL are presented in Table 3-5 (KOCOAL, 2016c)

Table 3-2 Current Issues of AHR in KOCOAL

Detailed tasks	Current Issues of AHR	
	2015	2016
Job analysis	• Compensating job analysis • Managing mid-term organizational and workforce planning • Updating job analysis to reflect new duties	• Continuing job analysis • Conducting job analysis for new jobs • Re-estimating proper number of people to reflect industrial environmental change
Organizing	• Organizational design reflecting strategies/core business/ environmental changes • Enhancing coal production and safety managing organizations • Strengthening supply management through adjusting jobs • Strengthening implementation for current issues and government policies • Founding growth engine organization	• Constructing organizations appropriate for strategy achievement • Resetting core business to reflect changes in the environment • Expanding the number of employees in core business departments • Restructuring organization and personnel workforce-associated strategies
Delegation and adjusting jobs	• Adjusting jobs to reflect reorganization and environment change • Applying business change for organizational units reflecting reorganization • Revising work division with establishment/abolition/ adjustment	• Enlarge delegation • Expanding delegation provisions and authority to reflect reorganization • Continuously collecting opinions about work, able to delegate efficiently

Hiring and fostering system	• Conducting consultation for NCS-based ability-centered recruitment • Enlarging socially equal recruitment for men of national merit and the challenged • Examining vitalization methods for core skill human resources	• Enforcing NCS-based skills centered hiring • Enhancing socially equal recruitment for men of merit and the challenged • Providing vitalization methods for core skill human resources
Human resource management	• Analyzing current conditions and effectiveness of ability and performance-based personnel recruitment and management program for low performers • Managing introduction of effective career development program (CDP) • Enlarging flexible workplace	• Training key experts, thematic education, strengthening performance management • Supplementing introduction of effective career development program (CDP) • Reinforcing operation of flexible workplace
Personnel evaluation	• Frequent monitoring for personnel evaluation process • Enlarging measurement of the goal setting ratio, enhancing assessor-assessed evaluation interviews and reinforcing education for fair assessment	• Renewal for core competencies system • Increasing acceptance rate of achievement assessment for inducing outcome creation, enhancing assessor education for fair evaluation, connecting with personnel systems and increasing application of evaluation result
Core expert nurturing program	• Developing and enlarging future-oriented professional training programs • Expanding ability development program for women managers • Continuous reinforcement of special leadership development process • Expanding education for people in promotion list	• Reinforcing members' abilities by conducting future growth-related special programs • Increasing the number of in-company instructors • Enhancing education related to future business strategy • Fostering education for leaders of the next generation (energy leader, etc.)
Thematic education program	• Introducing training courses for high performers • Introducing women's talent development program • Introducing specialized in-company instructor course	

Enhancing performance-based system	• Management training for high performers • Performance-based corporate culture (training courses for high performers, etc.) • Introducing incentive system for license acquisitions	• Management training for low performers • Improving competence, conducting programs for improvement of job ability • Establishing CDP-based education system
Public specialized program	• Continuous expanding of training programs in cyber-training institutes • Certification courses, management, leadership, professional job field, etc.	• Expanding innovation lectures Developing programs for benchmarking, business innovation, self-improvement, developing a CS mindset • Enlarging in-company instructor development programs • Placing in-company professional instructors

2.1.4. Implications for VINACOMIN

VINACOMIN needs not only infrastructure but also quality human resources to improve its competitiveness. For this, human resources development, especially increasing advanced-level managers' competencies is needed, especially. VINACOMIN Business School is a unit directly under the VINACOMIN providing training programs for the employees. Although it has provided a variety of training programs employees, but there is a growing need to develop better training programs for the managers. To provide suggestions for VINACOMIN, the case of KOCOAL is suitable. KOCOAL has worked to strengthen its performance management and evaluation systems. Following KOCOAL's example, VINACOMIN should try to construct systematic performance improvement systems based on assessment of current employees' performance and rational compensation strategies. For low performers, a systematic management program of coaching and consulting based on cause analysis and assessment is needed. For high performers, additional compensation such as position benefits or the opportunity of study abroad is needed. To provide proper training and education programs, VINACOMIN should find the needs of the organization and its members, not only through satisfaction surveys, but also using competency-based questionnaires.

However, these individual programs and policies may not be systemic nor sustainable without institutional and structural reform. Institutional reform includes establishment of a professional AHRD department with clear roles and responsibilities and expert HRD practitioners and policy makers. Structural reform means the development of extensive curriculum or a roadmap that is composed of series of courses and programs. AHRD is a long-term project and cannot be achieved by short-term, isolated interventions. As observed in the case of KOCOAL, development of a competency-based curriculum which identifies and prioritizes the development of interventions should serve as a guiding light to long-term innovation.

2.2. ICT industry in Korea – Korea Telecom (KT)

VNPT provides quality products and services in the telecommunication industry. To meet customers' increasingly diverse needs, VNPT has to innovate and develop its technological capability. Although VNPT has a good educational environment equipped with a high-tech infrastructure such as e-learning systems, advanced and qualified experts in management and systemic AHRD are not available. KT, a leading corporation in the IT industry in Korea, also has needs for sustainable and systemic AHR fostering systems. Thus, we analyze KT's AHR systems and draw implications from them.

2.2.1. Overview of Industry

The Korean ICT industry maintains high competitiveness when measured against advanced countries. It shows a strong export competitiveness in the IT manufacturing sector, where active investments in R&D and infrastructure have borne fruit. However, there have not been sufficient improvements yet in the areas pointed as comparatively vulnerable. Korea has a rather big growth imbalance across the industry sub-sectors, and it still has a long way to go in terms of the qualitative levels of technological innovation, talent training and the labor market environment. Qualitative performances in R&D and venture investments have failed to keep up with quantitative growth. Moreover, Korea may lose its competitive advantages to latecomers who are catching up fast in the areas where it currently commands a strong lead over its competitors. This is already happening as China is beginning to overtake Korea in export values and patent counts for ICT equipment and services. However, Korea's ICT competitiveness remains relatively high and can serve as the foundation for further improvement in the future. Therefore, it is believed that Korea should continuously strive to enhance its competitiveness in the ICT industry with balanced growth policies and countermeasures against risk factors (KISDI, 2015).

2.2.2. Overview of Organization

2.2.2.1. Role

Established as Korea Telecom in 1981, KT is Korea's largest comprehensive communications operator. It merged with its subsidiary, KTF, in 2009 and is leading the smart era by introducing smartphones in Korea. KT focuses its capability in establishing GiGA wire and wireless network infrastructure and differentiating the Media/IT platform by utilizing its core technology. Based on its advanced infrastructure, the company also finds and nurtures ICT convergence service in various industrial sectors (KT, 2015).

2.2.2.2. Mission

The mission of KT is to be 'the best national company that provides the fastest and most innovative ICT-based telecommunications and most innovative ICT-based telecommunications and convergence services for the convenience of customers' (KT, 2015).

2.2.3. AHR Features of KT

2.2.3.1. General AHR system

With the belief that fostering talent leads to corporate competitiveness, KT recruits the best and most talented people to work as the company's exemplary employees who fulfill the basics and principles, communicate continuously to realize customer value, and face challenges with perseverance. The company places recruited employees in suitable positions and assesses their performance using a fair personnel system. KT has also established a corporate culture in which employees can fulfill their potential by completing education based on the company's talent development program. To encourage all members of the company to work together, KT pursues a corporate culture of mutual cooperation and trust so that both management and onsite employees can communicate and cooperate with each other (KT, 2015). Figure 3-3 shows the KT's competitiveness about AHR in 2015(KT, 2015).

Table 3-3 KT's Competitiveness in AHR

Core Competency	Performance Index	
Securing and Maintaining Talent	Average years of continuous service	Male: 18.8 years, Female: 16.9 years
	New employees	208 persons
Fair AHR Policy	Request for objection to assessment result	Reduced by 7% (Number of requests compared to 2013)
Reinforcing Capability of Executives and Employees	Hours of education for each person	50 hours
Balance between Work and Life	Rate of returning to the office after parental leave	Male: 92%, Female: 87%
Communication Management	Satisfaction level for online grievance handling center	4.78 (out of 5)

2.2.3.2. Program for promoting capability of executives and employees

KT provides various and systemic programs to encourage executives and employees to grow into the best KT members they can be, who can find new opportunities for growth and take the lead in the rapidly changing technology environment and intensively competitive communications market.

KT accelerates efforts for change and innovation to become a 'KT for the talent'. With the aim of fostering 'members with initiative and endurance', 'leaders leading change and performance', and 'experts whose performance is recognized in the market', the company has reestablished and implemented three major systems: core value education, leader fostering education, and job expert fostering education. In the education sector, KT as an ICT company has enhanced professionalism and convenience in business by reinforcing the 'Mini Course', a smart mobile program to strengthen timeliness and mobility, and met various executives' and employees' needs for growth by increasing the number of e-learning courses from 187 in 2013 to 1,246 in 2014. Through these efforts, the company saved direct and indirect expenses worth 526 million won, including expenses for business trips by trainees. The company plans to achieve other subsidiary effects of saving a comparable amount in costs in 2015(KT, 2015). Figure 3-6 shows the various programs in KT (KT, 2015).

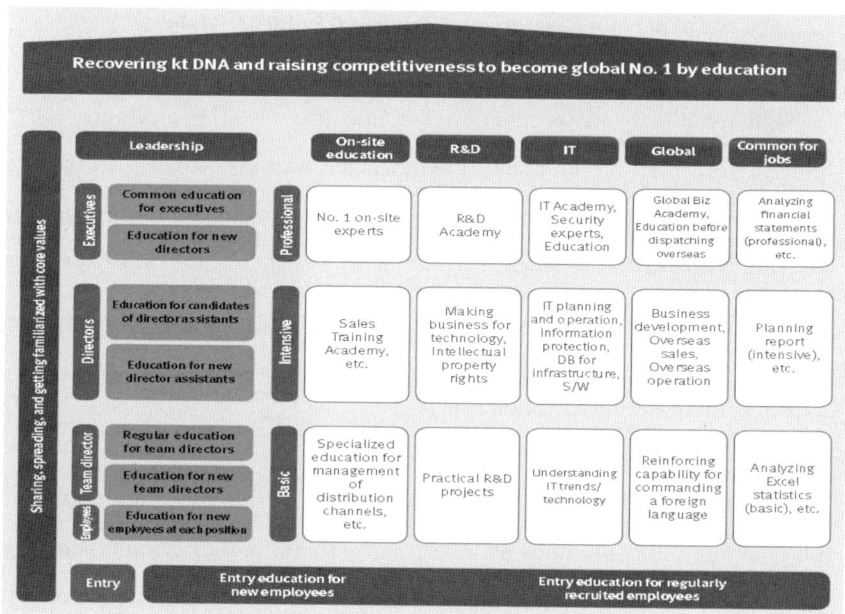

Figure 3-6 Program for Executives and Employees in KT

2.2.3.3. Strengthening on-site education directly leading to business performances

Considering customers as its top priority, KT reinforces on-site education based on on-site cases that directly lead to business performance by addressing discussion-based issues. The company also contributes to improving services by repeating drills until the service quality by employees at customer contact points is improved. To support these efforts, 275 employees were selected as professional lecturers on professionalism and loyalty. These employees carried out on-site education with the aim of sharing and applying know-how (KT, 2015).

2.2.3.4. Continuing and Reinforcing Global and Future Capability

To preemptively foster manpower conducting global projects to realize 'global No.1 KT,' the company has reflected various requests from each business sector. And KT developed and administered 17 customized courses covering business development, overseas sales and conducting on-site projects overseas (KT, 2015).

2.2.3.5. Human Resource Management

KT offers fair wages in accordance with the relevant regulations on job position and continuous service years without any discrimination. The company's current level of remuneration for newly recruited employees is 172% compared to the legal minimum wage.

KT's TM (Talent Market) program, an IT-based open AHR system, was launched in 2009 to allow employees to choose their own assignment and voluntarily begin work. The TM program discloses assignment information that ranges from staffing plans to current status and necessary job qualifications. This improves the transparency of workforce supply and demand and enables KT to promptly assign the right people to the appropriate position. The company encourages employees to reinforce their professionalism and career management by allowing them to move to the appropriate position by considering their work experiences, expertise(KT, 2015).

AHR history for Advanced-Level Managers in KT is as follows;

AS KT finished equitization in 2002, it started a campaign for management innovation, demonstrating its will to show that it would become a more customer-centered and field-centered organization. New plans for training employees were established in response to the changes. Multiple training programs for advanced-level managers were started to improve their competencies.

In 2005, A career development program was initiated as many employees had requested. The program includes outplacement and life-long education for employees over 44 years old to prepare for their retirement.

In 2006, As Korea's telecommunications market reached its saturation point, KT struggled to be the key player in the industry. One of its efforts made was making a new organization called the "Value Innovation Center" to drive innovation and change in the company. The organization was open to new ideas and trends, and advanced-level managers had opportunities to embrace them.

A systematic competency framework with training programs was developed, and new programs transforming the company into a learning organization were initiated in 2007.

In 2009, KT changed its seniority-based pay system into a performance-related pay system and declared an "end of hierarchy" which aimed for flexible environments. It triggered a big change in the organization that motivated everyone to perform at their best.

In 2014, The organizational structure returned to hierarchy, so training programs for each level were started again. Many programs were provided for newly promoted supervisors. KT also implemented training programs for top young talents in order to manage talent effectively and systematically.

2.2.4. Implications for VNPT

To respond to the rapidly changing nature of the IT industry, KT saw management innovation as a crucial point. This is similar to VNPT. Because of the characteristics of the telecommunications industry, it is important to have the capacity to innovate and seize new opportunities.

General management skills have utmost priority in the AHRD reform initiatives of VNPT, since the telecommunications industry is facing strong competition in the domestic and global market and undergoing rapid changes in technologies and customer needs. Technological advancement and efficient manufacturing are necessary conditions to be a player in this hyper competitive market. Timely and market-oriented decision making along with financially efficient AHR operation capability will serve as strategic leverage for VNPT. KT's early experience of development and wide implementation of manager training programs for AHRs and junior managers utilizing internal and external resources should be a practical lesson to learn. E-learning as a primary tool for AHRD initiative should also be recognized. KT has established a good e-learning system as an ICT company and has maintained a high level of satisfaction with its education programs. Its technology-enhanced work environment, computer-friendly organizational culture and technologically savvy employees have facilitated KT's innovative e-Learning system. VNPT, which enjoys similar advantages to KT's and which needs rapid and cost-effective delivery of new ideas and knowledge among employees scattered over a large area, may find huge benefits in AHRD reform. E-learning can be considered a profitable future business of VNPT as well as a tool for internal use. In Korea, and specifically in KT, e-learning has become a rapidly growing knowledge-intensive business. VNPT's know-how and solutions learned from internal use of e-learning for AHRD should serve as valuable business assets in this promising industry.

2.3. Agriculture Banking Industry in Korea – Nonghyup

Agribank is a commercial bank whose focus is rural development. It is the largest bank in Vietnam in terms of capital, assets, workforce, operating network and customer base. The main agenda of Agribank is to implement agricultural modernization. To achieve this, Agribank is utilizing information technology and providing better services and financial products. Since Agribank's services are diverse, experts in diverse industries (agriculture, banking, services etc.) should be part of its operation. In Korea, Nonghyup has had a similar challenge implementing training programs for prospective experts in regional areas. In this study, we will cover the training strategies of Nonghyup and their implications for Korean economic development supporting the Saemaeul Movement (SMU).

2.3.1. Overview of Industry

The Korean banking industry has undergone substantial structural reforms since the 1997 financial crisis. A number of banks merged or exited, and foreign banks were permitted to enter the banking industry. Perhaps most significantly, there have been fundamental changes in the behavior of banks; they are now focusing much more on profitability and competitiveness than they did in the past. They are also assuming an increasingly important role as comprehensive asset managers. The structural and managerial reform effort has indeed improved banks' solvency and profitability. Banks have performed better in nearly every respect and in a relatively short period of time. There has been especially marked improvement in productivity, risk management, and business process innovation. The long-held belief that "banks never fail because the government will bail them out" has nearly faded away completely. People in the financial sector are beginning to consider their occupation separately from their workplace. There has been considerable progress in financial opening and liberalization with an eye toward efficiency. Korea is widely acknowledged to possess qualified human resources in the financial industry who have a mastery of the latest information technology in addition to a high level of competence in taking on broad changes in global industry trends. It is primarily thanks to these resources that banks have been able to stage a remarkable turnaround and revitalize their management so efficiently after the crisis. The financial industry is a high value-added industry with great potential to create jobs and to grow quickly. Now is the time to capitalize on the progress that has been made thanks to the reforms. Banks must continue to improve efficiency and sharpen their competitive edge if they hope to prosper in the fiercely competitive global market.

2.3.2. Overview of Organization

2.3.2.1. History/Background of Nonghyup

In 1907, the Korean government accepted the proposal of a Japanese financial advisor to establish a local financial cooperative based on Kye, which is a traditional Korean mutual aid organization. The Local Financial Cooperative was renamed the Financial Cooperative in 1918. It featured urban financial Cooperatives for small and medium-sized industrial business customers, ordinary people and the Do-federations as a local united organization. It soon became a nationwide organization covering both urban and rural areas.

The movement for Agricultural Cooperatives by the private sector was carried out since 1920s and it was recognized by young people who expected construction of a new nation as an important mission. The successful nationwide organization for the Agricultural Cooperative campaign owes much to such social capital already formed.

Korea was liberated from Japan on August 15, 1945 but the US Armed Forces and the Soviet Armed Forces made an entry into Korea for the reason of disarmament of Japanese Military Forces. This resulted in the separation of Korea into South Korea and North Korea. In 1948, the Korean government was established but the Korean War lasted for 3 years and devastated the entire land and the economy of Korea. North Korea invaded South Korea on June 25, 1950, two years later. The Korean War ended with the Armistice Agreement on July 27, 1953. During the war that lasted for three years, more than three million people died and the fighting effectively destroyed industrial facilities and most cities. The Korean War further hampered reunification into one nation in addition to the huge loss of lives and destruction properties. The Korean War is currently under cease-fire.

In 1970s, the Saemaeul Movement (SMU) was launched by the Korean government to stimulate the economic development of Korea. SMU was an initiative based on the idea of self-governing and collaboration of farmers as a way to improve living conditions. The government assessed outcomes in order to give incentives to successful villages. This incited inter-village competition and spread SMU all over the country in a short time. Thus small financial support by the government significantly changed entire rural districts. The Agricultural Cooperatives were the center of the SMU. The most important key to continuing SMU was to train leaders, and the Agricultural Cooperatives were in charge of this. It also constructed income associating systems for town units, expanded the capability of association members, improved the education system and nurtured a cooperative organization system for Saemaeul village. The governance structure of the Ri-Dong Agricultural Cooperatives, the Shi-Gun Cooperatives and the specialized Agricultural Cooperatives in the Agricultural Cooperative Act in 1958 and the Agricultural Cooperative Act in 1961 was made to follow the principle of Cooperatives while the government controlled the governance structure of the Nonghyup Such selection by the Korean government was negatively evaluated in terms of self-regulation and damaged the identity of the Cooperatives but was based on the calculations of the situation that a voluntary and self-help organization of Cooperatives by farmers was not expected. The Agricultural Cooperatives made steady progress while expanding business with legal and institutional protection and the support of the government. Meanwhile, the Agricultural Cooperatives participated in the Green Revolution for self-sufficiency of food in the 1970s and led SMU, which is a rural development initiative, to further enhance the close relationship with the government. The government could effectively enforce, monitor and supervise policies even in rural districts through the Agricultural Cooperatives.

The strategy for operating the Agricultural Cooperative system, which focused on cooperation between the government and the Agricultural Cooperatives, can be a good lesson to developing countries that have similar issues. It should be noted that dependence of the Agricultural Cooperatives on the financial support of the government might potentially result in a negative effect of too much financial burden rather than improving the policy effect. It is necessary to also fully contemplate the opposite side effect that such a system may impede the normal development of Cooperatives with respect to self-help, independence and self-regulation thereof (Park. *et al*., 2012).

2.3.2.2. Roles and Missions

Nonghyup has three major roles of (Nonghyup, 2016):

Supporting Education: Nonghyup carries out training for cooperative members to enhance their rights and interests and promotes new technologies related to the R&D of both improved and new crop breeds.

Economic section: Nonghyup supports various marketing and supply initiatives concerning production, distribution, and consumption so that farmers may devote their time and energy to farming activities. The marketing and supply business is generally divided into agriculture and livestock sectors and focuses on boosting rural household incomes and decreasing production costs via the expansion of the agricultural and livestock product markets.

Financial Services: Nonghyup's aim is to obtain funds and profits requisite for the successful implementation of its activities and to provide differentiated financial services, including credit cards, insurance, cooperative banking, foreign exchange, stock, etc.

2.3.3. AHR Features of Nonghyup

2.3.3.1. Extension Service for Training Staff

As the management basis of the Primary Agricultural Cooperatives stabilized and business expanded in the early 1970s, there was a request for systematic, high-quality training to improve the practical business ability of the Primary Agricultural Cooperatives and the specialized Agricultural Cooperatives. During the period from 1976 to 1980, more Do-based training facilities were constructed in each region, and the previous Gun-based training was abolished in 1978.Table 3.4 shows the outcome of mid-and long-term training according to the extension service for training staffs for 20 years from 1961 to 1980.

Table 3-4 Outcome of Extension Service for Training ACK staffs (1961~1980)

(Unit: persons)

	1961~1965	1966~1970	1971~1975	1976~1980	1961~1980 Total
NACF-based training	7,722	6,911	12,057	14,489	41,179
Do-based training	10,917	12,973	38,309	41,679	103,878
Gun-based (B)	228,023	97,664	110,029	12,119	447,835
Total	246,662	117,548	160,395	68,287	592,892
Share of Gun-based training (B/A, %)	92.4	83.1	68.6	17.7	75.5

2.3.3.2. Qualities of AHR management for employee education in Nonghyup

According to the training place or methods, Nonghyup conducts institute training, commissioned education, study abroad and other educational programs.

ⅰ. Collective training

(ⅰ) Rank by process

- Normal half-courses: Employees in level 5 or lower
- Advanced half-course: Employees in level 4
- Administrator courses: Employees in level 3
- Senior management course: Employees in level 2 or higher

(ⅱ) Specific functional process: Employees in the certain sectors

(ⅲ) Special Courses: Employees in special sector or etc.

ⅱ. Commissioned Education

In order to acquire the knowledge and skills necessary for performance in the field or in closely related business, employees are commissioned by the professional staff at schools and educational institutions in the country.

iii. Study Abroad

To acquire the knowledge and experience which are necessary to perform the job, send employees to study abroad and to receive training in the field (Kim, J. H., 2005).

2.3.4. Implications for Agribank

Agribank does not seem to conduct systematic, continuous education and training that covers new employees, middle managers and executives, though it has adopted specific centralized training for performance improvement in such topics as international payment, IPCAS (financial systems), money laundering, credit cards business and training for newly recruited staff. The early system Nonghyup used can be adopted in the manner of government-led approaches. Nonghyup had divided the country into small and large units in a hierarchy. Eventually, this division gave each regional area the responsibility for autonomous education and training from small regional units to large ones. It is important to consider whether the country and its society are ready for a self-regulated hierarchy. In Nonghyup's case, it was much more effective and efficient for regions and their farmers to be controlled by the government rather than to have autonomous power at first because they did not have enough capital, knowledge, and attitude to see to themselves. With deficient economic and social structural conditions which are typically considered for developing countries, the very first step may be to turn to the government to enact stable, powerful and integrated approaches (Park *et al*., 2012).

The development of Nonghyup with SMU can be good model for stepwise empowerment. Autonomous, independent actions and rights can be practiced only after the moral and socio-economic infrastructures are set. The goal of SMU training was to achieve mutual dependence based on the belief that if there is no motivation for independence and then there will be no achievement. SMU training was meant to inspire the goal to identify the belief through presentation of cases and small group discussion. Participants returned to their villages to implement the outcome of training. This training scheme was rapidly diffused throughout the country. This developed into a nationwide movement with parallel promotion of rural SMU, urban SMU and enterprise SMU (Park *et al*., 2012). Both socio-economic innovation with a 5-year economic development plan and moral innovation with SMU paved the way for stable conditions for economic development as well as preparation for accepting democratization. In other words, the government laid the foundation for equitization with standardized training and education which fostered leaders' ability to self-regulate in each regional unit. Eventually, local self-governmental and democratic education in agricultural development as well as increased regional competitiveness would be expected by practical implementation and management which would be operated autonomously by each regional unit.

Although Vietnam has a socialist economic system, there is a need for equitization of SEOs. Nonghyup's democratic and independence-fostering decentralization method can be effective for applying capitalist economic principles in Vietnam.

The suggestions for Vietnam HR so far can be summarized as table below.

Table 3-5 Target Corporations in Korea

Linked Vietnam SOEs	VINACOMIN	VNPT	AGRIBANK
Selected Korean Corporation	대한석탄공사 KOCOAL	kt KT	NH NongHyup NONGHYUP
Industry	•Coal Mining industry	•ICT industry	•Agriculture Banking industry
Status/History	•State-owned company (1950~)	•State-owned company (1981~1993) •Private company (2002~)	•National Agricultural Cooperative Federation (1961~)
Roles	•Developing coal mines and managing coal production	•Providing ICT-based telecommunications	•Promoting a balanced development of the national economy
Implications for HR	•Implementing Management Training Programs •Training key experts, thematic education •Strengthening performance management and evaluation systems	•Regarding the management innovation as a crucial point •Establishing good e-learning system •IT-based open HR system	•A nationwide movement with parallel promotion of rural Saemauel movement •Extension Service for Training Staffs •Local self-governmental and democratic education for agricultural development

3. Productivity Organization in Korea: Korea Productivity Center (KPC)

3.1. Reasons for selection

The Korea Productivity Center (KPC), a government bureau under the

Ministry of Knowledge Economy, is the leading provider of sustainability information and services in the Republic of Korea. Korea was able to successfully accomplish national economic development plans in the early stages because a system which consistently administered the government's economic development plans for industrial growth was established. KPC, which was established mainly by the private sector, played a leading role in promoting the government's industrial policy and cultivating management and technical skills for national industry as a central organization. KPC achieved consensus on the nation's industrialization targets and distributed the knowledge and skills required to revitalize industry (KDI & MOSF. 2011).

3.2. Overview of Organization

3.2.1. Role

KPC has led the development of South Korea into an advanced country with diversified approaches, including research on different types of productivities such as total factor productivity and labor productivity, training, consulting, release of index surveys, and qualification certification. KPC has played a pivotal role in increasing the productivity of various industries to promote the rapid growth of the national economy (KPC, 2016b).

3.2.2. Basis of establishment

KPC was established as a foundation with the government's approval in 1957, but its status as an organization has undergone some changes. The Manufacturing Development Act sought to expand the industrial base, improve productivity, promote the effective utilization and development of resources, develop human resources, balance international payments and strengthen the foundation for fostering self-supporting industries. Under Article 22 of this act, KPC was reestablished as a special corporation on July 1, 1986. The act provided momentum for fundamentally changing the basis for industrial policy by avoiding government-led support for particular industries, establishing a base for autonomy of the private sector and seeking support for industries according to functions (SaKong, I., &Koh, Y., 2010).

Korean industries demanded a new strategy to respond to the changing market environment in the wake of the WTO and the financial crisis of the late 1990s. To this end, the government replaced the Manufacturing Development Act with the Industrial Development Act to strengthen the competitiveness of Korea's industry and to upgrade the industrial structure in 1999. Presently, the legal status of KPC is as a special corporation under the Ministry of Knowledge Economy under Article 32 of the Industrial Development Act (KDI & MOSF, 2011).

3.2.3. Main Project (Korea Productivity Center, 2016)

Productivity statistics research: National Productivity Award, PMS (Productivity Management System) certification, state certified statistics, productivity research and surveys, APO (Asian Productivity Organization), collaboration projects

Release of index survey: National Customer Satisfaction Index, National Brand Competitiveness Index, Dow Jones Sustainability Management Index

Education & training: Management and job tasks training, ranks, leadership, and competence training, online & mobile training, CEO training, employment & career move training, overseas training

Consulting: CS, brand, IT consulting, Innovative manufacturing consulting, Management consulting

Qualification certification: State certification (ITQ, GTQ, ERP), private qualification (IEQ, UTQ), international qualification (ICDL, CompTIA)

3.2.4. Organizational Structures

The organizational structure of KPC is shown in Figure 3-7 (KPC, 2016c).

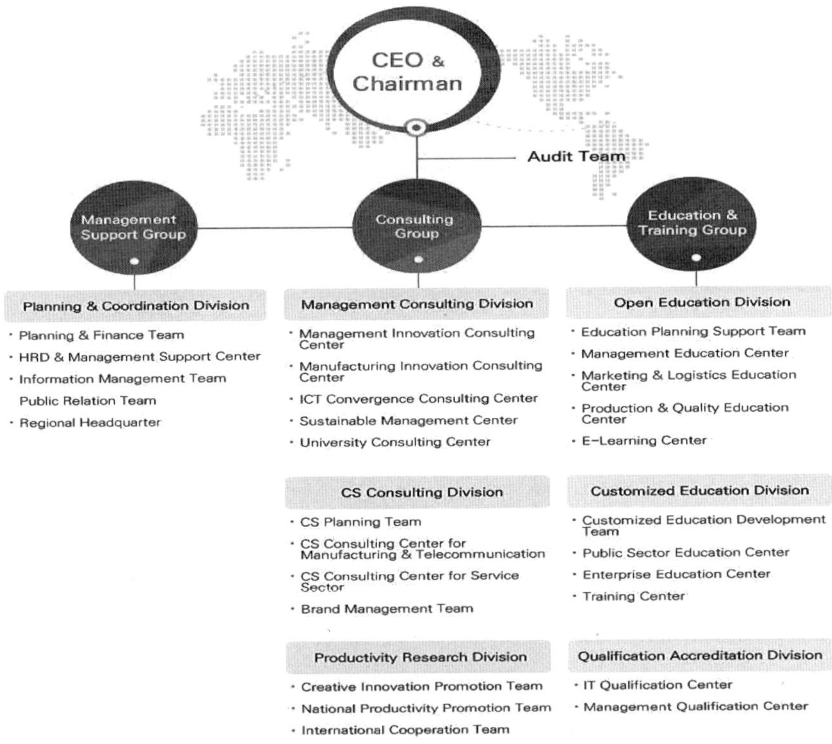

Figure 3-7 Organizational Structures of KPC

3.3. History and Role of KPC

KPC's role has changed as Korea's economy and government have changed. Its core roles are presented in Table 3-6 (KPC, 2016a). More detail about these roles is given in Appendix3.

Table 3-6 History of Government's Policy and performance of KPC

Year	Economic Condition and Government's Direction	Performance of KPC
1950s	• Investment in import substitution industries • Created policies to increase productivity	• Established a long-term plan to drive the productivity movement • Focused on the transfer of modern economic and business concepts
1960s	• Export-led industrialization strategy in labor-intensive light industries • 1st and 2nd Five-Year Economic Development Plans which led to the construction of industrial infrastructure	• Corporate consultancy work, education and industrial training to utilize new management techniques
1970s	• Nation's exports changed to durable consumption goods and labor-intensive medium goods • Needs for production machinery, automobiles, steel and petrochemicals were growing	• Productivity movement was ignored due to growth of monopolistic enterprises (government decreased its support)
1980s	• Exports slowed in the aftermath of the second oil shock in 1979, so government adopted productivity enhancement as a major policy task for the 1980s • Technology and function-intensive industries were developed • Suppression of labor rights weakened productivity movement	• In 1986, KPC restarted with the purpose of clarifying the role of government and the direction of government policies • Focused FA/OA diagnosis, distribution of performance & rationalization

1990s	• Due to the foreign exchange crisis in 1997, domestic demand rapidly fell • More attention was put on productivity enhancement to strengthen the competitiveness of the manufacturing industry	• "Productivity doubling movements" played a central role in the 1990s • After crisis, KPC focused on factory rationalization, standardization and quality enhancement to overcome the crisis
2000s~	• Government implemented policies to move toward a knowledge based economy by investment in state-of-the-art technology development, exploration of new growth engines and environmental management	• Supported industrial development and strengthened competitiveness of companies though offering new management innovation technique and programs

3.4. AHR in KPC

Since 1958, when it offered a "practical management course," Korea's first industrial training program, KPC has been Korea's first, largest, and best industrial training institute, offering 1,600 training courses and training 150,000 people each year. In order to reinforce the competitiveness of enterprises and meet diverse needs, KPC provides systematic and professional training solutions to help customers grow, including training courses for each competence area such as detailed tasks, ranks, and business skills, qualification certification courses, e-learning, CEO training, customized training to meet organizational needs and global benchmarking (KPC, 2016d).

3.4.1. Types of AHRD programs

Various AHRD programs in KPC are shown in Table 3-7 (KPC, 2016d).

Table 3-7 KPC's Educational Programs

Type	Description
Public training	Program that imparts management knowledge and techniques by planning and designing training programs for employees.
Customized commissioned training	Program after designing training customized to the needs of the customer in case of commissioned training
Specialized training for the public sector	Training service per requests from the government and public institutes
CEO training	CEO training school to improve management's will to innovate and innovation competence for CEOs of small- and medium-sized enterprises
Overseas training	Training program to reinforce competitiveness of domestic enterprises and organizations for benchmarking other organizations
Online and mobile training	Self-directed and autonomous learning programs that utilize web-based and mobile-based multimedia contents

3.5. Implications for AHRD of Vietnamese SOEs

Korea's experience in productivity movements, which have been promoted specifically by KPC, offers some implications for the establishment of a national productivity organization, ways to fund and operate such an organization, and measures for step-by-step implementation.

First, the establishment of KPC as a public foundation by individuals and private organizations has its pros and cons. The merits are that it allowed KPC to maintain a nonpolitical, non-profit and unbiased stance, and thus, to promote fair and rational productivity movements without influence from enterprises, workers, and the government. KPC was established as a foundation by private organizations, but this worked against it when it sought to intensively promote the policy of nationwide productivity enhancement. Thus, it is recommended that a productivity enhancement organization should be set up free from politics and influence, though its activities to enhance productivity should be promoted with support from the government.

Second, the strategies for productivity enhancement movements should be planned according to the nation's stage of economic development. Considering Korea's experience, long-term government policy for productivity enhancement should be established when economic policy is set up at the national level. The growth of industries may occur only when enterprises' productivity improvement movements occur through long-term productivity policy. It is also important to view people as the vehicles for productivity enhancement through the whole process of improving productivity, and thus, human-centered productivity movements should be promoted. In addition, productivity movements are currently changing from being manufacturing field-centered to consumer-centered.

The KPC has been able to achieve outcomes over the past 50 years because it was able to facilitate autonomous productivity enhancement in a way that benefited enterprises, workers, and customers together. Figure 3-8 presents a timeline of Korea's economic development alongside the corresponding history of the KPC (KDI & MOSF, 2011).

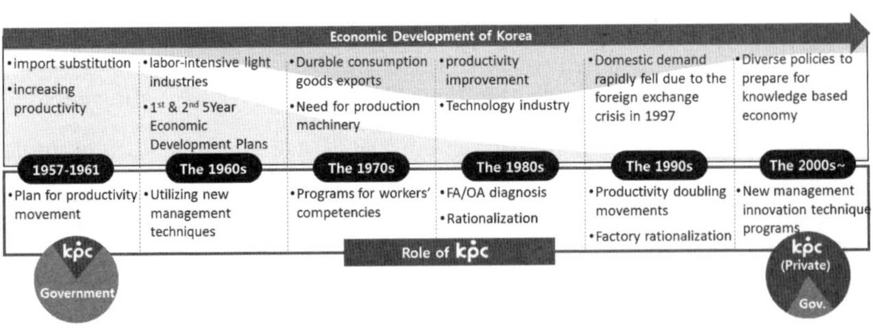

Figure 3-8 Co-evolutionary History of KPC and Korean Economic Development

V. Policy Recommendations and Imperatives

1. Summary of suggestions

To arrange the growth of targeted SOEs and create visible outcomes, the conditions (e.g., input resources of time, professional manpower, finance, etc.) should be considered. This study suggests short-medium-long term third five-year and so forth promotion strategy through the three task domains of organization establishment, securing contents, and professional manpower training. Table 3.8 presents a summary of suggestions for the innovation of AHRD in Vietnamese SOEs.

The indirect goals of the impact on SOEs and private corporations in the process of utilizing the accumulated organizational and human resources were considered. The direct goal of this 3(organization, content, manpower) by 3(short-, medium-, long-term) strategy is to strengthen the AHRD ability of targeted SOEs. The huge changes in national economic and social development need the ecological co-evolution of the balanced growth and productive interaction of every element in the economic system of Vietnam. Improving the infrastructure of AHRD through enacting this plan will be a strategic lever for improving productivity and consolidating the competitive power of the main agents of production in Vietnam's domestic economy through a vertical trickle-down effect of fostering AHRD professionals in the organization and a horizontal ripple effect which will promote AHRD in other SOEs and private corporations or privatized SOEs.

Figure 3-9 presents the effects of the proposed strategies in graphical form.

Table 3-8 "3 Year X 3 Domain" AHRD Innovation model

	Implantation & Implementation (2016-2020)	Localization & Revision (2021-2025)	Take-off Diffusion (2026-2030)
Institution	• Establish VPC (Vietnam Productivity Center) by reforming VNPT • Restructure HRD functions of 3 target SOEs • Establish collaborative relationship with 3 benchmark SOEs in Korea	• Enlarge VPC to independent R&D group • Install training centers for 3 target SOEs • Establish consulting service function for other SOEs	• Spin-off VPC into self-sustaining special organization • Install training centers for other SOEs • Begin offering technical aid to neighboring communist countries
Contents	• Implant and implement MTP • Develop and implement 3 key management programs (accounting, financing, marketing) • Develop competency models for SOEs • Implant e-learning system infrastructure	• Vietnamese MTP into VMTP • Develop and implement 5 key management programs (HR, procurement, logistics, project management, business planning) • Develop competency-based training curriculum for 3 target SOEs • Develop and acquire e-learning contents	• Operate HRD consulting business for other SOEs • Develop competency-based training curriculum for other SOEs • Develop mobile-based blended learning system • Outsource and curate e-learning contents from the global market and open-source community
Expertise	• Develop general competency courses for HRD & ISD • Dispatch Vietnamese HRD practitioners to Korean institutions (short-term intensive courses + degree-seeking programs) • Develop HRD specialists development roadmap	• Install professional masters programs for HRD and ISD in Vietnamese academic institutions • Develop specialized competency courses for HRD & ISD with the aid of KPC	• Co-found Corporate University • Expand bachelors-masters-doctoral programs for HRD and ISD • Put national certificate for HRD Experts in operation
Prime Mover	HCMA	3 Target SOEs	Individual SOEs

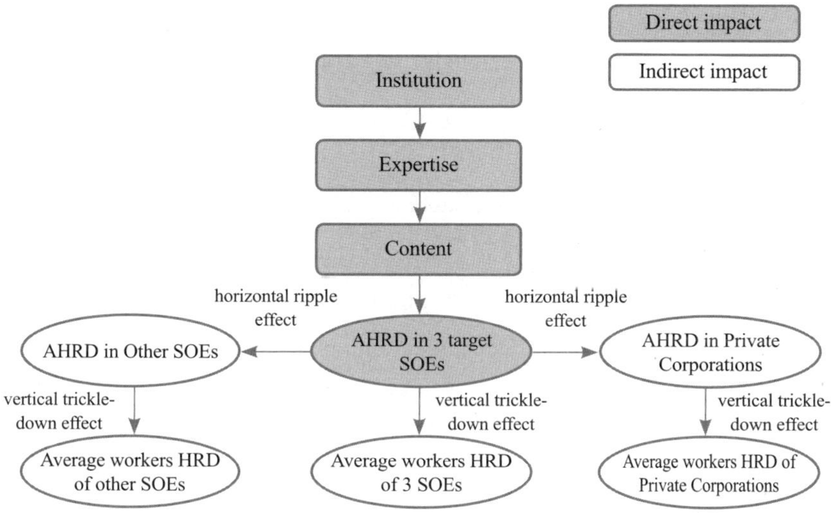

Figure 3-9 Concept map of the proposed strategies related the direct and indirect effects

2. Promoting strategies by steps

2.1. [Stage 1] Implantation & Implementation (2016-2020)

As suggested in Vietnam 2030, it is an urgent matter to improve the productivity of SOEs which are the driving forces of economic and social development in Vietnam and which have responsibility of providing the power for development of the state. The development of AHRD is possible through the construction of a total AHRD system of institutionalization, provision of excellent contents provided from secure of professional manpower, and so forth. Therefore, the short-term approach of putting fish (i.e., contents) on the table to fulfill an immediate nutritional deficiency should be conducted simultaneously with medium- and long-term projects of training professional fishermen (i.e., AHRD professionals) in advanced methods and adjusting organizations (i.e., institutions).

The goal of the first 5-year AHRD plan, which began in 2016, is to install institutions that will eventually promote and carry out the third 5-year AHRD project by 2030 by launching early development of administrative manager's general abilities. Core specialized abilities (accounting, finance, marketing) of Socialist SOE managers who are familiar with planned economy systems, also need to be developed in addition to the basic courses.

2.1.1. Establishment of institutions

An official institution, (i.e. VPC: Vietnam Productivity Center) is needed for long-term projects to systematically improve AHRD in SOEs. Some changes of policies are needed for this: related laws should be enacted, the ministry in charge of this institution should be organized (or chosen) and budget or foreign capital should be allocated. Korea had a similar experience in the 1960s when the KPC was founded. Vietnam can refer to the contents of the laws and organizational structures of KPC but they should always keep the Vietnamese context in mind. Cooperation between the KPC and the Party and government of Vietnam will be helpful for this (Appendix 3).

The proposed institution can be compared with the truck producing diverse contents and delivers them to the students since after. By actively benchmarking and following the example of strong, durable and performance-confirmed experiences in other countries (i.e., Korea), the early danger should be minimized and early operation should be possible. The organization can evolve in the original form of domesticated organization, after the accumulation of operation of organization know-how and the analysis of training needs of Vietnam.

2.1.2. Developing/Implanting learning contents

Learning achievement depends not only on the training institution, but also on the contents. The quality and quantity of the training program contents are important factors for AHR to develop their competencies. In the first stage, a Management Training Program (MTP) should be developed or implanted to create fundamental competency in the three subjects (e.g., accounting, finance, and marketing) which are the core of a market-oriented economy.

The effectiveness and efficiency of MTP have already proven through its adoption in the US, Japan, and Korea. The contents contain all of the managerial competencies necessary to manage a market economy. MTP should be adopted and spread at first in a package form which cannot be changed by each instructor (Appendix 4). It is better to acquire Korean contents with minimum modification rather than develop a new program in-house because MTP already contains the necessary and common contents for every manager in a market economy in a standardized package program.

Accounting, finance, and marketing are essential core competencies needed to be able to make rational decisions in a market economy. Competencies in these areas are also expected to be very effective for changing perceptions and attitudes of the majority of public AHR. These three subjects should be newly developed according to ISD (Instructional System Design) method including needs analysis-design-development-evaluation steps, considering Vietnam AHR's knowledge, skills and attitude and conventional working practices. Instructional designers and AHRD practitioners in Korea can support this new development project effectively.

2.1.3. Securing Experts

HRD experts are needed to establish the organization and develop, secure, and operate contents. If there is no one driving the truck, the hunger of consumers cannot be satisfied, even if it is full of fresh groceries. Similarly, if there is no nutritionist or food manufacturing professional, the whole nation will fall into a state of malnutrition. Experts will be expected to operate programs and give lectures in the short term and engage in R&D in the medium-long term by conducting needs assessments, developing, acquiring and implementing content and creating evaluation tools. In light of these various duties, experts should be developed not as individuals but as a team having rich experience and various kinds of expertise step by step over a long period. Thus, to secure the workforce in the early stage who are majoring in HRD, psychometrics, educational technology, or business management and having consulting experience in Vietnam or Korea, the support from outside of Vietnam is necessary. Advice from the KPC will be useful in deciding on professional experts' qualifications and composition. Securing minimum manpower for the operation of initial organization through dispatch of Korean experts will be desirable. And Development of general competency courses for HRD & ISD is needed to start fostering experts (Appendix 5).

2.1.4. Prime Mover - HCMA

The first 5-year period for AHRD in SOEs is crucial in determining the success of the whole plan to 2030. Thus, we propose that HCMA, which has a deep understanding of government policies and qualified research capacity, should handle the entire project in collaboration with the general managers in charge of human resources of the three target SOEs, the general manager of international relations at the KPC as an implementation agency, and KOICA as a support organization. Establishing a VPCS (Vietnam Productivity Center for SOEs) and the Research Centre for Governance for SOEs as dedicated/affiliated organizations within HCMA in the initial phase is desirable.

2.2. [Stage 2] Localization & Revision (2021-2025)

The goals of the second stage are continuous improvement of dedicated organizations as well as diversification and domestication of contents based on the infrastructure built in the first 5-year period. In this stage, the primary agents should change from the State and Party to SOEs and the private sector, gradually utilizing human-physical infrastructure in the three target SOEs and promoting a horizontal ripple effect to support SOEs' or equitized corporations' AHRD projects and a vertical trickle-down effect to educate employees.

2.2.1. Strengthening Dedicated Organization

Separate center in HCMA as a VPC (Vietnam Productivity Center), and strengthening organization and manpower. To maximize the ripple effect, courses fostering outstanding instructors, instructional designers, and AHRD practitioners should be developed and put in place. An AHRD consultant group should be formed to provide commissioned education for workforces in other SOEs or private enterprises. AHRD activity can be accelerated by establishing consulting team to boost the ripple effect.

2.2.2. Contents Development

Develop VMTP by modifying and supplementing MTP adjusted to conditions of Vietnamese SOE with reference to domestication case of JMA, KPC, and KMA (Korea Management Association) (Appendix 4).

Develop additional courses that include human resources, distribution, project management, purchase, business administration.

In addition to hierarchical management competency model, job competency model, AHRD competency model for general SOEs and assessment systems for each competency should be developed (Appendix 5).

Also, establishing e-learning infrastructure and contents development organization through improvements of IT infrastructure and dissemination of smart device are objective of the second period plan. By combining developed e-learning contents, service industry, LMS (Learning Management System) and MOOC (Massive Open Online Course) platform development competency and know-how, Vietnamese fast growing IT infrastructure, and Korean IT competency, Vietnam can maximize last-mover advantage, and realize high-level e-AHRD comparable to Korea.

2.2.3. Fostering Experts

When the second stage starts in 2021, the training capacity of Vietnamese universities and government-funded research is expected to have improved significantly compared to the current conditions. For example, SOE-AHRD related majors such as business management, educational technology and AHRD will be in place and degree programs (e.g., bachelor, master and doctoral levels) will be equipped. Thus, the AHRD professionals fostered by

VPC in the first stage can take advantage of regular degree courses.

To achieve these objectives, VPC should actively expand the base of AHRD experts by constructing conjunct research-education systems and developing curriculum suitable to industrial needs. These AHRD experts can contribute to improvements in AHR and the growth of productivity, interacting not only with SOEs but also with private enterprises and FDI (Foreign Direct Investment).

2.2.4. Prime Mover – 3 Target SOEs

In Stage 1, HCMA played the role of prime mover for implementing policies and procedures efficiently. This was beneficial in that it allowed efficient and consistent decision-making. In the second stage, some important issues and challenges related to diversity and context will emerge, so the prime mover should be the three target SOEs. HCMA will remain an important player as it provides support for the targeted SOEs to prevent some of the frustration and inefficiency that result from constantly changing decision patterns and overlapping investments.

2.3. [Stage 3] Take-off & Diffusion (2026-2030)

The goal of this stage is to make AHRD a market-oriented industry and a knowledge industry for the future. This will be achieved in three steps: equitization, liberalization and modernization. In Stage 3, key outcomes will be realized as the results of national development plans such as Vietnam 2030 and SEDP. Many privatized companies in Vietnam for improved efficiency will have more competitiveness in the markets. If they implement some AHRD strategies designed by this project, they can start quality training programs for their advanced-level managers without difficulties.

Furthermore, Vietnam can play an important role in the world by sharing its own experiences related to AHRD development in SOEs with other developing countries, as Korea did with Vietnam. Sharing its experience as a change maker from a socialist-oriented market economy to a market-oriented economy will be a good model for other countries in Asia.

2.3.1. Institution

After 2030, when most of the SOEs will be privatized, VPC will continue to play a critical role in the country by leading AHRD in SOEs and cooperating with private AHRD consulting firms. At this point, VPC should be transformed into a self-sustaining special organization. This is similar to the KPC's current situation in that the leader of the organization is nominated by the government but the organization raises its own funds. VPC is still partially owned by the government because certain parts including infrastructure in the country require more stable and consistent needs and supports.

2.3.2. Contents

More companies will choose to source more of their training activities from external suppliers to stay competitive. Therefore, advanced learning strategy frameworks like content planning and evaluation will needed when choosing outsourcing training. Curating content is helpful for this because it utilizes some good sources for learning such as MOOC, Flipped Learning and OCW (Open Course Ware). Vietnamese SOEs can utilize Korean sources like K-MOOC, KOCW and e-learning contents shared by companies. These will guide Vietnam to a more advanced and knowledge-based economy.

2.3.3. Expertise

As content curation continues, AHRD professionals will be focused on planning, evaluation and outsourcing rather than management and development. Using online learning programs will provide an opportunity to analyze learners' behaviors and needs because it leaves a lot of information about learning and learners. AHRD professionals in learning analytics will be required to train and develop of employees to make informed decisions about learning and more advanced AHRD.

2.3.4. Prime Mover – Individual SOEs

In this period, various agents such as HCMA, training institutions in each industry, training institutions within each SOE and private consulting firms will emerge as the providers of AHRD. This highlights the dual characteristic identity of a socialist-oriented market economy which simultaneously features public ownership and market efficiency at the same time. This mixed approach will be effective in that there is a public part which is more stable as well as competition between the agents that will lead to efficient decisions and quality services.

2.3.5. Using e-Learning for AHRD

In Vietnam, e-learning has become a widely use tool for education (Peeraer& Tran, 2015). e-Learning is useful since many learners are able to take courses whenever and wherever they want as long as they have access to the internet. Plus, since e-learning is based on an online platform, abundant data including log data can be accumulated and this could be a source for analysis. By analyzing learning data, personalized learning for human resources management can be achieved. Therefore, introducing e-learning to AHRD systems in Vietnam would be very helpful in providing adequate training programs for advanced-level managers.

CHAPTER FOUR:

ADVANCED HUMAN RESOURCE DEVELOPMENT IN RESEARCH AND DEVELOPMENT (R&D) IN VIETNAM

Sam Youl Lee

Professor & Chair, Department of Public Administration

Chair, Science, Technology, and Policy (STP) Major, Underwood Int'l College (UIC), Yonsei University

Ⅰ. Introduction

Ⅱ. Human Resources in R&D in Vietnam

Ⅲ. Policy Issues Related to AHRD Systems for R&D in Vietnam

Ⅳ. Korean HRD Policy for R&D

Ⅴ. Policy Recommendations

CHAPTER FOUR:

ADVANCED HUMAN RESOURCE DEVELOPMENT IN RESEARCH AND DEVELOPMENT (R&D) IN VIETNAM

I. Introduction

This chapter will present the current status of personnel development and supply in research and development in Vietnam and offer an assessment of the current advanced human resource development (AHRD) in research and development. Since the role of human capital is especially important in R&D, it will be meaningful to understand the current status and problems in Vietnam that need to be overcome so that it can catch up with developed countries.

This chapter will analyze the advanced human resource (AHR) policy in R&D in Korea and enumerate the characteristics of Korean policies that can be applied in Vietnam. Based on the analysis of Vietnam and Korea, this chapter will suggest actionable items for AHRD policy for Vietnam.

II. Human Resources in R&D in Vietnam

1. The General Status of R&D and Analysis in Vietnam

Since the adoption of the doi moi (renovation) policy in 1986, Vietnam has transitioned from a centralized planning to a socialist market-oriented economy. This has translated into strong economic growth (see Figure 4-1) and transformed Vietnam from one of the world's poorest countries in the 1980s to a lower middle-income country in 2010 (World Bank, 2013).

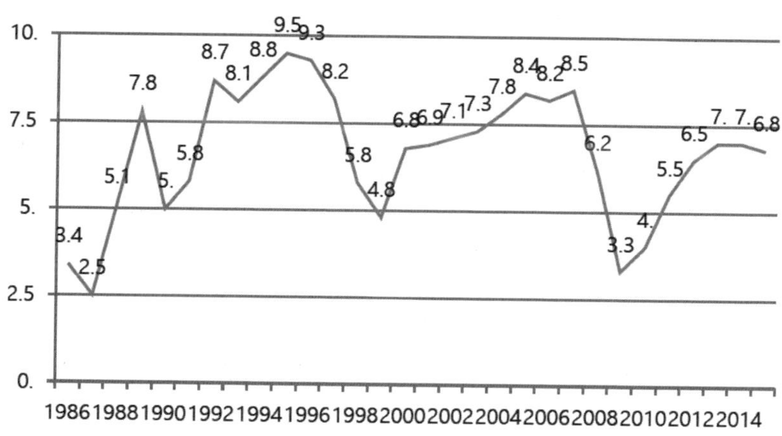

Source: General Statistical Office (2016)

Figure 4-1 Vietnam real GDP Growth

This long-term growth has been attributable to three main factors: the doi moi policy, cheap labor cost, and availability of natural resources. As the country's economy has shifted to a lower middle-income one, these factors have weakened or gradually disappeared. The science and technology (S&T) field is considered the driving force for social and economic development and restructuring the national economy. However, in terms of research and development (R&D), there are some weaknesses. Figure 4.2 shows historical data on patents granted in Vietnam between 1990 and 2014. The number of patents granted in a country is one of the indicators for R&D output. However, the figure shows that in Vietnam, most of patents are granted to non-residents. In 2014, 1361 out of 1397 patents granted were to non-residents, which is more than 97%. This implies that the growth in R&D capacity in Vietnam is not as strong as its economic growth.

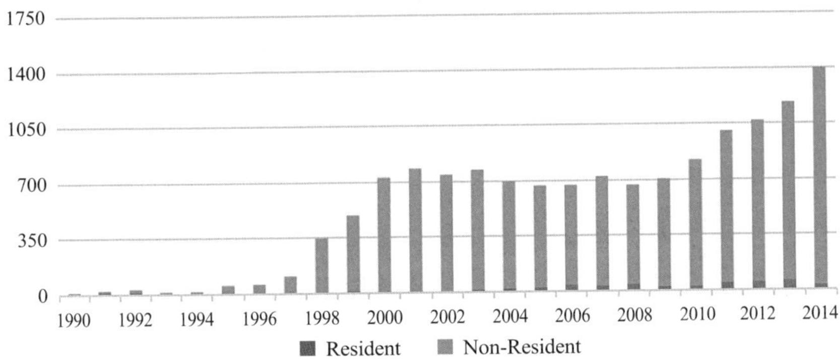

Source: World Intellectual Property Organization statistics database, Accessed on August 8, 2016.

Figure 4-2 Patents granted in Vietnam (1990~2014)

In addition, R&D expenditure as a percentage of GDP is low. In 2013, the gross expenditure for R&D was only 0.37% of GDP (Ministry of Science and Technology [MOST], 2016 – forth coming), of which 56.7% is from government expenditure; 41.8% from enterprises; and 1.5% from foreign sources (see Table 4-1). This implies that Vietnam's innovation system is still quite dependent upon government initiative and therefore, the government's R&D strategy is expected to have a strong impact on innovation system in Vietnam compared to other countries. For example, in Korea, the government and public share of R&D expenditure went below 50% in 1977 and stayed that way except in 1979. In 2014, the share was 24%.

Table 4-1 Gross expenditure for R&D in 2013

Sources of Expenditure	GERD (billion VND)	Percentage
Government	7591.6	56.7
Enterprises	5597.3	41.8
Foreign	201.7	1.5
Total	13390.6	100

Source: MOST, 2016 (forthcoming)

Based on the Sciences Technology's Law 2013, organizations of sciences and technology include: (1) organizations focusing on research and development; (2) training institutions such as universities, colleges and academies; and (3) service organizations of sciences and technology. According to a Ministry of Science and Technology (MOST) survey, there are 1055 S&T organizations in Vietnam. Out of these, there are 505 (47.9%) research institutes, 338 (32.0%) universities, and 212 (20.1%) science and technology services organizations (MOST, 2016).

In the national innovation system, the linkages between academia and industry are weak and sometimes nonexistent. Technology transfer from research institutes and universities to enterprises is insignificant, and Vietnamese universities focus mainly on pure basic research. Enterprises' demand for technology is a vital driver of applied research from research institutes and universities. However, there is a shortage of demand from the enterprise side; domestic enterprises rely much more on import technology than on technology created by domestic research institutes and universities. Furthermore, technology development from domestic R&D institutions is limited and does not meet the demand from enterprises.

MOST considers human resources in R&D to a critically important factor for economic development in general and S&T development in particular. As shown in Table 4.2, there are 164,744 R&D personnel in Vietnam and 84% of them belongs to government. Only 12.7% belongs to non-governmental and 2.6% to foreign funding personnel. As you can see R&D personnel in Vietnam heavily relies on government funding. Out of 164,774 R&D personnel, 128,997 are categorized as researchers, which 78.3% and about 87% of researchers are working for government. However, according to the survey that MOST has done, the R&D personnel as full-time equivalent (FTE) is much lower than the number of people participating in R&D activities; and number of R&D (FTE) over 10,000 people is approximately 7.

Table 4-2 R&D personnel in Vietnam

	Total	%	R&D Position			
			Researcher	Technician	Support staff	Other
Government	139,531	84.7	112,191	8,898	12,829	5,613
Non-government	20,917	12.7	15,076	2,837	1,569	1,435
Foreign funded	4,296	2.6	1,730	1,064	751	751
Total	164,744	100	128,997	12,799	15,149	7,799

Source: MOST, 2016 (forthcoming)

Table 4.3 shows how R&D human resources are distributed among types of organizations. Most work in universities and research institutes, with 17.4% enterprises.

Table 4-3 Distribution of R&D personnel by organizations

Sectors	Total	%	R&D Position			
			Researcher	Technician	Support staff	Other
Total	164,744	100	128,997	12,779	15,149	7,799
Research institutes	37,481	22.8	29,820	1,895	3,852	1,914
Universities	74,217	45	63,435	2,524	6,131	2,127
Administrative organizations	10,926	6.6	8,460	978	979	500
Other governmental organizations	11,989	7.3	7,495	2,580	1,386	528
Enterprises	28,708	17.4	18,553	4,745	2,705	2,705
Non-profit organizations	1,423	0.9	1,234	68	96	25

Source: MOST, 2016 (forthcoming)

2. Detailed Statistics on R&D Organizations

2.1. Human Resources in Government-Affiliated Research Organizations

According to the MOST, in 2012 Vietnam had about 1,600 Organizations of

Science and Technology, including: 1,001 Central Organizations of Science and Technology (433 Organizations of Science and Technology under Ministries/ Boards or Organizations - Ministry level; more than 340 Organizations of Science and Technology under the Vietnam Union of Science and Technology Association (VUSTA) and other member associations) and 512 Organizations of Science and Technology at provinces.

Table 4-4 Number of S&T Organizations (Divided by Scientific Sectors)

No	S&T Sectors	No. of Organizations		
		Nationwide	Central	Provincial
	Social Sciences and Humanities	149	108	41
	Natural Sciences	124	95	29
	Agricultural Science	327	184	143
	Health Sciences - Pharmaceutical	103	57	46
	Sciences Technical and Technology	810	560	250
	Total:	1.513	1004	509

Source: MOST. Conference on "Human Resources Development Policies for Sciences and Technology," Hanoi, July 3, 2012.

Moreover, the percentage of organizations of R&D established by Ministries / Boards or Ministry-level organizations (52.5%), by Universities (22.4%) and 0.5% by People Provincial Committee / People City Committee. On the management-side, the organizations under Government are 0.7%; under Ministries / Boards or ministry-level organizations are 54.8% and under Universities are 44.5%.

Table 4-5 S&T Organizations divided by Central and Provincial/City

	Organizations		Number of Officials		Average number of personnel / the number of Organizations of Science and Technology
	Quantity	%	Quantity	%	
Central	1004	66,35	49,393	81.58	49.2
Provincial/ City	509	33,65	11,150	18.42	21.7
Total	1,513	100.00	60,543	100.00	40.0

Source: MOST. Conference on "Human Resources Development Policies for Sciences and Technology," Hanoi, July 3, 2012.

The average number of personnel was 40 officials per organization overall. There were an average of 49.2 officials per organization at the central level and 21.7 officials per organization at the provincial/city level.

As you can see from the statistics above, Ministry of Agriculture and Rural Development has the biggest number of boards and Ministry-level departments followed by Vietnam Academy of Science and Technology, Vietnam Academy of Social Sciences.

In addition, National Assembly has 2 and National University has 9 and Ho Chi Minh National University has 2 Organizations of Research and Development.

Table 4-6 Organizations of Research and Development under Government

Ministry/Board or Ministry-level departments	Number of R&D departments
Vietnam Academy of Social Sciences	35
Vietnam Academy of Science and Technology	34
Ministry of Industry and Trade	10
Ministry of Education and Training	3
Ministry of Transport	2
Ministry of Planning and Investment	3
Ministry of Science and Technology	10
Ministry of Labour - Invalids and Social Affairs	3
Ministry of Home Affairs	1
Ministry of Agriculture and Rural Development	65
Ministry of Finance	1
Ministry of Natural Resources and Environment	4
Ministry of Information and Communications	2
Ministry of Justice	1
Ministry of Culture, Sports and Tourism	4
Ministry of Construction	8
Ministry of Health	25
State Bank of Vietnam	1
Government Inspectorate	1
Committee for Ethnic Affairs	1
Vietnam Agency News	2
Voice of Vietnam	1
Vietnam Television	1
Vietnam Social Insurance	1
Ho Chi Minh National Academy of Politics	17
Management Board of Ho Chi Minh Mausoleum	1
Total:	**237**

Source: MOST. Conference on "Human Resources Development Policies for Sciences and Technology," Hanoi, July 3, 2012.

Table 4-7 Quantity of Universities, Academies and Colleges (2012-2013)

Type	Quantity
University	207
College	214
Total	421

Source: MOST. Conference on "Human Resources Development Policies for Sciences and Technology," Hanoi, July 3, 2012.

2.2. Vietnam's Human Resources in R&D

The data for this section come from two main resources: one is data from the National Research about Human resource of Research and Development implemented by MOST gathered from organizations of research and development, universities, administrative agencies and the other is from research data on nationwide enterprises gathered by Vietnam's General Statistics Office.

Table 4-8 shows the breakdown of different positions held by employees, especially women, in R&D. According to the definition from OECD, a Researcher is a R&D Officer with a Diploma or Bachelor's degree, Master's, or Ph.D. who spends at least 10% of working time on R&D activities. Based on the research's result about Research and Development 2014 and research about Enterprises 2014, in 2013, Vietnam had 164,744 people working on R&D including: 37,481 researchers working at Academies, Research centrals. The divide of Human resources of Research and Development by functions as follow: 128,998 researchers (Diploma, Bachelor), 12,798 Technical officers; 15,250 Support officers and 7,800 other function officers.

Table 4-8 Human Resources of R&D by Performer and Gender in 2013

(unit: person)

	Total	Work functions			
		Researchers	Technical officers	Support officers	Other
Human Resources	164.744	128,998	12,798	15,150	7,800
Government	139,531	112,190	8,898	12,829	5,613
Non-Government	20,917	15,076	2,837	1,569	1,435
FDI	4,297	1,730	1,063	752	752
Female Human Resources	73,700	56,846	5,033	8,412	3,409
Government	61,862	48,497	3,833	6,964	2,568
Non-Government	9,772	6,972	958	1,171	671
FDI	2,066	1,377	242	277	170

Table 4-9 shows that that the Human resources in Research and Development mainly work in the academic sector. The Enterprises sector has 28,708 people working on R&D, which accounted for 17% of total human resources in R&D.

Table 4-9 Human Resources in R&D by Working Sectors

(unit: Person)

Working sectors	Total	Work functions			
		Researchers	Technical officers	Support officers	Other
Human Resource (Total)	164,744	128,998	12,799	15,149	7,799
Academies, Research and Development Centrals	37,481	29,820	1,895	3,852	1,914
Universities	74,216	63,435	2,524	6,131	2,127
Administrative Agencies	10,926	8,460	987	979	500
Other Agencies	11,989	7,495	2,580	1,386	528
Enterprises	28,708	18,553	4,745	2,705	2,705
Nonprofit organizations	1,424	1,234	68	96	25

Table 4-10 shows the degrees held by instructors in higher education in Vietnam. The number of Ph.D.s at tertiary education is relatively low. In 2011~2012, there were only 8,519 Ph.D. holders in Universities. In colleges, there were only 633 Ph.D. holders. The master degree holders dominate universities (27,594) and colleges (8,766).

Table 4-10 Personnel in Tertiary Education by Degree

(unit: person)

Type	University		College	
Year	2010-2011	2011-2012	2010-2011	2011-2012
Ph.D.	7,338	8,519	586	633
Master	22,865	27,594	7,509	8,766
Specialist	434	443	-	-
Bachelor, Diploma	20,059	22,547	14,939	14,696
Other Qualification	255	569	588	342

Source: MOST, 2013

2.3. General Evaluation of Performance of Vietnam's Human Resources in R&D

The research capacity and creativity of scientific research workers in Vietnam show some limitations based on the data on international publications and patented inventions, although there has been some progress. To be specific, the number of applications for patents, a crucial indicator of innovation, is far below expectations, and although international publications have increased over the years, there is still a lot of room for further improvement.

The data for invention patent granted by the nationality of owners shows that the total number of patents granted period 1996-2000 is 1,486, of which only 32 were granted to Vietnamese citizens a rate of 2.2%. In addition, the total number of patents granted in the period 2006-2010 was 3,588, of which only 175 were granted to Vietnamese citizens (4.9%). In 2013, the total number of patents granted was 1,171 of which only 53 were granted to Vietnamese citizens (4.5%).

The Web of Science database for the period 2006-2013 reports 10,983 published articles originating in Vietnam. 2013 was the first year that Vietnam had more than 2,200 scientific publications reported in Web of Science database; compared to 1,563 in 2011 and 1,929 in 2012, this was quite an increase. In terms of total published articles in the period 2006-2013, Vietnam ranked 62nd in the world, after Thailand (43rd) and Malaysia (42nd) and higher than Indonesia (64th) and the Philippines (69th). For comparison, in 2012, 1,868,974 articles were registered worldwide in the Web of Science, of which Vietnam has 1,929 posts (representing 0.103%). Vietnam ranked 60thin the world in terms of scientific research output in 2012.

In addition, there is a lack of researchers in research institutions. According to the Ministry of Education and Training, there are 56,000 academic staff members at universities and colleges, but only about 1,100 of them (3%) participated in scientific research. For example, Vietnam National University - Ho Chi Minh city (VNU-HCM) is one of two leading universities in Vietnam. In the period 2006-2010, VNU-HCM professors published 2,300 scientific articles, of which 720 papers were published in scientific journals with an average impact index of1.8. Funds earned from technology transfer activities was 344.5 billion Dong (Ministry of Education and Training), up by 1.25 times compared to the previous 5 years.

The real problem is that there is a lack of researchers dedicated to scientific research activities. In 2012, at VNU-HCM there were only 777 scientific research staffs out of a total of 5,514 employee-civil servants. Among 787 articles published in scientific journals in September 2012, only 188 were published in international journals, of which 147 were in the ISI list. This gives a ratio of ISI scientific papers per lecturer in VNU-HCM of only 0.06.

A large part of S&T manpower is not highly qualified, even in universities the lecturers does not directly work with the process of research and development. The majority of R&D personnel are currently working in the public sector. Since the spirit of cooperation in research and teamwork skills of S&T staff is not high, it is difficult to form strong interdisciplinary research teams. To make matters worse, in recent years, universities have failed to recruit excellent students to study basic sciences, social sciences and humanities, leading to a lack of good students who will be trained to become talented scientists in the future.

Another serious problem is limited research capacity, passion and sense of responsibility by researchers. Some researchers fail to stay up to date on the new achievements of science and technology in the world and end up with obsolete knowledge; others are working on scientific issues but lack enthusiasm to build up scientific study in Vietnam for catching up with the advanced countries in the region and are less concerned about real-world application:

> *A part of the science and technology intellectuals who has research capacity, with passionate and devoted to research activities, tend to decrease, while lazy expression, (they tend to) lack of professional pride and to not regularly improve knowledge, pragmatic and opportunity thought, chasing personal interests. (Assessment of the Ministry of Science and Technology on implementation of Resolution 27)*

Furthermore, the foreign language ability of many intellectuals is limited and cannot meet the requirements of global research, scientific exchanges and international integration. Unfortunately, some young intellectuals seem to have little interest in overcoming these difficulties by learning and improving their professional qualifications.

The uneven distribution of R&D personnel between regions and fields of activity is another serious problem. While human resources in R&D have increased quantitatively, improvement in terms of quality and capacity has been limited. Nearly 60% of R&D personnel are concentrated in the Red River Delta region and Southeast (23.38%), while Mekong delta has only 9% and Highland has just over 2%. In addition, large numbers of highly qualified scientists trained abroad are approaching retirement age. The prospect of the next generations of R&D workers in research institutes is quite uncertain, and the number of competent personnel presiding over major scientific and technological tasks has decreased although the size of universities has increased.

Distribution of R&D workers over sectors is also disproportionate. Vietnam is still an agricultural country, with 67% of the population living in rural areas. Production from the sectors of agricultural, forestry and fisheries have the largest scale, but these sectors have only 15,302 R&D workers which is 25.25% of the total R&D workers in Vietnam. Professors and associate professors specializing in these sectors are aging and have passed the peak of their careers.

In general, the scientific and technological capacity and innovation of Vietnam are still weak, and the system of national innovation is still fledgling and fragmented. R&D activity remains a supplemental activity in enterprises as well as in government agencies. Since the level of competition is increasing in the world, Vietnam needs to invest in developing its capacity for advanced science and technology, including R&D activities. It is imperative for businesses to enhance their creative capacity in order to enhance the country's position in the global value chain. Meeting these needs requires a strong investment in science, technology and innovation as well as strengthening, evaluating and adjusting the innovation system.

Vietnam has established a legal basis for the fields of science, technology and innovation as well as some new institutions that can manage R&D financing, but the process of establishing the modern institutional framework should further be strengthened to ensure fast progress. If government agencies are professional, autonomous and engaging in a greater range of activities, these policies will be implemented more effectively. Human capital is a key issue for innovation. The nation's capacity for innovation depends on the quality of education and training for scientists, technicians and other professionals along with coverage of the education system. Vietnam has made efforts to improve the quality of education and skills but must do more to increase the quantity and quality of human resources in science and technology.

3. National Strategy for Science and Technology Development 2011-2020

Vietnam established laws and plans for R&D human resources development, especially in terms of national law and strategy on S&T. Vietnamese law enacted in 2013 specifies that the government must implement high-priority policies for development of human resources in R&D (Article 6) and defines key rights and responsibilities of R&D workers (Article 23).

To implement the regulations and incentives related to human resources development in R&D, the Vietnamese government passed Decree No. 40/2014/

ND-CP on utilizing and putting R&D individuals in important positions. The main principles of this policy are to create favorable working environments for individuals in the R&D sector and to provide enough resources to implement the policy.

Corresponding to the Socio-Economic Development Strategy 2011-2020, the National Strategy for Science and Technology Development 2011-2020 (SSTD) was formulated. Since the SSTD is most closely related to R&D personnel policy, it is analyzed in depth. The main objectives of the SSTD are shown in Table 4-11

Table 4-11 Main Quantitative Objectives of the SSTD

Main objectives of the SSTD	2015	2020
The value of high-tech products as a percentage of GDP		45%
Technological innovation rate	10 – 15%	> 20%
Total expenditure for science and technology as a percentage of GDP	1.5%	2%
Government expenditure for science and technology in the total government budget	At least 2%	At least 2%
Number of researchers per 10,000 people	9 -10	11 – 12
Development of the World's standard engineers	5000	10000
Number of international level research institutions	30	60
Number of science and technology enterprises	3000	5000
Number of high-tech incubators	30	60

Source: Synthesis from Decision number 418/QD-TTg

The SSTD addressed the development of important technologies including information and communication technology, new material technology, machinery manufacturing and automation technology, and environmental technology. Strategic measures to achieve these objectives are as follows:

Focus on national science and technology programs for making connection between research and innovation (e.g., Technological Innovation Programs, National High-Tech Development Program, Technology Market Development Programs…);

Reform R&D expenditure mechanisms of the government funding;

Develop policies for attracting and retaining R&D personnel;

Stimulate the development of the technology market;

Integrate Vietnam's S&T sectors into international S&T sectors;

Enhance the social awareness of science and technology development.

The SSTD has achieved the following results. First, the value of high-tech as a percentage of GDP increased from 11.7% in 2011 to 19.1% in 2012 and 28.7% in 2013. However, the recent increase in the high-tech products value depends a great deal on FDI companies, notably Samsung Electronics. Secondly, the average growth rate of international publications during the period 2011-2015 is 19.5% per year, which is higher than the strategy objective. Table 4-12 presents the numbers of publications and growth rates each year.

Table 4-12 Increase in International Publications 2011-2015

Years	Number of Publications	Growth rate
2011	1584	
2012	1964	23.99%
2013	2509	27.75%
2014	2759	9.96%
2015	3137	13.70%
Total	11953	

Source: Ministry of Science and Technology, 2016

For technological innovation rate, according to computation by State Agency for Technological Innovation (SATI) and MOST has shown that the technological innovation rate has achieved 10.68% as almost a minimum target of the strategy. The number of science and technology enterprises reached 2800 in 2015, a little lower than the given objective. In sum, although there are variations in achieving the target, SSTD is on the right track to achieve its goals. However, in order to reach the target, there are several issues that need to be taken care of. First, setting priorities in R&D policy sometimes becomes a political issue rather than an evidence-based approach. For example, SSTD is setting the value of high-tech products as a percentage of GDP at 45%. Therefore, the numerical objective of SSTD must not be confusing compared to the socio-economic objective. Second, there are discrepancies between S&T laws and regulations and other laws and regulations on government budget, taxes, labor and salary. Third, line ministries and provincial governments have not paid much attention to the implementation of the SSTD. Finally, a lack of competition in the national market means there is little pressure on domestic enterprises to apply technological innovation. This explains why enterprises spend little on R&D and most R&D personnel work in the government sector.

III. Policy Issues Related to AHRD Systems for R&D in Vietnam

1. Issues with National Innovation System in Vietnam

This report cannot evaluate the entire national innovation system in Vietnam due to lack of space. However, since AHRD for R&D is an integral part of a national innovation system, it is crucial to briefly discuss it in order to handle issues with AHRD for R&D.

Lee *et al.* (2010) listed several problems in Vietnam's innovation system. First, Vietnam suffers from low demand for industry and industrial research capability. The innovation capability of government-owned enterprises (GOEs) is limited, and technology transfer from multinational corporations (MNCs) is minuscule and weakly connected to the rest of the economy. Second, Vietnam's innovation system is not working as expected since there is little coordination between plans and industrial policies for the science and technology industry. Third, there is a fundamental gap between research institutes and industry, and R&D policies to promote close cooperation between them have not been successful.

The World Bank (2016) recently made very similar diagnoses of the national innovation system in Vietnam, highlighting the weak research output from research institutes and universities. In particular, the R&D personnel educated in these institutions are not as competitive as expected in terms of research capacity. The report also mentioned that there is weak logical linkage between diagnosis and the programs prescribed.

Many studies have provided very similar observations, which implies that the problem is not the fact that we do not know what the problems are. Rather, the problems are how to set goals to solve the problems and achieve them via effective implementation.

2. Main Issues: What Are the problems?

The following is a summary of the main problems associated with a national innovation system in Vietnam regarding human resources in R&D.

2.1. Fragmented Innovation System

R&D systems in Vietnam are severely fragmented. Although there are more than 500 research institutions, the division of labor among them is not clear and the productivity and quality of R&D is not as high as it could be. R&D institutes are not well connected to ministries, provinces, universities, and business, and cooperation among them is scant since there is little incentive for them to collaborate with others. This leads to unsuccessful policy attempts to connect them. Such fragmentation in a national innovation system makes planned education and supply of advanced human resources more difficult since supply cannot meet demand efficiently and effectively.

2.2. Weak Research Capacity and Weak link between R&D Institutes and Business

This is a subset of the fragmented innovation system. In order to make R&D relevant to the national economy, it is very crucial to have the outcomes of R&D institutes transferred to business for creating and producing new products and upgrading production processes. However, since the link between R&D institutes and business is quite weak in Vietnam, research output is not well transferred from R&D institutes to private companies. Furthermore, there is little collaboration between universities and business, which leads to a mismatch in human resources supply and demand.

Most of the policies in the 1970s focused on strengthening the link between R&D institutes and business. However, ministries acted as intermediaries so that there was no direct link between them. When Vietnam's economy rapidly moved away from the centrally planned economy model, R&D institutes were forced to sell their research results to the market, but they lacked marketing skills and desired technologies to be sold in the market.

Since 1997, there have been various policy efforts to strengthen the link, but Vietnam's government is still having difficulty creating a successful ecosystem for cooperation between R&D institutes and business. At the same time, lack of competiveness in the national market leads to low pressure on domestic enterprises to apply technological innovation. This explains why enterprises spend little on R&D and most R&D personnel belong to the government sector. Since there is little demand from enterprise for advanced R&D personnel, the supply is limited and not focused and as a result, the majority of R&D workers look for jobs in government R&D institutes.

Although enterprises' demand for technology is a vital driver of applied research from research institutes and universities, there is a shortage of demand from the enterprise side; domestic enterprises usually rely on imported technology rather than on technology created by domestic research institutes and universities. At the same time, the ability to develop technology in domestic R&D institutions is limited and does not meet the demand from enterprises. There are problems from the demand-side as well as supply-side and therefore the issue should be approached from the ecosystem perspective, not as separate issues.

2.3. Weak Technology Transfer from FDI

Technology transfers from companies associated with FDI are quite limited in terms of quantity as well as quality. Since FDI is one of the main sources of technology adopted by catching-up countries, Vietnam needs to emphasize and increase adequate technology transfer from FDI-related companies. For that, Vietnam's government needs to be selective in accepting FDI if possible and set up systematic support for maximizing technology absorption from FDI. Since human capital plays an integral role in technology transfer, the human capital strategy should be the main agenda for technology transfer from FDI at the same time. Policies to promote brain-power circulation need to be included.

2.4. Ineffective Implementation and Evaluation of R&D Basic Plans

There are various plans for R&D development and promotion, but the implementation and evaluation of them have been neither proper nor effective. There are three main reasons for this. First, there are discrepancies between S&T laws and regulations and other laws and regulations on government budgets, taxes, labor and salary. Second, line ministries and provincial government have not paid much attention to the implementation of national strategies such as the National Strategy for Science and Technology Development 2011-2020. Third, the logic between problems and policies has been weak and it has not been clear how policies are to accomplish the goals set for the plans. The plans contain rhetorical components and "ought-to" but are short on "how-to".

Although the plans are very systematic and organized, they cannot produce any result unless they are properly executed, which is one of the most serious problems associated with the national innovation system in Vietnam. Since evaluation is quite political, it often faces political resistance from stakeholders. However, it should be noted that only proper evaluation can lead to policy learning and improvement, which are seriously lacking in Vietnam.

2.5. Lack of a Central Organization for Coordinating R&D Policy and Statistics

The Ministry of Education and Training and the Ministry of Science and Technology are closely involved in making policies and preparing budgets for R&D. In addition, the Ministry of Planning and Investment and Ministry of Finance take primary responsibility for balancing and allocating the annual budgets for R&D and higher education. There is National Institute for Science and Technology Policy and Strategy Studies(NISTPASS), which is an S&T organization under the Ministry of Science and Technology, which assists the Minister to fulfill functions of studying S&T management strategies, policies and mechanisms, for policy planning. The policy-making process needs more participation from business and better statistics on economic status and R&D investment and human resources since accurate statistical data are the foundation for informed policy-making process.

In order to transform Vietnam's economy to a R&D-based economy, the issues mentioned above should be addressed systematically and consistently with the help of adequate funds.

2.6. Ineffective Coordination among Various Laws and Regulations

The legal environment for the development of S&T human resources has not really synchronized. For example, law relating to S&T businesses are not compatible with land-use law. Thus, S&T businesses do not enjoy the privileges in accordance with the law. In particular, many S&T businesses are not eligible for incentives related to land use rights, land lease and infrastructure with the lowest price within the price bracket of the State in the locality where they are leasing outside the high technology area. In addition, the State's tax policy for some sectors is still ineffective for encouraging the development of S&T enterprise. For example, the tariff on imported materials is higher than the tariff on imported products for some goods that the majority of enterprises in Vietnam cannot produce. Therefore, domestic products (higher tariff rates on imported material) face unequal competition with imported products (tariff rates are very low, even at 0%).

2.7. Lack of Entrepreneurship-Related Incentives and Regulation based on R&D

Vietnam now has around 421 universities/colleges, and 375,000 active businesses but only 500 S&T enterprises, this is not much a big ratio of S&T businesses. In recent years, the government of Vietnam has issued documents and policies to create favorable conditions for developing S&T enterprises, including incentives related to taxes, fees and charges, credit and the use of S&T services. However, so far, the number of S&T enterprises and incubators of science and technology business are smaller than their growth potential. The quality and service of the S&T incubator is limited in facilitating promotion of

S&T enterprise.

There are several reasons for this problem. First, there is a lack of guidelines for implementation of mechanisms and policies in the industry and thus, the incentives are not applied in practice as planned. Second, the capital market in Vietnam is not entirely developed, especially the formation and attraction of venture capital. Stock markets have only been trading shares of businesses that lacks of technology unlike those of countries with advanced economy, thus, fail to raise funds for S&T start-ups and incubators. Third, although a program called “Supports for development of science and technology enterprises” was enacted in 2014, it was only just launched because for the program was not provided with written instructions. The program also has a number of points not in line with the needs and practices of most of the local government and enterprises, especially provisions relating to support of S&T business incubators. Fourth, Vietnamese enterprises are mainly small and medium enterprises that are limited in self-innovation, and the government does not have the mechanisms and policies to effectively create a linkage between research institutes, universities and business or to help businesses receive the results of science and technology to form new enterprises. Fifth, the enforcement of intellectual property law in many localities is not serious. Violations persist in many places, which limits the attraction of investment in R&D. Finally, MOST has too many agencies performing the function of state management of S&T enterprise, but it has not taken the drastic measures needed to develop S&T business. According to Decree 115, MOST needs to transform public S&T organizations into autonomous, self-responsible businesses or being establishing S&T enterprises, but the implementation of the conversion is very slow and is not controlled. The Government’s Decree 115 which guides the implementation of the 2014 Law on Social Insurance requires all Vietnamese workers abroad to pay compulsory social insurance from January 1.

IV. Korean HRD Policy for R&D

Korea's experience in HRD policy for R&D can be a good reference for future policy in Vietnam. Since HRD is a part of economic policy and R&D policy, it is necessary to explain the economic policy and R&D policy first and then the explanation of HRD for R&D in Korea will follow.

1. Korean HRD Policy in R&D[16]

1.1. R&D Personnel in Korea

As shown in Figure 4-6, the number of R&D researchers in Korean has steadily increased over the years, from 20,718 in 1981 to 437,447 in 2014. Total R&D personnel also increased from 35,805 in 1981 to 605,604 in 2014, which is about 17 times increase. This increase has been especially sharp since 2000, which shows that the Korean economy has shifted to a more R&D-centered economy. Total R&D expenditure has sharply increased during this time as well.

16 This part is mainly dependent upon a publication titled "Future Direction of HRST Policy: Lessons from History" (KISTEP 2013).

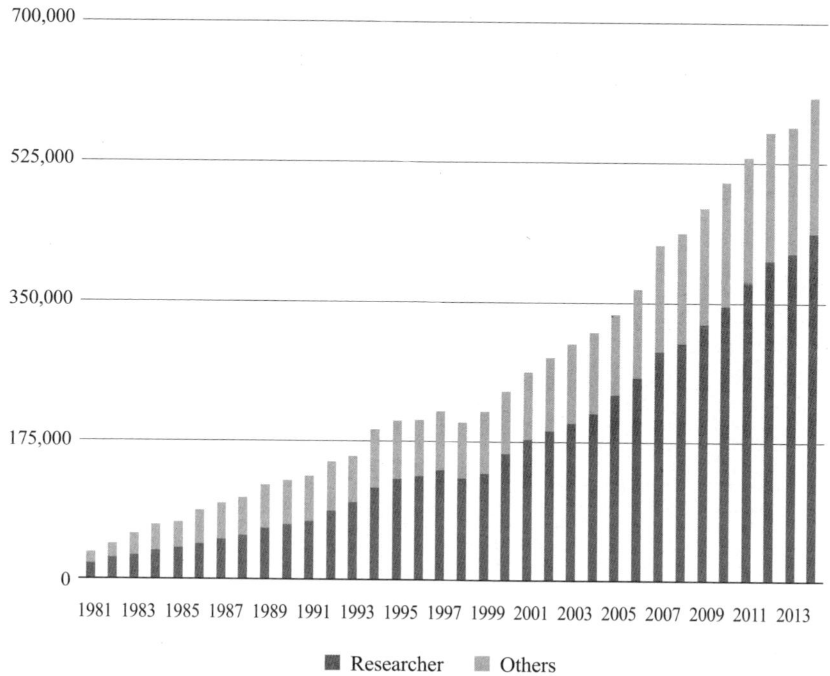

Source: Korea Institute of S&T Evaluation and Planning (KISTEP), R&D Activity Investigation Report. Each Year.

Figure 4-3 R&D Personnel in Korea (1981~2014)

1.2. Korean HRD Policy in R&D

Korean HRD policy in R&D before 2000 can be categorized into four periods: 1960s, 1970s, 1980s, and 1990s. A breakdown of each period is presented in Table 4-13

Table 4-13 Korean S&T HRD Policy between 1960 and 2012

	1960s	1970s	1980s	1990s	2000-2004	2003-2007	2008-2012
Policy Goals	Secure light industry-focused capabilities and manpower	Focus on training first-line scientists and technicians for heavy chemical industrial development	Focus on advanced S&T for future high-tech industries	Develop S&T training for technical innovation and core technology	Design S&T training to respond to private sector needs	Conduct periodic training on creative talents	Conduct convergence creative talent training and functional training
Key Features	Train skilled workers Control quantity of students in University for quality management Raise needed funding	Expand the scale of university personnel and strengthen universities' competitive-ness Establish standardized qualifications for skilled workers	Attract graduate and doctoral-level human resources and get international support Promote status of Scientists	Strengthen university research capacity Strengthen linkage between university and industry Utilize scientists for national R&D projects	Encour-age superior students to study S&T Enlarge activities of science and engineer-ing workforce	Establish HR policy to cover the whole life period Recruit civil engineers	Integrate STEAM education and research policy Attract overseas scholars through programs such as WCU

Source: Korea Institute of S&T Evaluation and Planning (KISTEP) (2013) "Future Direction of HRST Policy: Lessons from History"

1.2.1. 1960s: Securing light industry-focused capabilities and manpower

In the 1960s, the Korean government focused on securing light industry-focused capabilities and manpower through law and planning. Specifically, it focused on initial training and formulating a base for application policy. The 1st Five-Year Plan for Technology Promotion (1962-1966) and the 2nd Five-Year Plan for Science and Technology Promotion(1967-1971) were passed successively.

For programs and institutions, the Korean government conducted full-scale supply and demand forecasting, set up career training for skilled workers, worked to attract overseas Korean scientists and allocated supporting funds for universities. Programs for attracting overseas Koreans scientists and technologists were quite successful, bringing 493 scientists to Korea between 1968 and 1979.

To build infrastructure, the Korean government established the first administrative organization for R&D and specialized research institutions. It established KIST (Korea Institute of Science and Technology) in 1966 and a Human Resource Department in the Ministry of Science and Technology in 1968. Table 4-14 presents detailed information about the development of S&T HRD policy in the 1960s.

Table 4-14 Korean HRD Policy in S&T in the 1960s

	Law / Plan	Program/ Institution	Infrastructure
Characteristics	Initial training and formulating base for application policy	Conduct full-scale supply and demand forecasting Offer career training for skilled workers Attract overseas Korean scientists Provide support funds for universities	Establish the first administrative organization for R&D and specialized research institutions
Key Examples	1st Five-Year Plan for Technology Promotion (1962-1966) 2nd five-Year Plan for Science and Technology Promotion(1967-1971)	Develop program for attracting overseas Korean scientists and technologists (1968) (attracted 493 scientists from 1968 to 1979)	Establish KIST (Korea Institute of Science and Technology) (1966) Create HR department in MOST (1968)

Source: : Korea Institute of S&T Evaluation and Planning (KISTEP) (2013) "Future Direction of HRST Policy: Lessons from History"

1.2.2. 1970s: Focusing on training first-line scientists/technicians for heavy chemical industrial development

The Korean government focused on training first-line scientists/technicians for heavy chemical industrial development to meet the demand from the heavy and chemical industries.

For law and planning, the government established technical qualification standards and built supply strategies for human resources by work force demand types (Scientist, Technician, skilled workers). The National Technical Qualifications Act (1973), the 3rd Five-Year Plan for Science and Technology Promotion (1972-1976), and the 4th Five-Year Plan for Economic Development: Science and Technology (1977-1981) were all enacted.

For program and institution, the government focused on quantitative expansion and qualitative strengthening of university personnel and established the requirements for technical personnel qualification standards. A national technical qualification system was put in place in 1975.

For infrastructure, the government fostered institutions for supporting science and technology personnel and established education and research facilities in various disciplines. The Comprehensive Science and Technology Council operated 1973-1997, and KAIS (Korean Advanced Institute of Science) was opened in 1971, Korea Science Foundation in 1977 and Changwon Technical University in 1977.

Table 4-15 Korean HRD Policy in S&T in the 1970s

	Law / Plan	Program/ Institution	Infrastructure
Key Features	Establish technical qualification standards Build supply strategies for human resources by work force demand types (Scientist, Technician, skilled workers)	Quantitative expansion and qualitative strengthening of university personnel Establish requirements for technical personnel qualification standards	Foster institutions for supporting S&T personnel Establish education and research facilities in various disciplines
Key Examples	National Technical Qualifications Act (1973) 3rd Five-Year Plan for Science and Technology Promotion (1972-1976) 4th Five-Year Plan for Economic Development: Science and Technology (1977-1981)	National technical qualification system (1975)	Comprehensive Science and Technology Council (1973-1997) KAIS(1971) Korea Science Foundation(1977) Changwon Technical University(1977)

Source: Korea Institute of S&T Evaluation and Planning (KISTEP)(2013) "Future Direction of HRST Policy: Lessons from History"

1.2.3. 1980s: Focusing on advanced science and technology for future high-tech industries

In the 1980s, the Korean government focused on advanced science and technology for future high-tech industries to prepare for new industrial growth.

For law and planning, the Korean government tried to enhance the quality of S&T personnel for the future high-tech industries and established and implemented the 5th Five-Year Plan for Economic Social Development: Science and Technology (1982-1986) and the 6th five-Year Plan for Economic

Social Development: Science and Technology (1987-1991).

For program and institution, the government planned to attract and strengthen training for advanced science and technology personnel and promote the status of scientists. It started the International Postdoctoral Research Support Program in 1982 and the Recruitment Program for foreign scholars in Advanced Science and Technology in 1985. The Korean Science Award was established in 1987.

For infrastructure, institutions for gifted students were established and the function and scope of policy administration system in HRD for S&T were expanded. Various Government-funded Research Institutes (GRIs) were also formed, including KAIST (Korea Advanced Institute of Science and Technology) in 1981, the Korea Science Academy in1983 and the Human Policy Review Committee in 1984. A Deputy Director General for Human Resources was appointed under the Ministry of Science and Technology in 1985 and operated the Council for Promoting Science and Technology between 1989-1991.

Table 4-16 Korean HRD Policy in S&T in the 1980s

	Law / Plan	Program/ Institution	Infrastructure
Key Features	Enhance the quality of S&T personnel for the future high-tech industries	Attract and strengthen training for advanced S&T personnel Promote status of scientists	Establish institution for gifted students Expand the function of the HR policy administration system
Key Examples	5th Five-Year Plan for Economic Social Development: Science and Technology (1982-1986) 6th Five-Year Plan for Economic Social Development: Science and Technology (1987-1991)	International Postdoctoral Research Support Program (1982) Recruitment Program for foreign scholars in Advanced Science and Technology (1985) Korean Science Award (1987)	Establish various Government-funded Research Institutes (GRIs) (1980-present) Establish KAIST (Korea Advanced Institute of Science and Technology) (1981-present), Korea Science Academy (1983-present), Human Policy Review Committee (1984) Appoint Deputy Director General for Human Resource Department in Ministry of Science and Technology (1985) Form Council for Promoting S&T (1989-1991)

Source: : Korea Institute of S&T Evaluation and Planning (KISTEP) (2013) "Future Direction of HRST Policy: Lessons from History"

1.2.4. 1990s: S&T training for technical innovation and core technology development

In the 1990s, the Korean government focused on S&T training for technical innovation and core technology development.

For law and planning, a temporary special law established a pan-governmental-level performance evaluation system. The Special Law for Science, Technology and Innovation was passed in 1997 and the Comprehensive Plan for Science, Technology and Innovation was set up in 1992.The 7th Five-Year Plan for Economic Social Development: Science and Technology (1992-1996) and Science, Technology and Innovation Five-Year Plan (1997-2001) were implemented.

For program and institution, the government expanded support for higher education institutions of science and engineering and utilized talent through national R&D projects and industry-university-GRI linkages. A Doctoral degree program was begun based on academic-industry-GRIs cooperation in 1991, along with the Brain Pool program in 1994 and the BK21 (Brain Korea) program (1999-present) which was designed to support graduate students in universities.

For infrastructure, the Ministry of Science and Technology was upgraded it to the ministry level from the sub-ministry level in 1998. Intermediaries between talents and industries were identified and institutions for gifted young students were established in universities, including the S&T Advisory Council in 1991, the Korea Institute for Advanced Study in 1996 and the KAIST Center for the Gifted in Science (1997).

Table 4-17 Korean HRD Policy in S&T in 1990s

	Law / Plan	Program/ Institution	Infrastructure
Key Features	Establish temporary special law Establish pan-governmental-level performance evaluation system	Expand support for higher education institutions of science and engineering Utilize talent through national R&D projects Utilize talent through industry-university-GRIs linkage	Empower the Ministry of Science and Technology Establish intermediaries between talent and industries Establish institutions for gifted young students in universities
Key Examples	Special Law for Science, Technology and Innovation (1997) Comprehensive Plan for Science, Technology and Innovation (1992) 7th five-Year Plan for Economic Social Development: Science and Technology (1992-1996) Science, Technology and Innovation five-year plan (1997-2001)	Doctoral degree program based on academic-industry-GRIs cooperation (1991) Brain Pool program (1994) BK21 program (1999-present)	Ministry of Science and Technology promoted to ministry status (1998) S&T Advisory Council (1991) Korea Institute for Advanced Study (1996) KAIST Center for the Gifted in Science (1997)

Source: : Korea Institute of S&T Evaluation and Planning (KISTEP) (2013) "Future Direction of HRST Policy: Lessons from History"

1.2.5. 2000~2004: Independence of S&T from General Industrialization and Economic Policy

Entering the new millennium, S&T policy in Korea became independent from general industrialization and economic policy. The Korean government established Science and Technology Basic Law and basic plan for Science and

Technology and provided support for gifted young students and women in the S&T field. The Framework Act on Science and Technology (2001), the Act on Fostering and Supporting Women Scientists and Technicians (2002) and the 1st Science and Technology Basic Plan (2002-2006) were all passed. For program and institution, the Korean government started the BK21 program for world-class graduate school and human resources in 1999. An independent institution for gifted students in science was made part of the infrastructure.

Table 4-18 Korean HRD Policy in S&T between 2000 and 2004

	Law / Plan	Program/ Institution	Infrastructure
Key Features	Establish Science and Technology Basic Law and basic plan for Science and Technology Provide support for gifted young students and women in science and technology field	Promote programs for world-class graduate school and human resources (BK21)	Establish an independent institution for gifted students
Key Examples	Framework Act on Science and Technology (2001) Act on Fostering and Supporting Women Scientists and Technicians (2002) The 1st Science and Technology Basic Plan (2002-2006)	BK21 program (1999-present)	Establish Korea Science Academy (2001-present)

Source: Korea Institute of S&T Evaluation and Planning (KISTEP) (2013) "Future Direction of HRST Policy: Lessons from History"

1.2.6. 2004~Present: Independence of S&T from General Industrialization and Economic Policy

Since 2004, there has been a major shift in S&T human resources policy in Korea from quantity-based policy to quality-based policy. By setting up a series of Basic Planning for the Science and Engineering Workforce (1st, 2nd and 3rd), the Korean government has tried to adjust the policy to meet the changes in the environment and policy orientation.

The 1st Basic Planning of Science and Engineering Workforce (2006~2008) focused on strengthening S&T Universities through management reform, educating Core R&D personnel, developing a demand-based personnel supply, and improving welfare for personnel in the science and technology fields.

The 1st Basic Planning of Science and Engineering Workforce: modification plan (2008~2010) was based on the 1st basic Plan but stressed policies related to gifted young students and overseas human resources.

The 2nd Basic Planning of Science and Engineering Workforce (2011~2015) expanded the scope from the elementary school to higher education as the Ministry of Science and Technology became merged with the Ministry of Education under President Lee Myung-bak and focused on the relationship between education and R&D and the promotion of the R&D capability of private companies.

The 3rd Basic Planning of Science and Engineering Workforce (2016~2020) under President Park Geun-hye focuses on strengthening the capacity of S&T human resources and helping their career development. Plans are in place to tap into foreign scholars and female S&T personnel to make R&D investment more effective.

Table 4-19 Korean HRD Plans in S&T since 2004

Title	1st basic planning for science and engineering workforce	1st basic planning for science and engineering workforce: modification plan	2nd basic planning for science and Technology workforce	3rd basic planning for science and Technology workforce
Period	2006-2008	2008-2010	2011-2015	2016-2020
President / administrative system	Roh Moo-hyun / Science, Technology and Innovation Division	Lee Myung-bak / Ministry of Education, Science and Technology	Lee Myung-bak / Ministry of Education, Science and Technology	Park Geun-hye / National Science and Technology Council
Key Features	Strengthen S&T universities through management reform Educate core R&D personnel Demand-based personnel supply Improve welfare for personnel in S&T	Based on the 1st basic plan but stresses gifted young students and overseas human resource	As the Ministry of Science and Technology merged with the Ministry of Education, extended the range from elementary school to higher education	Strengthen the capacity of S&T human resources and help their career development Tap into foreign scholars and female S&T personnel

Source: Korea Institute of S&T Evaluation and Planning (KISTEP) (2013) "Future Direction of HRST Policy: Lessons from History"

2. Environment Change and Problems in S&T Policy in Korea

There have been three significant changes in the environment surrounding the S&T domain: the growth of private companies, the development of universities, and globalization.

As mentioned earlier, the research capability of private companies has significantly advanced over the last 30 years and excelled beyond the GRIs and GOEs. Therefore, it is no longer necessary for private companies to depend upon these organizations for technicians and engineers since universities can provide enough qualified entry-level human resources and private companies are now able to train their employees by themselves.

In addition, the research capability of Korean universities has been strengthened with the help of increased R&D investment. Since there were few research facilities in universities, advanced-level human resources sought positions in GRIs, which paid higher salaries. However, with increased revenue from R&D investment and tuition, Korean universities equipped themselves with decent research facilities and building. Moreover, as a result of the Asian financial crisis in 1997~1998, the tenure of researchers in GRIs was shortened to 61 years old from 65 years old, which led to the exodus of high-profile researchers to universities. The concentration of GRIs in the Daejeon area became an obstacle to recruiting advanced Ph.D. holders since they tended to prefer to live in Seoul, the capital of Korea. The reorganization of GRIs became a policy problem since GRIs have been criticized due to their inefficiency and ineffectiveness. In addition, the mission of GRIs became dubious because of changes in the research and policy environment.

Since the 1990s, the Korean economy became liberalized and globalized. Korean companies became globalized at the same time. For example, Samsung is no longer a domestic company; instead, it has become a global player with production facilities and research centers all over the world. Due to globalization, the scope of government S&T policy no longer matches the targets of the policy, which seriously limits the effectiveness of R&D policy.

2.1. Recent Adjustments in S&T Policy in Korea

2.1.1. Continuing Investment in R&D and R&D Personnel

Entering the 2000s, the Korean government had increased R&D spending and the supply of researchers by expanding universities. After Korean companies successfully caught up with foreign competitors in major industries, they faced the limit of the "catch-up model." They could not find any examples to follow and could not utilize the "me too" strategy which used to work effectively. Such limits led the government to increase the R&D budget in Korea since it was not possible to create any breakthroughs and realize technological opportunities in promising areas (see Figure 4-7).

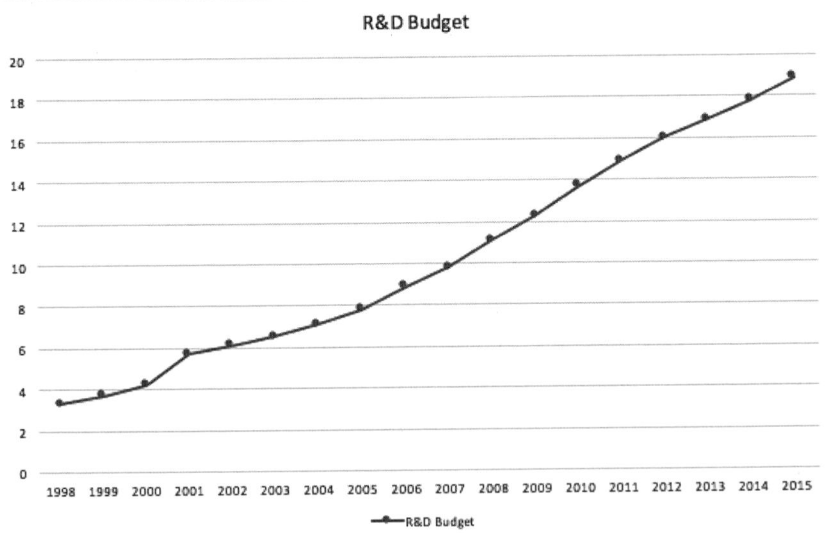

Source: Korea Institute of S&T Evaluation and Planning (KISTEP), R&D Activity Investigation Report. Each Year.

Figure 4-4 Government R&D Budget in Korea 1998~2015 (Unit: Trillion Won)

The supply of researchers in R&D have also increased consistently over the years. As shown in Figure4.8, the number of researchers in R&D per million increased from 2,345 in 2000 to 4,175 in 2006 and 6,457 in 2013.

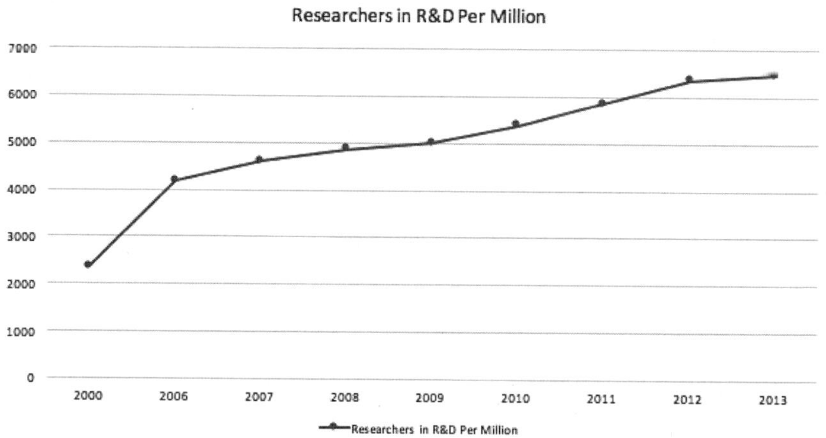

Source: Korea Institute of S&T Evaluation and Planning (KISTEP), R&D Activity Investigation Report. Each Year.

Figure 4-5 Researchers in R&D per Million in Korea

Facing the limits of the "catch-up model", the Korean government frequently changed the strategic areas as well as the governance structure of R&D policy.

2.1.2. Path Dependency: Expansion of Universities and GRIs

Table 4-20 presents the changes in expenditure on R&D by different types of institutions between 2009 and 2013.

Table 4-20 R&D Expenditure by Institutions, 2009~2013

(Unit: 100 million won)

	2009	2010	2011	2012	2013
Total R&D	124,145	136,827	148,528	159,064	169,139
GOR	6,683	7,090	7,319	7,701	8,198
GFRI	49,718	55,113	57,099	64,286	69,923
University	30,120	33,956	37,672	37,214	39,718
Other	37,624	40,668	46,438	49,863	51,300

Note: GOR: Government ; GFRI: Government Funded Research Institute.

Source: Korea Institute of S&T Evaluation and Planning (KISTEP), R&D Activity Investigation Report. Each Year.

The earlier choices the Korean government made became rigid R&D structures that needed to be reformed. The government tried several times to reform GFRI and increase their productivity but were only able to make minor changes since the resistance from GFRI was quite strong and the direction of the reform was not agreed upon among stakeholders. Each new president set the reform of GFRI as the first agenda for S&T. However, although there is wide consensus that reform is needed, it has been impossible to agree on the directions and details of the reform, which resulted in frequent minor changes that were ineffective.

With the liberalization of university establishment in the 1990s, the number of universities drastically increased, which opened the door to higher education wider. However, since a decrease in total population is forecast, it is expected that some of these universities will fail to recruit students and eventually go bankrupt. Such insolvency and bankruptcy may lead to the instability of higher education and a decrease in the quality of education. Some universities are heavily dependent upon government financial support and tuition.

These are current primary policy issues in Korea since the government cannot fix the problems even though they have been known for a long time. Therefore, it is very crucial to note that policy choices made in the coming years in Vietnam will have a lingering impact on Vietnam's future.

2.1.3. Population Change and Its Impact on R&D and R&D Personnel

Figure 4.9 shows that the total population in Korea is expected to decrease in 2030,with the percentage of people older than 65 expected to be 24.3% and the percentage of people between 15~64 years old decreasing to 63.1% in 2030. When this happens, the Korean economy will face a fundamental structural shift, and S&T-based economic growth will be needed even more than before since Korea will no longer be able to depend on the increase in production factors such as labor. The Korean government needs to focus on increasing its Total Factor Productivity(TFP) and quality of human capital, which are complexly related with educational and cultural institutions. This requires a more focused and systematic plan for strategic R&D investment in potential sectors and industries.

As shown in Figure 4.10, the number of graduate students in Korea rapidly increased from 1996 till 2003. It hit a ceiling in 2010 and has stayed flat since. Most of the increase had been driven by national universities. Since it takes a sizable investment to increase the number of graduate students especially in S&T areas, it is not plausible for private universities to do the job. Therefore, the Korean government played a crucial role in increasing the supply of R&D personnel from universities. As shown in Figure 4.11, the percentage of engineering and science degrees of total degrees awarded in Korea is very competitive compared to other countries including Taiwan, Japan, China, and Singapore.

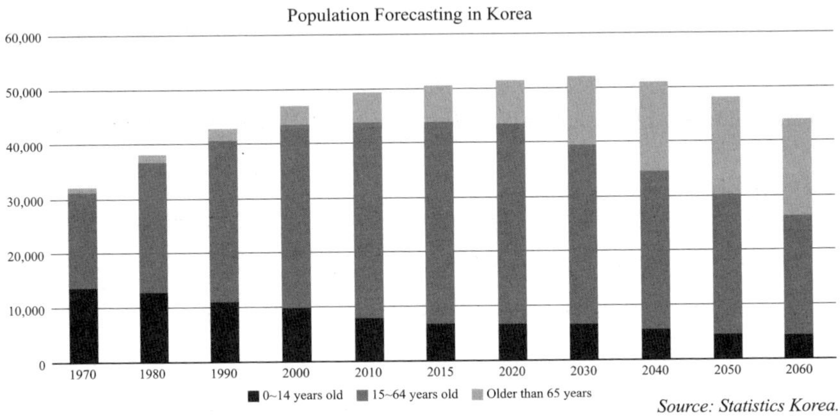

Source: Statistics Korea.

Figure 4-6 Korean population forecast, 1970~2060 (unit: thousands)

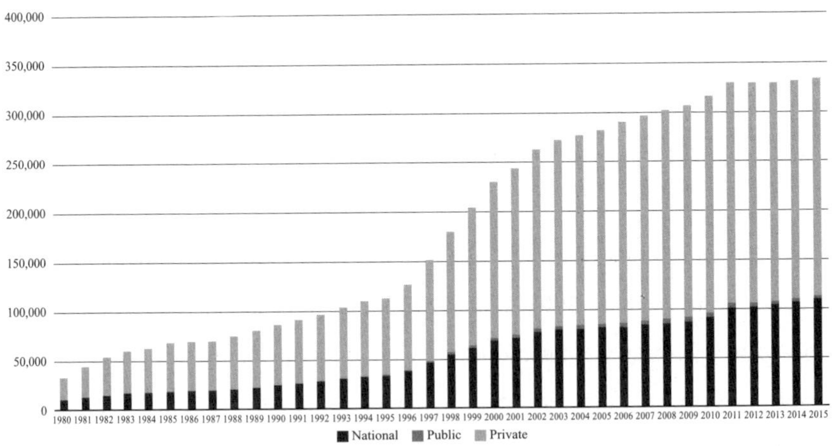

Source: Korea Educational Statistics Service, Number of Graduate Students. Retrieved August 8, 2016 from: http://kess.kedi.re.kr/kessTheme/timeStats?itemCode=03&menuId=m_02_03_02

Figure 4-7 Number of Graduate Students in Korea (1980~2015)

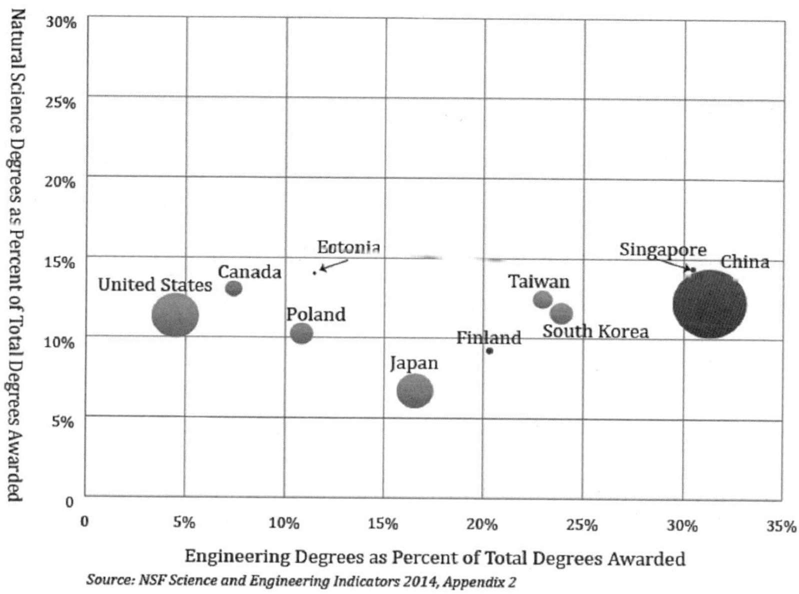

Figure 4-8 Engineering Science Degrees Awarded by Country (2010)

The ample supply of graduate students has been a huge asset for the Korean economy when it has been expanding. At the same time, the quality of graduate education also increased as evidenced by global university rankings and numbers of publications in international journals. However, since the Korean economy has been shifting from quantity-based growth to quality-based growth, companies are paying more attention to quality of R&D personnel. Therefore, current policy focusing on the number of R&D personnel is starting to change to policy focusing more on quality of education and research. However, this policy shift is not easy because it means a "select and concentrate" policy will be needed. This is not good for second- and third-tier universities because it will lead to a decrease in the financial support they receive. Since such universities are located mainly in provincial areas, these policies are tightly connected with political issues too, which make reform even harder.

In summary, the issues mentioned above indicate that there will be unprecedented change in the R&D environment for Korea. The 3rd Basic Planning of Science and Engineering Workforce (2016~2020) is an effort to adjust the Korean innovation system to meet these challenges. However, it is not easy to change such a rigid system.

V. Policy Recommendations

Science and technology have progressed at unforeseen speed. The prospect of a fourth Industrial Revolution as well as the impending development of Artificial Intelligence make the environment for catching-up countries worse than before. Unstable world politics threaten free movement of goods and services. This means that Vietnam is in a quite different and in some ways more difficult position from that Korea faced during its economic development era.

The biggest challenge is that the time window for the catching-up countries is rapidly shrinking. For example, automation is wiping out the cost advantage catching-up countries had enjoyed during economic development. The future economy is expected to demand less and less labor and require more and more advanced human resources.

Vietnam does not have much time to catch-up. The following recommendations are policy suggestions based on analysis and discussion with experts in Vietnam. It should be noted that these recommendations do not cover all topics related to the issues but rather focus on the main agenda only.

Recommendation 1. Vietnam's government needs to restructure the role and capacity of government-affiliated R&D organizations.

There are 1055 S&T organizations in Vietnam, but their R&D productivity fails to meet expectations. It is highly recommended to have a so-called "select and concentrate strategy" in order to nurture prestigious R&D institutes and make the division of labor among R&D institutes more clear. Although enormous political and administrative resistance is expected, the longer it takes, the more it will cost. The point of restructuring is to make the R&D budget more efficient and make R&D organizations more attractive destinations for top-talented people. As shown in Korea's case, a development strategy centered on GRIs has potential. The Vietnamese government needs to make the best use of the existing institutions by restructuring them.

The Vietnamese government considers mechanisms to create autonomy to be the most crucial mechanisms for S&T development after the renovation of GRIs. However, the autonomous mechanism designed in Decree 115/2005/ND-CP seems to contain mistakes. The policy indicates that an autonomous mechanism for public research institutions is the "self-financed" mechanism, policy equates autonomy with self-financing. Instead, new autonomous mechanisms have to focus on autonomous R&D personnel and autonomous utilization of funding.

Recommendation 2. Vietnam's government needs to renovate its economic growth model.

There must be a change in the current economic growth model to rely more on science, technology and innovation (STI). In order for S&T to be a driving force for industrialization and modernization of the country, the central government should request its departments and provincial governments to take actions for actions to promote STI. For example, each ministry and provincial government has to incorporate some STI indicators or measures in their development plans or strategies. The central government should also ask its departments and provincial governments to regularly report their achievements or failures relating to STI. Korea's experience shows that the timely change of the country's growth model from production factor-based to innovation-based has been crucial for the continuous growth of the Korean economy.

Recommendation 3. Vietnam's government needs to invest in empowering the research capacity of GRIs and universities and increase salaries to attract more competent researchers.

The research capability of major R&D organizations suffers from lack of qualified personnel, adequate funding and able students. Since human resources are the core for the innovation-based economy of the future, it is very crucial to empower main R&D institutions by investing in them on conditions of internal reform of related institutions.

The current government salary system for researchers can be considered as a hindering factor in STI. It contains too many levels of payment for researchers and is not attractive to talented researchers. A change in the government salary system should focus on the following perspectives: (1) the number of levels should be reduced and each researcher category might contain several levels; (2) research institutions should have autonomous rights to pay for their researchers according to the given budget or to bring a researcher from one category to another once (e.g., from "common" researcher to "principal" researcher");

(3) the government should give funding, supervision and evaluation of public research institutions according to their R&D performance.

The successful creation and operation of KIST can be referred to as a good policy example in empowering GRIs and universities in Vietnam.

Recommendation 4. Vietnam's government needs to strengthen collaboration among GRIs, universities, and business.

Currently there is a severe lack of collaboration among GRIs, universities, and business. The Vietnamese government needs to facilitate cooperation by creating joint R&D projects, education and job training programs. Universities need to shuffle their curricula to meet the demands from business. New plans and strategies are not enough to bring changes. more active interventions geared toward fostering cooperation programs geared toward cooperation among institutions are necessary.

Recommendation 5. Vietnam's government needs to bring more competition to the domestic market in order to make business more innovative and more attractive for R&D workers.

Since there is a lack of competition in the domestic market, there is less incentive for businesses to invest in R&D. Rather they tend to import technology from foreign companies for the domestic market, which limits their innovation capacity and job opportunities for university graduates. By bringing more competition into the domestic market, it is expected that businesses will pay more attention to their own R&D. At the same time, government needs to help businesses to engage in R&D by providing them with administrative support, tax incentives and R&D budget. The step-by-step liberalization policy in Korea which made Korean business more competitive globally can be referred to as a policy example.

Recommendation 6. Considering that the main driver of technology transfer is the talent, Vietnam's government needs to make technology transfer more efficient by promoting brain circulation and using strategic FDI policy.

The technology transfer from FDI in Vietnam is limited. Since the main driver of technology transfer is the talent, the Vietnamese government needs to focus on attracting talent from foreign companies and countries. It is very important to make Vietnam attractive to skilled expatriates.

Vietnam's government needs to develop customized training programs for foreign companies. Since the curriculum in Vietnamese universities fails to satisfy the demands of foreign companies and it takes huge resources to reshuffle the whole curriculum, it will be more practical to set up special programs for training students and workers customized for foreign companies. These can be co-financed by the government and the foreign companies.

Since automation based on robotics and artificial intelligence is proceeding faster than before, Vietnam might not have enough time to accumulate the necessary technological capacity. The government needs to pay more attention to technology transfer before it is too late. It is advised to use FDI more strategically and selectively. The Korean government initially focused on the import of capital goods and later shifted to investing in R&D and actively recruiting Korean scientists and engineers abroad. This shift helped the Korean economy stay competitive.

Recommendation 7. Vietnam's government needs to strengthen its implementation and evaluation capacity by creating a new R&D governing system including HRD and setting up a policy-learning mechanism.

Although there are strategies for R&D governing system, implementation and evaluation are not as effective as expected. HRD-related policies experience similar problems. By creating a governing system for R&D, the Vietnamese government will strengthen its capacity to execute and evaluate the plans. One of the strengths of Korea was the effective implementation of government plans and strategies. Korean government officials worked very hard to accomplish the goals in their plans, and they learned from their experiences. The Vietnamese government needs to strengthen the implementation capacity of the bureaucracy and learn from policy based on strict and systematic evaluation. Evaluation should not be a way to place blame but an opportunity for learning.

Recommendation 8. Vietnam's government needs to recommend and facilitate entrepreneurship at GRIs as well as universities by streamlining laws, regulations and incentives.

Vietnam's government has set up several measures to promote entrepreneurship, but there is a lot of room for improvement. The legal system must be evaluated to complete mechanisms and policies to create synchronization and ensuring enforcement in order to encourage the development of scientific and technological enterprise. A model of R&D business incubators needs to be built in line with local conditions and R&D

management majors should be fostered in universities, especially in the engineering and technology university, to establish and develop an expert team specializing in technology incubators, assessment, technology evaluation, promotion of technology transfer, consultancy and technology transfer.

Active entrepreneurship based on R&D in universities is expected to provide more incentive for talented student to major in S&T fields and more funding opportunities for universities. The Korean government recently started to emphasize and support entrepreneurship by university students and faculty members. Vietnam can refer to this recent policy development in Korea in order to learn what works and what does not work.

CHAPTER FIVE :

THE WAY FORWARD FOR AHRD IN VIETNAM

M. Jae Moon

Professor, Department of Public Administration, Yonsei University

CHAPTER FIVE :

THE WAY FORWARD FOR AHRD IN VIETNAM

Vietnam is a country of dynamism and energy which has already demonstrated an extraordinary record of economic growth as well as promising prospects for continued social and economic development in the future. Vietnam 2035, prepared by the World Bank and the Ministry of Planning and Investment, highlights six critical pillars which are required to drive new a visions for Vietnam by 2035. They include 1) enabling economic modernization with a competitive private sector firmly in the lead; 2) improving the country's technological and innovative capacity; 3) reshaping urban policies and investments for more dynamic cities and urban centers; 4) charting an environmentally sustainable development path with increasing adaptation and resilience to changing climate patterns; 5) promoting equality and inclusion among marginalized groups for the development of a harmonious middle-class society; and 6) establishing a modern rule of law state and democratic society. We believe that the Government of Vietnam needs to build a stronger and more capable state that is firmly supported by more competent personnel in key areas including government, SOEs, and R&D in order to effectively pursue the more prosperous and inclusive future defined *in Vietnam 2035*.

To supply high-quality human resources in key strategic areas, the Government of Vietnam needs to improve in both human resource management (i.e., recruitment, selection, career development path, promotion, pay, ethics, performance evaluation, and retirement) and human resource development (training and development), particularly for middle- and high-level management. This four-part report reviewed key issues and imperatives in three selected areas, identified the current status of AHRD and offered lessons and policy suggestions based on cases studies in AHRD of government, SOEs, and R&D.

In terms of AHRD in government, limited progress has been made in introducing the principle of meritocracy, advancing a position-based system, increasing salary and compensation, improving training capacity and de-politicizing AHRD by normalizing the relationship between the state and the Party. Similarly, several key limitations are identified in the AHRD of SOEs, including slow transformation of AHRD, lack of HRD capacity, and politicized recruitment of top management. For AHRD in R&D, there is a paucity of competent and qualified faculty members in universities and R&D managers in government research institutes as well as an insufficient supply of high-quality R&D personnel in the private sector.

In order to diagnose compelling AHRD issues in the government, SOE, and R&D sectors, Part I presents a review of official documents issued by the Government of Vietnam, such as SEDS 2011-2020, SEDP 2011-2015, and SEDP 2016-2020 and major development reports recently published by various international organizations such as the World Bank, OECD, and ADB. Based on the comprehensive review of these documents, Part I offered a systematic assessment of the current status of AHRD systems in Vietnam and identified a set of HR imperatives that should be seriously considered in dealing with the HR issues facing each area.

Part II examined HRD in the Vietnamese government and offered a detailed review of the contextual and environmental (i.e., external and internal conditions) circumstances of the Vietnamese government. Drawing mainly from the Korea's hands-on experience and know-how on leadership development through advanced HRD approaches, this part also mapped out the implementation and adoption of AHRD and offered specific recommendations in terms of AHRD systems, agencies, and programs. The policy recommendations specifically include: 1) institutionalized HR(M/D) systems, 2) integrated/Internalized HRD agencies, and 3) interactive HRD programs.

Part III assessed the current status of Vietnamese SOEs and recommended policy for their AHRD systems. To draw practical and compelling implications for various SOEs across various industries, three SOEs were selected as representative samples for analysis: VINACOMIN, VNPT, and Agribank, which represent primary, secondary, and tertiary sectors of industry, respectively. Comparable Korean cases were also selected as benchmarks: KOCOAL, KT, and National Agricultural Cooperative Federation or Nonghyup. Based on the comparative studies of selected cases from both countries, the part offered specific policy recommendations for each SOE along with general policy suggestions including 1) integration of HRM and HRD initiatives, 2) development of HRD professionals, and 3) modification and improvement of proven standardized training programs.

Part IV investigated the HRD system in the R&D area. In conjunction with the analysis of the current status of the supply and demand of R&D personnel in Vietnam, this part analyzed AHRD policy South Korea and identified major characteristics of Korean policies to identify policy recommendations for Vietnam. Various policy recommendations were offered in four dimensions: 1) universities and government research institutes; 2) FDI and business; government; and 4) collaboration among university, GRIs, and business. Specific policy recommendations include: 1) restructuring the role and capacity of government R&D institutes; 2) promoting more competitive environments to facilitate investment in R&D personnel; 3) strengthening collaboration among university, GRIs, and business; 4) promoting efficient technology transfer; and 5) creating R&D governing system to strengthen the capacity to implement and evaluate R&D programs.

While the Government of Vietnam has been making progress in improving its AHRD by introducing a position-based system and cultivating a performance culture in various sectors, this progress has been somewhat slow and limited. Based on various policy recommendations and suggestions by priority and urgency presented in four different parts of this report, we propose four key policy pillars that need to be considered by the Government of Vietnam to modernize the state and particularly to improve AHRD in the government, SOE, and R&D sectors in order to build a foundation for sustainable and inclusive economic and social development. The policy pillars of AHRD include the following: 1) promoting meritocracy in AHRD; 2) establishing new institutional arrangements to strategically promote AHRD; 3) enhancing institutional capacities of AHRD organizations; and 3) integrating fragmented AHRD systems.

Four Policy Pillars of AHRD in Government, SOEs, and R&D Sectors

Pillar	Policy Measures
Principle: The Principle of Meritocracy for AHRD	• Apply the principle of meritocracy to AHRD in government, SOEs, and R&D sectors • Eliminate nepotism and non-merit factors in recruitment and selection of new employees and shifting from seniority-based personnel system to merit-based personnel system • Depoliticize the appointment of top management in various sectors, particularly in SOEs
Institution: Establishment of AHRD Institution	•Establish central NAtional Advanced Human Resource Development Institute of Vietnam (NAHRDI) •Establish the Vietnam Productivity Center (VPC) as an official training institute for SOEs and private companies •Restructure government-affiliated R&D organizations to maximize their potential contribution to sustainable development
Capacity: Institutional Capacities of AHRD Organizations	•Improve the quantity and quality of trainers and faculty members in AHRD organizations, SOEs, government research institutes and universities •Strengthen institutional capacities of AHRD in curricular development, needs assessment, and feedback systems for effective training programs •Increase the number of AHRD specialists and R&D managers
Alignment: Structural Alignment of Fragamented AHRD Systems	•Eliminate fragmentation and duplication between the state and the party as well as between the central government and provincial governments in AHRD to build a complementary AHRD system •Align vertical and horizontal AHRD systems to make optimal use of limited AHRD training resources •Coordinate AHRD functions between government research institutes and universities

Promoting Meritocracy in AHRD

First of all, the Government of Vietnam needs to strengthen and apply the principle of meritocracy to various stages of human resource management and development. In order to attract talented and competitive personnel to government, SOEs, and R&D, recruitment and selection of new personnel should be administered based on merit rather than nepotism or any other non-merit factors such as political, family or other personal and relational background. Key human resource decisions (i.e., promotion, job assignments, performance evaluation) need to be made based on performance and merit and move away from seniority-based and nepotism-based HR decisions. In SOEs, the intervention and influence of government and party often hampers a merit-based human resource system. The board of directors in SOEs also need to be reconstituted to ensure long-term planning and professional management. Short-term and often non-merit-based appointment of board members weakens the meritocratic and professional foundation of SOEs and eventually damages competitiveness in the global market. Meritocracy also helps to attract talented youth to the R&D area

- *Apply the principle of meritocracy to AHRD in government, SOEs, and R&D sectors*
- *Eliminate nepotism and non-merit factors in recruitment and selection of new employees and shifting from seniority-based personnel system to merit-based personnel system*
- *Depoliticize the appointment of top management in various sectors particularly in SOEs*

Building New Institutional Arrangements for AHRD by Establishing New AHRD Institutes to Supply Competitive Human Resources to Various Sectors

Vietnam is at a crossroads. The quality of human resources in various sectors determines success or failure in pursuing and realizing the strategic goals of SEDP 2016-2020 and Vietnam 2035. Despite partial and slow improvement of existing HRD institutes, they are not ready to be fully transformed into new AHRD institutes which can not only provide various training programs to meet the current demand for human resources in various sectors but also supply high-quality human resources in the future. While the Vietnamese government needs to conduct comprehensive evaluation of existing HRD institutes and find ways to transform them into innovative and comprehensive AHRD institutes, it also needs to consider establishing new AHRD institutes for government, SOEs, and R&D.

- *Establish the National Advanced Human Resource Development Institute of Vietnam (NAHRDI) for central government officials and later AHRD Institutes for provincial and local government officials*
- *Establish the Vietnam Productivity Center for SOEs (VPCS) as an official training institute for SOEs and possibly private companies to strategically meet their training needs in various areas then strengthen its research capacity and maximize spin-off effect to various organizations*
- *Establish a central R&D institute such as V-KIST (Vietnam version of Korean Institute of Science and Technology) to supply high-quality advanced R&D personnel to R&D institutes and private companies to enhance the potential and competiveness of the Vietnamese economy while restructuring existing government research institutes (GRI) to maximize their potential contribution to the sustainable development of Vietnam*

Enhancing Training Capacities of AHRD Organizations by Developing Quality of Trainers, Training Curricula, and HR Professionals

Given the increasing future demand for competitive human resources in government, SOEs, and R&D in the next two decades, strengthening the institutional capacity of AHRD organizations is surely critical. Despite continued progress in AHRD organizations in the three selected areas, their institutional capacity has been limited due to lack of competitive trainers, effective training curricula, learning needs analysis and post-training feedback, among other issues. The Government of Vietnam needs to enhance both the quantity and quality of trainers as well as improve training curricula and training capacity of various training institutions under the Central Committee for Organizations (CCO), Ministry of Home Affairs (MOHA), Provincial Department of Home Affairs, and Department of Organization and Human Resource Management (DHRM). Dealing with the labor shortage in SOEs and R&D, enhancing the institutional capacity of AHRD organizations is not optional but required to supply skilled employees and competent high-quality R&D personnel. While each SOE needs to increase the number of AHRD managers and strengthen the institutional capacity of its own AHRD organization, it is also critical to supply enough skilled labor through a general skill training organization such as VNPT. Weak performance and teaching capacity in research institutions and universities are also problematic and have constrained the innovativeness and competitiveness of the Vietnamese economy. The quality of government research institutions as well as vocational and tertiary education will need to be increased in order to meet the demand for more competent and talented personnel in R&D. A sufficient supply of qualified faculty members in universities and R&D managers in government research institutes is critical.

- *Improve the quantity and quality of trainers in AHRD institutions in government and SOEs as well as ensuring qualified and competent faculty members in government research institutes and universities*

- *Strengthen institutional capacities of AHRD in curriculum development, training needs assessment, and feedback mechanisms for effective training programs*
- *Increase the number of AHRD specialists for governments and SOEs and R&D managers for R&D sectors as well as bridging the gap between talents needed and talents supplied*

Alignment of Fragmented AHRD Systems

It has been argued that state institutions are highly fragmented. Overlap and confusion in rules and roles between the State and the Party, between the central government and provincial governments, and even among central agencies are presented as one of the major obstacles to building a stronger state (World Bank and the MPI, 2016). Fragmentation and duplication are also common in AHRD when the center of the AHRD system is not strong and capable enough. The fragmented AHRD systems need to be unified and the overlaps and confusion which often pose obstacles to timely deployment of capable personnel in the right place need to be eliminated. The main targets for NAPA and HCMA need to be coordinated and various AHRD organizations for SOEs also need to be strategically aligned and coordinated for various skill-based and problem-based training programs. The division of labor between government research institutes and universities in training and educating R&D personnel needs to be coordinated and strategically aligned.

- *Eliminate fragmentation and duplication between the Party and the state and between the central and provincial governments to build complementary AHRD systems*
- *Align horizontal and vertical AHRD systems among various AHRD*

organizations and skills-based training programs for optimal use of limited training resources in the nation

- *Coordinate division of labor between government research institutes and universities in recruiting and educating competent R&D personnel*

As the government enacts these recommendations, AHRD systems will be put in place that will ensure a more capable and accountable state which will drive a post Doi Moi reform for continued realization of modernity, industrialization, and a high quality of life envisioned in the Vietnam 2035.

APPENDICES

APPENDICES

Appendix 1. Policy, Legal System, Actual Status and Evaluation, and Proposed Policy Directions for AHR Recruitment and Appointment

Policy and Viewpoint

The ninth conference of the 10th Central Executive Committee on continuing to promote the implementation of Staff strategy from now until 2020 made a request: "Improving the quality of staff planning, ensuring the initiative, visionary view, meeting all immediate and long term tasks. Building staff planning at all levels, especially strategic level; combining leading and managerial staff planning with planning professional staff, business and production managing staff, leading staff in the armed forces, scientific research staff, leading experts; innovating the staff introduction process to planning sources of leader and manager positions, especially for young staff, female staff, and staff of ethnic minorities".

The documents of the 11th National Party Congress defined: "Good implementation of staff strategy in the time of promoting industrialization and modernization; innovating thinking and operating methods, overcoming weaknesses in each stage of the staff organization. Building and strictly implementing mechanisms and policies to detect, recruit, train and foster staff; appointing people with talent and faith to important positions".

The 4th Resolution of the Central Conference in the 11th term on "Some urgent issues in building the Party at present" proposed a solution: (1) experimenting on empowering the secretary of executive committees to select, and introduce the process for the selection of the members of the standing committee; (2) responsible for selecting, introducing to elect and appoint juniors; experimenting on the system of promotion, leadership and management probation; and (3) implementing personnel introduction process towards action plans, or schemes being presented by staff expected to be promoted or appointed before the consideration and decision of competent authorities".

The conclusions of the 7th Conference of the 11th Central Executive Committee emphasized the importance of innovation and development of the political system from the central to grassroots requested measures to improve the quality of officials and public servants as follows: "Implementing examination for management positions at the central (to director level) and local (to the department director level) or equivalent".

Legal System

Article 6 of the Law on public and civil servants (2008) stipulates: "The State shall adopt policies to detect, attract, foster, use in important positions and have suitable treatment for people with talent. The Government shall have specific policies for people with talent". Clause 1, Article 51 stipulates: "The appointment of employees holding leader and manager positions must be based on: a) Demand and tasks of the agencies, organizations and units; b) Standards and conditions of leader and manager positions". The appointment competence, order and procedures for public servants as leader and managers are implemented in accordance with the law and competent authorities.

Resolution No.30c/NQ-CP of the Government dated 08 November 2011 on

Issuing overall program of state administrative reform in the period of 2011-2020, in section d, subsection 4 of Article 3 defined responsibilities: "Improving provisions of legislation on selection, arrangement, task assignment appropriate to the level, abilities, fortes of selected civil and public servants; implementing rank upgrading examinations on the principle of competition; organizing competitive examinations for the appointment to leader and manager positions from department head and equivalent level (at central), department director and equivalent level (at local) to lower ones".

The Project of "Promoting public service and servant regime reform" approved by the Prime Minister in Decision No. 1557/QD-TTG dated 18 October 2012 introduced key tasks (item 5, section II) on innovating methods for selecting leaders at department, office and division level. Leadership and management internship and probation are regulated as follows: a) Innovating in recruiting leaders of department, office and division level towards focusing on real talent principle, highlighting the responsibility of the leader, innovating methods and content of the vote of confidence. b) Completing regulations on conditions and criteria for appointment, re-appointment to leaders at department and division level at the Central and department and grassroots level at the local. c) Experimenting on implementing leadership and management internship and probation regime. And in Section 6, Regulations on regimes of promotion and policies on attracting, detecting, use in important positions and treating talented people in public service activities: a) Regulations on regimes of promoting, introducing talented people to recruit, appoint to positions in public service activities. b) Promulgating policies to attract and detect, foster, use in important positions and treat talented people in public service activities.

Actual Status of the Policy System on Advanced Human Resource Selection

This status is reflected through the system of policies and documents regulating advanced human resource selection. The content description of these relevant documents will contribute to reflecting the actual status of policy and subjects participating in the selection. The subject for advanced human resource selection in Vietnam is basically dependent on two systems-- the Communist Party and the State. These two systems are unified and complement each other, creating a unified institution of advanced human resource selection.

Current Government's Policy System of Advanced Human Resource Selection

a. The Prime Minister issued Decision No.27/2003/QD-TTG dated 19 February 2003 issuing Regulation on Appointment, reappointment, rotation, resignation and dismissal of staff and leaders of civil servants, including department level leaders and equivalents. The regulation has specified duration, criteria and conditions of appointment and the process and procedures for the appointment of local human resources and personnel from other places.

b. On the basis of the provisions of the Party and the State, the Minister of Internal Affairs with his functions issued Decision No.82/2004/QD-BNV dated 17 November 2004 on the "Standards for Department Director and equivalent positions under People's Committees of provinces and cities directly under the Central Government" and Decision No. 83/2004/QD-BNV dated 17 November 2004 on the "Standards for the Head of Departments under Ministries, ministerial-level agencies, governmental agencies".

c. To concretize the current regulations on staff organization in line with the conditions and characteristics of their agencies and units, heads of some ministries, departments, unions, provincial Party Committees and the People's Committees of provinces and cities directly under the Central Government have issued regulations on standards for the title of leader and manager and regulations on the appointment, re-appointment, resignation and exoneration of leaders, departmental-level, division-level managers and equivalent of their agencies and units. Specifically:

- Decision No. 33/2003/QD-BNV dated 20 June 2003 of the Minister of Home Affairs on regulations on the appointment, reappointment, transference, rotation, resignation and exoneration of staff and civil servants of the Ministry of Home Affairs;
- Decision No. 491/2012/QD-BNG dated 06 March 2012 of the Minister of Foreign Affairs issuing the Regulations on deputy director probation and standards for the promotion of Deputy Minister of Foreign Affairs;
- Regulation No.1956/QD-NHNN dated 19 August 2010 of the Governor of the State Bank on the issuance of the Regulation on the appointment, re-appointment, resignation, exoneration, transference and rotation of public servants in the Party Commission, the Governor of the State Bank and heads of management units;
- Decision No. 43/2010/QD-UB dated 06 September 2010 of the People's Committee of Hanoi City on promulgating regulations on the appointment, reappointment, rotation, resignation and exoneration of managerial staff and public servants.

Thus the policies of recruiting advanced human resources that we have described above on one hand reflect consistency and uniformity and on the other hand reflect the scientific and practical characteristics of each agency in staff planning and appointment.

Current status of Process on AHR Selection

Process on Planning

Step 1: Determine the demand and review, assess qualification of civil servants and officers under planned titles of leader and manager: Sub-committees, chiefs and deputy chiefs of agencies, organizations and units conduct the demand determination, review and assessment of qualification of current public employees and civil servants for planning job titles of leader and manager. Accordingly, 01 to 03 staff members will be appointed for each job title of leader and manager.

Step 2: Receive letters of introduction under job titles of leader and manager. Letters of introduction are received through organizing meeting with participation of leaders and managers of the units under and directly under the organization.

Step 3: Collect comments from party committee at all levels. Party committees at all levels include party cells and party committees of organizations where the appointed staffs will take part in the party's activities.

Step 4: Official section of Communist Party (Ministry and ministerial-level agencies) or Standing Committee (Provinces and City and Municipalities) approves the planning. Example: Planning titles of director general and deputy director general of Department of Personnel and Organization - Ministry of Home Affairs will be implemented as follows:

- Collective of Department of Personnel and Organization assesses planning demand, accordingly determines the number of positions to be planned for the titles of director general and deputy director general, then reviews and determines who should be removed from the planning list and the number of personnel added to the planning list. On that basis, civil servants and officials will be assessed in accordance with the essential standards under the planning for supplementing the planning list.

- Collect opinions on proposal of leader and manager positions at Department level in key meeting with Deputy Head of Personnel and Organization (or all of civil servants and officers under the Department).
- Collect opinions from party cells, party committees under party cell where the appointed staffs will take part in the party's activities or party committee under Department (if any).
- Party's Standing Committee under Ministry of Home Affairs will provide comments, then submit to Official section of Communist Party under the Ministry of Home Affairs for approval of planned personnel.

Process on Planning

Step 1. Request for objectives: In this step, agencies, units and organizations will submit authority (in writing) objectives, numbers, and assignment plan of appointed titles. On that basis, competent authority will approve the aforementioned objectives and plan.

Step 2. Introduction and nomination: Heads of agencies, organizations and units are responsible for introducing nominated staffs to board of leaders and sub-committees for review and approval. Board of leaders of agencies, organization and units and correlative sub-committees will jointly discuss to review, evaluate and select qualified personnel in planned resource in order to introduce them and collect opinions from officials, public employees and civil servants of the entire unit (or it is possible to collect opinion from representatives of the unit such as Head and Deputy Head of Department and Division). Organizations or introducer must make clear report and be responsible for biography of, comments and assessment on introduced staffs.

If staffs in in-place planned resources fail to meet the requirements on standards and conditions for appointment, it is necessary to introduce staffs from other resources (generally units at the same level, other departments under the Ministry or other Departments in the province, for example). Organization or introducer must make clear report and be responsible for biography of, comments and assessment on introduced staffs. In such case, Board of leaders and sub-committees also introduce staff nominated for appointment to get opinions from the key officials and public employees (through the meeting of key officials). The introduction must ensure excess number of staffs for selection.

Step 3. Collect votes of confidence from agencies, organizations and units: Organize meeting to collect opinions of officials, public employees and civil servants or key officials, public employees and civil servants (including chief and deputy chief of subordinate units and equivalent positions). Participants involved in collecting opinions: In accordance with general regulations in Decision No. 68-QD/TW of Ministry of Politburo Committee and Decision No.27/2003/QD-TTG dated February 19, 2003 of the Prime Minster promulgating the regulation on appointment, re-appointment, shift, resignation and removal from office of leading officials and public employees.

Procedure on collecting opinions:

- Make requests for and discuss about appointment of leader and manager positions and criteria required to the positions (for example, qualification, degree, career, training certificates, working experience);

- Announce list of introduced officials and public employees; summarize biography, education background and working period; evaluate strengths and weaknesses, prospects for development; Present plan on job assignment for each official and public employee;
- Vote for opinion poll: Opinion polls are printed and put in alphabetical order by name, clearly stating age, position and work place. It is a secret ballot. In each opinion poll, there are two options "agree" or "disagree" (counting of the polls is based on the percentage of agreement or disagreement for each person); and
- Polls are collected, counted, recorded and kept as confidential documents.

The result of counting polls and confidence votes which are "for reference" is only one of the basic components for review, but not the single and main factor to decide the appointment of officials. Therefore, a high rate of confidence facilitates the decision of appointment.

Step 4. Collect opinions from sub-committees of units, agencies and organizations: Collect opinions from sub-committees of units, agencies and organizations on personnel proposed for appointment. Opinions are collected through discussion, unanimous vote or confidence votes. The result of confidence will be announced right at sub-committee.

Step 5. Agencies, units and organizations jointly agree on the personnel selection to submit for the approval of the upper levels: Board of leaders and sub-committee jointly discuss and decide personnel to submit competent authority for appointment (generally the agencies are under management of upper levels such as Ministry, Ministerial-level Agencies; or People's Committee of province or municipalities).

Steps 6. Board of leader and sub-committee at upper levels are competent to decide on the basis of personnel submitted by the lower units. In case of appointment of director general upper under Ministry, upper competent authorities will collect opinions from board of leaders, Party Committee or Party's Standing Committee under competent authorities; Opinions from Official section of Communist Party (Ministry). Based on the summary of those opinions, Leaders of upper competent authorities will make the decision on appointment of personnel.

For appointment of Director of Department upper, opinions will be collected from Leaders of Provincial People's Committee, Standing Committee as well as specialized Ministries (in case of appointment of Director of Home Affairs Department, it is required to collect opinions from Ministry of Home Affairs, for example). Based on the summary of those opinions, the President of the Provincial People's Committee will make the decision on appointment of personnel.

Step 7. Announce and award decision: After competent person has signed decision on appointment, organization, agencies and unit organize ceremony to announce and award decisions for the appointed personnel.

Current Status of the Pilot Reform of Appointment Process

Recently, some agencies have conducted pilot innovation and reform of the appointment process. Accordingly, when collecting opinion polls and confidence votes, the candidates must present their work program at the meeting of key officials. This has offered a new feature in the selection of high-qualified personnel which has been available in none of the general regulations.

Some Ministries, Departments and provinces such as the Ministry of Justice, Ministry of Transport, Ho Chi Minh City, Da Nang City, Provinces of Quang Ninh, Long An, Binh Duong, Phu Tho, Bac Giang, and others have been assertively organizing pilot selection of leader and manager positions at departmental level or equivalent. The results are remarkable, initially creating competitive environments, expanding the scope and objects registering for selection; attracting qualified individuals to join in the group of leadership and management at departmental and division level and at the same time contributing practical experiences and innovation of methods for selection leaders at departmental level. Specific examples:

1. Pilot selection examination of leaders at departmental level under Ministry of Justice:

Candidates: Public employees and civil servants from units under the Ministry of Justice and the State's administrative agencies, political organizations, political-social organizations from the central to local levels, and workers in the enterprises or those who are not required to be in the planned resources.

Conditions to take part in the exam: Candidates must meet the branch criteria and standards on job title of leaders as prescribed: holding university degree or higher with the major suitable for the applied position; Candidates who are public employees and civil servants must have certificate of management issued by Government agencies as prescribed; Candidates who are workers serving in enterprises may submit the certificate later. Candidates must also satisfy the conditions on working experience and so forth.

- Candidates take part in an exam on writing general information about the state and law;
- Candidates establish and protect assigned project on solutions to improve operational efficiency of the state's organizations, units and management

sector. Candidates must present the project to the Council for evaluation. The Council is established with relevant party and chaired by the Minister;

Based on the results of the selection exam, candidates who got high marks will be appointed to the applied position.

2. Pilot selection examination of leaders at departmental level in Quang Ninh Province:

Pilot selection examination of Director of Ha Long Bay Management and Deputy Director of Department of Information and Communications.

a. Clarify the purposes, requirements, scope of objects, criteria and conditions for participating in the exam of each job title, method, procedures for selection exam and specific tasks of the relevant agencies and organizations.

b. Clarify candidates: Candidates including officials and public employees eligible for the job title required in exam; officials and public employees in power and officials selected for the job title of deputy secretary, president, vice president of People's Council and People's Committees of districts, towns and provincial cities, deputy director of provincial departments, divisions and union and equivalent (the agencies and units under the central government and provinces; leaders, business manager, Division officials under Department and equivalent).

c. Conditions to take part in exam: Officials must have at least 2 years of experience in leadership and management at division level or higher; were highly appraised for their good completion of tasks for2 years before the exam (compared to 4 levels of annual task completion of officials and public employees: Incompletion, Completion, Good completion,

Excellent completion); ensure the age for the first appointment and be healthy to perform their tasks; have profiles presented completely and clearly.

d. Candidates must establish and present assigned Project to the provincial Council for evaluation. Then the Council will ask the candidates questions about the project.

e. Members of Council: All of the Official section of the Communist Party of Quang Ninh province.

f. Results: Examination for selection of leaders and managers took place openly and transparently in accordance with the principles of competition and the 2 successful candidates are those who get highest marks.

3. Examination for selecting leaders at department level in Da Nang City

Da Nang is the first unit implementing the policy to expand the examination for selecting leaders and managers. After nearly 5 years of implementation, 283 candidates participated in the examination for selecting 92 titles, including 11 titles in the State Administrative Offices at levels of department and district. The process of examination is done through the following basic steps:

a. The local departments and agencies select and propose the business units that need the examination for selecting public servants, leaders, and managers, and plan and summit to the City People's Committee for approval.

b. The participants (very extended) include officials, public servants and employees on the payroll or employment contracts, including those who are admitted under the policy to attract human resources of the City People's Committees currently working in the administrative offices, business units and enterprises of all economic sectors inside and outside

Da Nang City.

c. The participants must write on the functions, tasks, organizational system and apparatus of the units that need the examination for selecting public servants, leaders, and managers; describe the position, authority, rights and responsibilities of the heads of units; forecast results, performance and growth of the units and protect projects of solutions to improve performance and develop the units in the future.

Evaluation of Selecting Advanced Human Resources

We use SWOT to evaluate this activity.

Strengths of Currently Selecting Advanced Human Resources in Vietnam

The implementation of selecting leaders at department level and equivalent and higher ensures the Party's leadership and complies with the provisions of the Party on officials work. The selection of advanced officials and public servants, leaders and managers is implemented in accordance with the principle of democratic centralism, impartiality and transparency; ensures proper procedures and orders; and contributes to creating incentives for people with qualifications and competence to strive to meet the requirements of themselves and the organizations.

The policies and specific regulations on the standards and conditions for each title of advanced leaders and managers, including levels of department and equivalent, are a basis for planning, training, fostering, creating and motivation of officials and public servants in general, gradually standardizing staff of officials and public servants in the spirit of the Central Resolution, contributing to build up staff of officials and public servants meeting the requirements of the era of industrialization, modernization and integration.

Processes, procedures and authority to appoint the titles of advanced leaders and managers has been specified and implemented uniformly. In this, the leadership of the Party for the officials working was assured: clearly define the roles and responsibilities of the committees, Party organizations and especially the responsibilities of the leaders. Besides, in the vote of confidence in the agencies, organizations and units also showed the principle of democratic centralism, objectivity, impartiality and transparency, and is an important channel for the competent authorities to consider before deciding whether the appointment is implemented or not. The term of titles of leaders and managers appointed is 5 years. After expiration, the re-appointment or non-re-appointment shall be reviewed; this is an important provision so that persons appointed must always train, strive and avoid psychological complacency and stagnation in the process of work of each official and public servant, leader and manager.

The pilot tests on selecting the officials at department level in the locality and central bring important experience in the innovation of this work. For the immediate future it has created a consensus in public opinion and shifted the appointment through practical capacity of the participants. It also detected and attracted people with capacity, qualification and good quality on the principle of public and equitable competitiveness for appointment to the proper titles of leaders and managers; ensured the leadership of the Party Committees in the work of officials; and contributed to providing a theoretical basis and experience for innovation in the selection and appointment of leaders and managers.

The participants are diverse and there are agencies that do not limit the participants. This requires planning, but expanding to the public business units and businesses. The examination includes writing on the functions and tasks of the agencies, organizations and writing and protecting projects to improve performance and develop the organizations and units in the near future (presenting solutions for development of organizations and answering questions from the project council).

Weaknesses

Some agencies and units are not fully aware of the position, importance, process and method for selecting advanced human resources. They confuse the selection between public servants and personnel and between the standard of titles appointed and the standard of planning, so they have difficulty in direction and implementation and have not yet associated selection with evaluation, training, fostering and use of officials and public servants. Awareness of all levels and sectors has been uneven; they are not highly motivated to change. The direction of the party committees and the heads of agencies and units has been weak and inconsistent. Decisions are still sometimes made based on reverence, affection and the ideology of "descendant of an influential family", and opportunists are proposed and appointed to the titles of leaders and managers at all levels.

There is no mechanism to encourage public servants, leaders and managers to resign if they do not meet the requirements and tasks; there are no alternatives of dismissal for public servants, leaders and managers who are not qualified and capable of handling the work. Thus, many organizations and units have leaders and managers who do not meet the job requirements. There is no mechanism for sharing information between participants and competent authorities for appointment of advanced human resources. According to current regulations, the people who voted for confidence shall not directly communicate or listen to presentations from people participating in the appointment process. Thereby, the evaluation of the qualities, qualifications and competence of the applicants is more authentic and more precise before the vote of confidence. Those who give votes of confidence as well as the authorities making the decisions sometimes base their decisions on the record only, without meeting the proposed person or evaluating his or her competence, qualification and qualities.

The structure of the vote for confidence is not scientific. The current regulations on the process of appointment show that though the vote of confidence is supposed to be seen as a reference only, it is in reality very important and decisive in the choice of whom to appoint or not to appoint. It is very rare that the person with the highest vote of confidence has not been appointed. The current structure of vote for confidence has only 2 criteria to select people who are entitled to vote, one of which is "agree" and "disagree". The roles and responsibilities of the heads as well as the party committees have not been presented and promoted.

The roles and responsibilities of the heads of the organizations, bodies and units have not been clarified in the selection of advanced human resources. Responsibilities and authorities of the heads or superiors who directly manage agencies and units have not been clearly defined for proposing and introducing human resources (at the level of Head, Director of Department) and deciding whom to include in the process of review and appointment. The responsibilities and authorities of the person with authority to make the final decision have not been clearly defined. Generally, the appointment is decided by collectives of the committees, and decisions are based on the conclusions and resolutions of the committees to sign the decision.

When the appointed person does not work well later or violates the law, the responsibility should belong to the collective and not a single individual.

Therefore, it is necessary to clearly define the responsibilities and authorities of the Party Committees and the heads in making decisions to appoint leaders and managers. That is, the heads or superiors should be directly assigned authority to appoint and take primary responsibility for the appointment of leaders and managers.

The appointment of leaders and managers does not meet the requirements of the management of each agency and unit. In some cases, sometimes even in the case of a director or head of the agency or unit, the appointment is made without assessing the actual qualification and capability of the proposed individual. The mode of collective decision about appointment of officials has not yet been clarified with respect to personal responsibility, especially of the head and of the advisory bodies on the work of officials (collectives of leaders and managers, collectives of Party committees). Because these rights and responsibilities have not been assigned, they are vulnerable to abuse.

The policy and structure of recruiting AHR fail to effectively attract and identify the right personnel with sufficient capabilities and personality for the organization. The process of personal credit evaluation and personnel appointment are executed within the organization only, and thus do not attract talented candidates outside the organization. In several cases, only candidates who have made no mistakes or faults are selected. Many highly capable and well qualified officials who are bold, straightforward and active receive low credibility because they only focus on quality and effectiveness in their work instead of building relationships and thus receive little support from their colleagues. As a consequence, a number of officials with limited professionalism and capacity are still appointed to managerial positions at department levels owing to their good relationships and tactics. In order to attain high credibility during the selection and appointment processes, many officials tend to avoid conflicts by making bad compromises, believing they are better than a good lawsuit, and thus do not dare to speak or take action.

The role of the Communist Party and the Government in appointing high-level personnel is ambiguous. The authority to appoint personnel at managerial levels has not been clearly stipulated, and co-operation between the leader and lower levels is not easy. The roles and responsibilities of the organization's leader in introducing and appointing candidates at managerial levels for higher levels of assessment and evaluation is limited.

The selection policy and structure are not actually based on AHR capabilities. The regulations and structures of the Communist Party and the Government regarding AHR appointment are being applied to different organizations with different typical features in a rigid, passive way which places too much importance on certificates rather than practical capabilities; performance evaluation is executed based on sentiment and dodging responsibility resulting in faulty appointments at managerial levels. The reason for this is the inability to identify the job requirements for managerial personnel at Department levels, which leads to qualitative evaluations.

The innovation of organizing tests to appoint managerial personnel has not been consistently applied, resulting in the inability to properly evaluate candidates' capacities or to select the most appropriate person. The test includes two parts: the first asks for the organization's functions and obligations and the second requires preparation and defense of a Project to enhance the effectiveness and development of the organization in the near future. However, this test is similar to the one for recruiting or upgrading normal officials, even though there are obvious differences in the personality, level of professionalism and capacity standards needed for the managerial and professional areas. These tests are acceptable when evaluating operational officials to relocate them into positions with higher professional expertise, but are irrelevant when considering and appointing managerial positions.

Opportunities

There have been sound changes in the Party's and Government's personnel policies, with strong contributions from the Party's resolution to study and follow President Ho Chi Minh's moral example and other resolutions in organizing personnel and preventing corruption. Furthermore, through the introduction of the Law on Cadres and Officials and Law on Government Officials, Vietnam's public service sector is transforming from business-based to position-based and standing on the officials' capacity, encouraging the enhancement of a high level of quality among the workforce. Vietnam's strong desire to cooperate and integrate with the global community serves as a robust motivation for the selection of high-level personnel.

Pilot projects in appointing leaders at Department levels are winning interest and consensus of both local people and international organizations. This draws the attention and support of local and international organizations in training and fostering high-level human resources.

Challenges

Create a consistent and single system of policies, regulations and processes in selection (planning, appointing) without overlapping the functions of the Communist Party and the Government by clearly assigning the functions, roles, obligations and rights to all stakeholders in the selection process. This process must be performed scientifically with high democracy and transparency, which increases the power of the related organization's leaders in making the nomination.

Build up a managerial capacity framework for AHR which will be the foundation for evaluating personnel planning and nomination. Restructure models and techniques in planning and nominating high-level personnel in which candidates' credit evaluation forms must be based on weighing their capacities and must be transparent to accurately reflect the candidate's credibility.

Eliminate the monopoly in selection. This will end bribery and corruption as well as the tendency to grant priority to officials' relatives or choose opportunists for high-level positions. Establish a transparent supervising structure in AHR selection. Build up a "resignation culture" in case the high-level official fails to accomplish his or her duty.

Continue to encourage innovations in recruiting AHR as piloted in some Ministries and Provinces in Vietnam. This is a good trend but may not be as effective when being implemented. Therefore, it is necessary to enhance innovations in selection methods and techniques to make them successful. Following are some challenges for innovations.

There needs to be a single concept and perception in reforming managerial officials at Department levels by organizing tests. This is an appropriate policy which guarantees the equality, publicity and transparency of selection and helps enhance the quality of governmental cadres, officials and managerial officials. However, there are faulty perceptions in seeing this as a solution to completely replace the normal selection process, by selecting the candidates with the highest test scores for the positions. In this way, the test is similar to official selection tests or up scaling tests.

The reform process must consistently abide by the principle by which the Communist Party solely monitors personnel arrangement. It must continue to consolidate current policies in personnel arrangement while supplementing or complementing them to improve the quality of the selecting and nominating processes.

It is necessary to reform the selection method to scientifically evaluate the capacity of high-level officials and thus select the right people. To accurately evaluate the candidates' qualities and managerial capacities, written tests alone are insufficient. There must be assessments and evaluations of their qualities and managerial capacities such as their vision, their abilities to make plans, organize, assign tasks, monitor and cooperate and their presentation and defense skill. All of these point to the need for selection reform.

The personal credit assessment among governmental officials should not be eliminated; instead it should be renovated in terms of the voting method and especially the structure and content of credibility so that the results truly reflect the community's views. This will turn this process into the foundation for higher-level review and selection. If the number subjects allowed to apply for selection is increased, the standards and conditions for application must abide by general and specific standards and conditions as stipulated by the Communist Party and the Government.

Some Proposed Policies for AHR Selection

Basing on the foregoing principles, we would like to propose solutions to reform the policies and structure in selecting AHR for Department and higher levels as follows:

1. *Innovation of advanced leadership assessment as competency framework:*

It can be said that the method of management leadership assessment for planning and appointing is mainly based on assessing the achievements and performance of the management leadership role rather than the manager's competency. According to Parry (1996), "Competency is a cluster of related knowledge, skills, and attitudes that affects a major part of one's job (a role or responsibility), that correlates with performance on the job, that can be measured against well-accepted standards, and that can be improved via training and development".

A competency framework is a description of the complete and necessary competencies to successfully execute tasks of a position, a team, a unit or entire organization. The competency framework consists of three components: list of competencies, definitions of competencies, and description of competency levels. Quan(2016, page 48), includes the following competency groups for the public administration sector of Vietnam:

- Ethics of public affairs
- Local understanding / knowledge
- Professional knowledge
- Management and administration
- Human resources management
- Self-management

Quan (2016) also divides the competency framework in Vietnam into 5 levels, of which level 5 is the highest. We believe that advanced leaders need to reach level 5, which Quan defines as "Performing competency at the expert level, individuals at this level can apply their competency in most various complicated situations, can provide new effective methods and approaches" (p. 20).The competency framework for assessing leaders and managers is the latest approach and is crucial in selecting advanced human resources and can serve as a basis to determine job positions in the current context of Vietnam.

2. *Decentralization of responsibility toward clearly and specifically regulating authorities and responsibilities of the leaders in the selection of advanced human resources:*

Authorities and responsibilities in staffing of the head in agencies under leader regimes should be clearly determined. These are different from those of agencies under the regime of collective leadership or individual responsibility. The regulations of the Party have always emphasized a focus on appreciating the head's responsibilities, but the implementation of this in practice has been still restricted in many aspects, and the responsibilities of the head have not been clearly determined and associated with the authorities. Public administrative agencies and servant organizations have been working under a leader regime model, therefore proposals of the head have been considered very important in the selection of human resources for appointment to leadership and management positions. The heads are responsible for the appointments of human resources referred and proposed by themselves, or the leaders at the appointing authority level have to take responsibility for their decisions. Thus, when problems occur to persons appointed based on capacity, quality, new level etc., there is the subject for to blame, to handle the current situation, or staff with poor capacity or breaking the legal regulations. It is difficult to blame for a specific person, although the appointment process shall undergo a lot of levels. Every level has certain authority, but when there is a problem occurring, no individual takes responsibility at all.

3. *Innovation of selection towards examination*

3.1. Expand the scope of those who can be nominated or apply for leadership and management positions.

The Party and the Government are currently encouraging the implementation of talent attracting policy, leading to the need to expand the selection objectives. If the selection for appointment to leadership and management positions of department and equivalent or above levels is limited to those who are in the planning of each agency and unit, the human resources will be restricted. According to current regulations, human resources come from two sources: (a) internal and external sources from other units of the Ministry and (b) from provincial and local government units. The selection should be expanded to officials, public servants and functionaries in the same or equivalent level positions but should not be limited to the scope of that particular agency and unit and should include officials and public servants who planned for similar positions or who are working in agencies, organizations of the Party, the Government, the Vietnamese Fatherland Front, socio-economic organizations and public non-business units.

This plan is consistent with the political regime in Vietnam: a Party governing and leading the entire political system, ensuring the principle of Party leadership on official tasks. Those in the planning must be considered for their ethical and political qualities, qualifications and competency, then approved and planned to be fostered and trained as leaders and managers by Party Committees.

3.2. Innovation of selection content

Selection content for candidates for advanced leadership positions should be approached based on the competencies needed of each position. Accordingly, the selection content includes not only criteria as set out but also competency standards of leadership, management, conduct and attitude. Specially, selection content should be aimed at competency in strategic self-planning in the candidate's sector, scientific thinking and problem solving in a positive and effective way. The examination content should stick to the competency framework of leaders and managers mentioned above.

3.3. Innovation of selection processes, methods and techniques

The examination processes for advanced leadership and management positions must be innovated. In addition to the writing step, applicants/candidates for leadership and management positions have to present plans for specific, novel programs if they are chosen for the leadership and management positions. They must also meet with and be interviewed by those who will cast a vote of confidence on their behalf.

Competency and professional skills can be assessed through such an examination process. However, the appointment of leadership and management positions is not merely based on the assessment of competency and professionalism, but also on the assessment of qualification, reputation and ability to gather and connect everyone in the agencies or units to accomplish their assigned tasks. It is necessary to have innovation of the examination process along with ensuring the leadership of the Party and compliance with the regulations on official tasks. Therefore, the examination result is just one reference channel in the vote of confidence and eventual signing of the appointment decision.

Votes of confidence are for reference only. They should be designed to include the capacity to assess the creditworthiness of the candidates on their (a) quality, ethics and attitude; (b) qualifications and (c) skills. Each content is evaluated at three levels: good, pass, not pass.

The individual or group who assesses and appoints candidates is usually an individual or institution at a higher level, as is the role of monitoring the process of selection of candidates. However, we believe that there should be an independent organization monitoring the selection process that is not part of the Ministries or the provincial or city people's committees. This will make the monitoring process more transparent and positive.

4. A New Proposal for a Probationary Process for AHR Positions

To ensure the quality of recruits for advanced human resources positions, there should be a probationary process for advanced HR positions. In other words, before the formal appointment of advanced HR positions, candidates should participate in probationary positions in which they are engaged in the role of advanced leaders and are challenged and tracked for a period of 6 months or longer. The appointing authorities shall monitor and assess the capacity and performance of the probationary leader and make the formal decision whether the person qualifies for the position of advanced leader or not based on this assessment.

Appendix 2. Outcomes of Official Rotation

Rotation of Officials

The job rotation of leaders and managers is meant to train, foster and challenge officials in real-world settings to provide them with further practical knowledge and help them grow more rapidly and comprehensively. The official rotation over the past years has achieved a number of remarkable outcomes. For instance, executive committees and party organizations have been well aware of the importance of experiential learning and had positive changes in implementing official rotation. Most of the executive committees and party organizations have realized that official rotation is aimed especially at young officials so as to actively provide official sources for both the short term and the long term, ensuring effective and efficient implementation of job rotation for training, fostering and stabilization and development of in-place officials. Consequently, the official rotation has gradually gotten into an orderly routine, creates new motivations among officials and is supported by most officials, party members and the public.

Up to now, over 42,000 rotations of leaders and managers at different levels have been circulated nationwide. At the Central level, 98 officials have been circulated in such positions as secretary, assistant secretary, chairman, vice chairman of a number of provincial and municipal people's committees. While in the 9th National Assembly, 11 officials at the deputy ministerial level and equivalents were circulated in localities; in Conclusion notice No. 127-TB/TW dated January 03, 2008 (the 10th NA), the Politburo and the Secretariat continued to circulate 35 officials including 12 deputy ministers and equivalents and 23 officials of general department, department and institute levels; in

Conclusion no. 146 - KL/TW of the Politburo (the 11th NA), 52 officials were circulated (24 officials in the positions of provincial and municipal committee's assistant secretary and 28 provincial and municipal people's committee's vice chairs). At the Provincial level, around 4,000 rotations of officials have occurred: 15,000 at the municipal level and over 19,000at ministry, department and branch levels. In the military branch, 23% of planning officials at the division level and equivalents have experienced rotations, 13% of whom are at campaign and strategy levels. In the public security branch, 14.8% of planning officials from department, departments' director and deputy director level have had rotations.

Through the implementation process, the circulated officials have accomplished their tasks, gained a great deal of practical experience and had deeper and more comprehensive leading and guidance methods; quite a few officials have made positive contributions in the locality's socio-economic development and are trusted by the local officials, party members and people; quite a few of them have been voted into the 11th and 12th Central Committees. 59.81% of the circulated officials have been appointed in higher positions and 22.47% in equivalent positions, 52.8% circulated at the provincial level in higher positions and 36.8% in equivalent positions, and only 0.15% have not accomplished their tasks. 54.95% circulated at the municipal level in higher positions and 8.06% in equivalent positions; only about 0.1% have not accomplished their tasks.

The rotation of officials has contributed to improving the partial, self-containing, stagnating and conservative thought patterns in official tasks and forces. Along with the rotation of young officials for training and practice in the real world, Politburo IX, X has directed the pilot implementation of guidelines arranging 6 provincial positions for non-local individuals: Provincial

Party Secretary, Chairman of the Provincial People's Committee, Director of the Police Department, Department of Planning & Investment, Department of Finance, and President of the People's Procuracy. For example, the Central Police Party Committee has arranged Police Directors of 20/63 provinces, cities and more than 67% Police Head of districts who are not local people. The Supreme People's Procuracy has rotated dozens of officials working as Presidents and Vice Presidents at the provincial level.

Implementing the policy of arranging some key leadership positions at provincial and district level for non-local people has allowed these areas to gradually improve the partial, self-containing problems in official tasks. Specifically, the rotation of officials created motivation in official tasks and forces; created a fresh working atmosphere in the leadership at the committee level as well as in the movement of the local units; created an environment for practice and taking on challenges of officials; allowed officials to be close to the people and experience real-life conditions in order to mature and grow faster and more comprehensively; helped the official management level to evaluate performance contributed to overcome the narrow and hidebound ways of thinking to official tasks. The comrades rotated have upheld the spirit of responsibility, strictly observing the decisions of superiors; being supported by committees, authorities, officials, Party members and people;being dedicated and loyal to local agencies and units they have rotated to and overcoming difficulties and being determined to strive to complete their tasks.

Appendix 3. AHRD Agencies in Vietnam

HCMA

HCMA is the country's largest training center of cadre and civil servants. HCMA is affiliated with the Party Central Executive Committee and the Government. HCMA has two major functions: (1) conducting research and making policy recommendations and (2) training and educating the middle and high-ranking officials of the whole political system. It is also among the most influential think-tanks and institutions for political education and is the leading research body of the Party and the Government on politics.

NAPA

NAPA and HCMA is one national centers of cadre and civil servant training. Established in 1959, NAPA is the national agency of CCT and PA research. NAPA is currently a PSDA of MOHA, headquartered in Hanoi. The briefings on the status change of NAPA is useful to know since it reveals partly the viewpoints of the Party and the viewpoint of policy intervention on the significance of training and approaches of organizing trainings for CCSs in general and AHRD in particular.

NAPA has undergone dramatic changes since the 1990s due to the increasing significance attached to PAR and the role of CCSs in the PAR process. It was originally established in 1959 as the school of public administration, responsible for training for district-level civil servants. In 1961, it was re-named the Central PA School. In May 1974 the School of Government Cadre Training in the South was founded. In 1977, the PA School in the North was transferred from MOHA to the Government Committee of Organization, which was then transferred to the Prime Minister's Office later that year. In 1980, the School was merged with the Central School of Economics to become the Central School of PA and Economics. In 1981, they were separated again. It was renamed in 1990 as the National School of PA. In 2002, NAPA was reorganized to be a member of MOHA. This movement is among the Government's efforts toward establishing a system of multi-functional ministries; reducing the numbers of Government organizations and responsibilities assigned to the Prime Minister and the Cabinet. In 2007 (officially in 2008), NAPA was merged with HCMA and separated again in 2015.

The contribution of NAPA to the PAR process involves three key areas including training, research and policy recommendations in the area of public administration.

Ministerial Schools for Civil and Public Servant Training

Each ministry has its own training and education institutions for the public and for its own CCSs. The key institutions to provide trainings for CCSs are called Schools and they provide short-term technical and professional courses for their own staff.

Provincial Schools of Politics (PSPs)

There is one school in each province, with a total of 63 nationwide. Almost all PSPs were established from the merging of the School of Public Administration, the School for Party's Cadres, and the School of the Youth's Union. The content on politics is decided by the HCMA, while the content on public administration and management is decided by NAPA.

District-level Center for Civil and Public Servant Training

Each district has one Center that is staffed and budgeted by the town or district authority. Centers are in charge of providing training courses for all the CCSs in the district. Given a very limited staff (usually four staff members per Center), Centers mainly operate as organizers, coordinating with other agencies or lecturers to provide lectures and talks.

Other Suppliers

Though they have not been considered as direct stakeholders in the training system, both public and private universities also take some part in training. They provide courses related to some aspects of business administration, office management, lower level administration and informatics and IT skills. Training activities are also undertaken by joint-ventures between domestic and foreign training institutions, ranging from workshops to short courses to courses leading to formal qualifications.

Donors are sometimes involved in training in accordance with PAR and among various donor-funded PAR-related projects. These donors then become stakeholders in the training process. Their involvement includes the provision of in-country and overseas courses.

Appendix 4. Development of Vietnam's HRD Institution

1) Introduction (1975-1986)

- Public Administration Background
  - National unification in 1975
  - Post-feudal, post-war society strongly imitated the Soviet Union model of public administration

- Goals of Training Programs
  - Understanding of the public administration system
  - Understanding of the mechanisms of the central-planning economy

2) The Dawn of change (1986-1993)

- Public Administration Background
  - "Đổi mới" initiated in 1986
  - 1992 Constitution
  - Rethinking the role of the state in growth

- Goals of Training Programs
  - Understanding of the political, socio-economic and social requirements for economic transition

3) Searching for a new model of training (1994-2001)

- Public Administration Background
  - Open up the economy
  - Nation-leading economic development
  - US trade embargo lifted

- First public administration reform initiative (one door, one stamp)
- High economic growth was well recognized by the world
- 1995: ASEAN member
- 1998: APEC member
- 1998: Ordinance on cadres and public servants
- 2000: Vietnam signed Millennium Development Goals (MDGs)

• Goals of Training Programs
- Understanding of political ideology and democracy
- Understanding of the socialist-oriented market economy compared to the original market economy and central-planning economy
- Overall understanding of national administration
- Acquiring administrative management techniques

4) Shape-up period (2001-2010)

• Public Administration Background
- Speed up public administration reform
- Masters Program of Public Administrations reform 2001-2010
- Poverty eradication- 2007 joined WTO

• Goals of Training Programs
- Understanding the essence and the needs of globalization and integration
- Understanding leadership and management skills in the context of integration, especially skills for economic management

5) Training for a constructive/social creation government period

(2016-onwards)

- Public Administration Background
  - New leadership term of the Party and the State
  - PAR deepened
  - Better business environment efforts needed
  - Increasing voice of the citizens and community, with the support of the mass media and the Internet

- Goals of Training Programs
  - Building capacity for shaping a new type of government-business relationship, emphasizing leading and managing change and innovation
  - To better listen, understand and respond to the needs of society, especially business
  - To attain knowledge and skills to take part adequately in protecting national sovereignty

Training Regimes	System of Officials' Training
Introduction (1975-1986)	- Focused on the middle and high ranking officials - Originally School for Public administration in 1959, National School of Public Administration in 1961, National School of Public Administration and Economics in 1980 - Strongly impacted and supported by the Soviet Union's system of training and education for cadres and civil servants
The dawn of change (1986-1993)	- National School of Public Administration and Economics in 1980, separate National School of Public Administration established in 1990, then National Academy of Public Administration in 1992
Searching for a new model of training (1994-2001)	- Founded the National Steering Committee for Public Administration Reform - 1992: first Training Program for High and Medium Experts (two-year term) - Knowledge exchange and creation on public administration and economic development models with strong support from international development agencies (e.g., ADB, WB, UNDP) and international training institutions from both developed and developing countries (e.g., Australia, France, Germany, Korea, Singapore, New Zealand, Russia, and the United Kingdom) - 1997: first Bachelor of Public Administration (part-time) offered for university graduates and current civil servants and public servants
Shape-up period (2001-2010)	- 2001: Action Plan 4 on improvement of the quality of cadres and civil servants within the Masters Program on PAR - Enhancement of training and education abroad using the national budget (Scheme 322 by MOET for potential leaders, managers and experts) - 2007: Restructuring of officials' training institutions: Merged the two national Academies (Ho Chi Minh National Academy of Politics and National Academy of Public Administration) - 2008: Law on Cadres and Civil Servants enacted, leading to greater regulation of training - 2010: Law on Public Servants - Decree 18/2010/ND-CP of the Government dated March 05, 2010, on training for cadres and civil servants (focus on decentralisation of training missions), in which the roles of provincial and ministerial schools are enhanced - More attention to training on institutional competence for institutional integration

Takeoff stage of public administration reform (2011-2016)	- 2014-2016: Designed and delivered training programs for potential strategic leadership (Politburos, General Secretary Committee and HCMA, details in section on AHRD Program) - First training programs introduced for (i) DG, DDG levels; (ii) Division level leadership, (iii) position-based - Regulation on compulsory annual training for cadres and civil servants for at least 40 hours - 2014: Newly designed advanced theoretical training programs and curriculum - January 2015: Restructuring of officials' training institutions: separated two national Academies (Ho Chi Minh National Academy of Politics and National Academy of Public Administration) - More attention paid to public service ethics and skills - Transition from duty-oriented to competency-oriented training
Training for a constructive/social creation government period (2016-onwards)	- More attention to training and position-based training - More leadership skills to be developed

Appendix 5. Process and Structure of Developing Training

After obtaining the direction of the Politburo on opening the training courses and the participants, the Academy has developed the program content. It is comprised of six modules, including the study visit and five basic modules.

a) The process of developing training programs

Step 1. The Academy actively consulted with scientists inside and outside, former leaders of the Academy and former senior leaders of the Party and the State on the content and the subjects to be included in training programs.

Step 2. Based on the comments given, the Academy built a draft framework and the thematic content.

Step 3. The Academy consulted scientists, former Politburo members and former leaders of the congress, the government, ministries, central agencies and the incumbent leaders of the Party, State, National Assembly and the Fatherland Front on the draft framework and thematic content of training.

Step 4. On the basis of these comments, the Academy edited the curriculum, the name of each topic and the construction of details.

Step 5. The curriculum framework was presented to the Evaluation Council. On December 18, 2012, the Council had a meeting to gain consensus of the members of the Council on several corrections and additions.

Step 6. Based on the conclusions of the Evaluation Council, the Academy invited scientists for adjustment, correction and supplementing of the details for each topic.

b) Structure of training and retraining programs

The program comprises of six modules, including the study visit and five basic modules as follows:

i . Marxism-Leninism and Ho Chi Minh Thoughts (6 subjects);

ii . Issues of the contemporary world (5 subjects);

iii. The direction of the Communist Party of Vietnam (10 subjects);

iv. Construction of the Party and State (7 subjects);

v . Science Leadership and Management (5 subjects);

vi. One module of complementary subjects, including 10 reports of domestic and foreign experts and visits to programs at the local provinces for 2 weeks.

Appendix 6. Foreign Experts and Study Visit Abroad

• *Reporting Contents of International Experts*

On the basis of the curriculum, the Academy agreed with international partners to ensure the correct time of retraining programs. Topics have been selected based on recommendations by the Academy and the strength of international experts. Experts selected to give lectures are senior officials and prestigious scholars. Selected themes involve issues of public servants and public service in the experience of Japan, South Korea and France, industrial policy, environmental protection, banking, finance, transport infrastructure development, human resource management, prevention of corruption, empowerment for women, and among others.

• *Study Visits*

Due to the high number of participants, all cannot be taken abroad for these projects, so at the end of each course, based on the test results and the needs of learners, the Academy selects a sufficient number as committed by projects and sends 22 students to Japan and 22 students to South Korea. Japan and South Korea have received 6 groups from 6 classes. In addition, Singapore has also received 2 delegations, and the UK and Israel each received 1 delegation. Joining the delegations are officials from the Academy, the Central Organizing Committee and the External Relations Commission. All delegations are covered 100% by the funds of the international partners.

• *Research Content*

For the delegations to Japan and Korea, the Academy and its partners have identified the theme trips and sites as well as partners working in the country associated with topics that the experts will present in the classroom. For the tours to other countries, research topics are determined on the basis of agreements with international partners.

• *Organizational Methods*

Before the trip, The Academy and international partners meet to discuss and organize all aspects such as program contents, activities, finance, logistics, and among many others.

• *Assessment and Monitoring*

After the end of the study program, all delegations write general reports on the results of the course, give recommendations for future programs, explain how they will apply their international experience and discuss how the knowledge gained applies in the specific conditions of Vietnam.

REFERENCES

Acuña-Alfaro, J. 2012. Incentives and Salaries in Vietnam's Public Sector. *Vietnam Law & Legal Forum.* January & February 2012. 11-15.

Acuña-Alfaro, J. and A. Tran. 2016. Vietnam's Public Bureaucracy and Implementation of two ASEAN policies. In J. Quah, *The Role of the Public Bureaucracy in Policy Implementation in Five ASEAN Countries* (pp. 370-430). Cambridge, UK: Cambridge University Press.

ADB. 2014. *Socialist Republic of Vietnam: Implementation of Civil Service Reform Plan*. Technical Assistance Report.

ADB. 2015. *State-Owned Enterprise Reform in Vietnam: Lessons Learnt and Future Directions.* Background paper for Public Finance Partnership Group High Level Meeting.

Agribank. 2012. *Annual Report.* Hanoi, Vietnam: Author.

Anand, Rahul, Kevin C. Cheng, Sidra Rehman, and Longmei Zhang. 2014. *Potential Growth in Emerging Asia.* [IMF Working Paper].Retrieved from http://www.imf.org/external/pubs/ft/wp/2014/wp1402.pdf.

Anh, Dang Nguyen. 2015. Restructuring Human Resources: Key for Sustainable and Fast Development of Vietnam. *Vietnam Social Sciences Review.* 2(166). 24-32.

Anh, N. T. T., L. M. Duc, and T. D. Chieu. 2014. *The evolution of Vietnamese industry*. UNU-WIDER Working Paper, 76.

Anh, Vu Thanh Ty, L. Chirot, D. Dapice, Huynh The Du, Pham Duy Nghia, D.

Perkins, and Nguyen Xuan Thanh. 2015. *Institutional Reform: From Vision to Reality*. Policy Discussion Paper Prepared for the Vietnam Executive Leadership Program (VELP) at Harvard Kennedy School.

Asia-Pacific Rural and Agricultural Credit Association. 2016. Member's Profile: The Vietnam Bank for Agriculture and Rural Development. Retrieved from: http://www.apraca.org/members_profile_detail.php?idmembers=26&namecountry=

Australian Trade and Investment Commission. 2015. *Vietnam – Cambodia 2015: Mining Opportunities* [Market Briefing]. Retrieved from: http://www.industry.nsw.gov.au/__data/assets/pdf_file/0006/66093/Vietnam-Briefing-Opportunities-in-the-Mining-Sector-13012015.pdf.

Bo Khoa hoc va Cong nghe – MOST. 2016. *Khoa hoc va Cong nghe Vietnam 2015*, Bo Khoa hoc va Cong nghe, Ha Noi.

Breu, M., R. Dobbs, J. Remes, D. Skilling, and J. Kim. 2012. *Sustaining Vietnam's Growth: The Productivity Challenge*. Retrieved from: http://www.mckinsey.com/global-themes/asia-pacific/sustaining-growth-in-vietnam.

Budiman, A., D. Y. Lin, and S. Singham. 2009. *Improving Performance at State-Owned Enterprises*. Retrieved from: http://www.mckinsey.com/industries/public-sector/our-insights/improving-performance-at-state-owned-enterprises.

Can, Ngo Thanh. 2013. Public Administration Reform in Vietnam: Current Situations and Solutions. *Scholarly Journal of Business Administration*. 3(5). 110-116.

Chia, S. Y. 2013. Comment on "Vietnamese Economy at the Crossroads: New Doi Moi for Sustained Growth". *Asian Economic Policy Review*. 8(1). 144-145.

Chinh phu – Government. 2004. *Nghi dinh so 204/2004/ND-CP ve che do tien luong doi voi can bo, cong chuc, vien chuc va luc luong vu trang,* Ha Noi.

Chinh phu – Government. 2005. *Nghi dinh so 115/2005/ND-CP ve co che tu chu, tu chiu trach nhiem cua cac to chuc khoa hoc va cong nghe cong lap*, Ha Noi.

Chinh phu – Government. 2012. *Quyet dinh so 418/QD-TTg cua Thu tuong Chinh phu phe duyet Chien luoc phat trien khoa hoc va cong nghe giai doan 2011 – 2020*, Ha Noi.

Chinh phu – Government. 2014. *Nghi dinh so 40/2014/ND-CP cua Chinh phu quy dinh viec su dung, trong dung ca nhan hoat dong khoa hoc va cong nghe*, Ha Noi.

Choi, S. O., and S. M. Park. 2013. *The Establishment of Career Civil Service System in the Korean Government*. Knowledge Sharing Program: KSP Modularization.

Chuan, Le Minh. 2011a. *Current Status of Coal Demand and Supply in Vietnam and Plan of VINACOMIN in the Coming Time* [PowerPoint slides]. Retrieved from: http://www.jcoal.or.jp/coaldb/shiryo/material/day2_session2_3.pdf.

Chuan, Le Minh. 2011b. *Perspective Development of Vietnam Coal Industry* [PowerPoint slides]. Retrieved from http://www.jcoal.or.jp/coaldb/shiryo/material/day1_keynote_b_en.pdf.

CHXHCN Vietnam – SRV. (2013*). Luat Khoa hoc va Cong nghe,* Ha Noi.

Clark, C. G. 1940. *The Conditions of Economic Progress.* London: Macmillan.

Commission on Growth and Development. 2008. *The Growth Report: Strategies for Sustained Growth and Inclusive Development.* Washington, DC: World Bank.

Cox, A. 2014. Human Resource Management in Vietnam. In A. Varma and P. S. Budhwar (Eds.), *Managing Human Resources in Asia-Pacific* (pp. 379-431). New York: Routledge.

Dang Cong san Vietnam – CPV. 2011. *Chien luoc phat trien kinh te xa hoi 2011 – 2020*, Retrieved from http://www.cpv.org.vn

Dang Cong san Vietnam – CPV. 2016. *Bao cao chinh tri Dai hoi dai bieu toan quoc lan thu XI, XII cua Dang,* Retrieved from http://www.cpv.org.vn

Dao Thanh Truong. 2015. STI System in Universities of Vietnam. *JSTPM*. 4(4).

Editorial Board. 2014. Vietnam Science and Technology Policy: Opportunities and Challenges. *JSTPM*. 3(2).

Five-year socio-economic development plan for the period 2011-2015.

Five-year socio-economic development plan for the period 2016-2020.

General Statistics Office. 2015. *Report on the 2014 Vietnam Labor Force Survey.* Hanoi, Vietnam: Author.

Global Methane Initiative. 2015. *Coal Mine Methane Country Profiles.* Retrieved from https://www.globalmethane.org/documents/toolsres_coal_overview_ch28.pdf.

Greenhaus, J. 1987. *Career management.* Hinsdale, IL: Dryden Press.

Hiep, Le Hong. 2015. *The TPP's Impact on Vietnam: A Preliminary Assessment.* Singapore: Yusof Ishak Institute.

http://www.logodi.go.kr/

http://www.nhi.go.kr/

International Bank for Reconstruction and Development/The World Bank. 1997.

World Development Report 1997: The State in a Changing World. New York: Oxford University Press.

International Labour Organization. 2008. *Skills for improved productivity, employment growth and development*. Proceedings of the International Labour Conference, Vancouver, Canada.

International Labour Organization. 2014. *Newsletter from ILO County Office for Vietnam*. Issue 9.

Kim, J. H. (2005). *A Study on Ways of Improving NACF's Performance Rating System* [Unpublished master's thesis]. University of Dong-A, Busan, Korea.

Kim, J.I., D. W. Kim, and I. C. Nam. (2012). Development Strategies and Role of the State. In *Supporting the Establishment of Vietnam's 2011-20 Socio-economic Development Strategy* (pp.35-194). Ministry of Strategy and Finance and Korea Development Institute.

Kim, J. I., D. Kim, I. C. Nam, M. J. Kim, and H. Lee. 2011. *Supporting the establishment of Vietnam's 2011-20 socio-economic development strategy*. Knowledge Sharing Program Report.

Kim, Linsu. 1997. *Imitation to Innovation: The Dynamics of Korea's Technological Learning*. Boston: Harvard Business Review Press.

Korea Coal Corporation. 2015. *Long-term Strategies for KCC (2016~2020)*. Retrieved from https://www.kocoal.or.kr/page/24

Korea Coal Corporation. 2016. *CEO's greetings*. Retrieved from:https://www.kocoal.or.kr/english/about/message.html.

Korea Coal Corporation. 2016. *History of KOCOAL*. Retrieved from: https://www.kocoal.or.kr/english/about/history.html.

Korea Coal Corporation. 2016. *Vision of KOCOAL*. Retrieved from: https://www.kocoal.or.kr/english/about/vision.html.

Korea Development Institute & Ministry of Strategy and Finance. 2011. *Modularization of Korea's Development Experience: Productivity Improvement*[in Korean]. Retrieved from http://www.kdi.re.kr/research/subjects_view.jsp?pub_no=12066.

Korea Educational Statistics Service. *Number of Graduate Students*. Retrieved from http://kess.kedi.re.kr/kessTheme/timeStats?itemCode=03&menuId=m_02_03_02

Korea Information Society Development Institute. 2015. *2015 ICT Industry Outlook of Korea.* Retrieved from: http://www.kisdi.re.kr/kisdi/fp/kr/board/selectSingleBoard.do?cmd=selectSingleBoard&boardId=GPK_RND_DATA&seq=31415&reStep=&ctx=

Korea Institute of S&T Evaluation and Planning. 2013. *Future Direction of HRST Policy: Lessons from History.*

Korea Institute of S&T Evaluation and Planning. *R&D Activity Investigation Report.*

Korea Legislation Research Institute. 2014. *Industrial Development Act*. Retrieved from: http://elaw.klri.re.kr/kor_service/lawView.do?hseq=31936&lang=ENG.

Korea Productivity Center. 2016. *KPC CEO Message.* Retrieved from: https://www.kpc.or.kr/eng/Info/CEO_Message.asp.

Korea Productivity Center. 2016. *PR brochure of KPC*. Retrieved from: http://www.kpc.or.kr/info/PR.asp.

Korea Productivity Center. 2016. *History of KPC.* Retrieved from: http://www.kpc.or.kr/info/Organiztion.asp.

Korea Productivity Center. 2016. *Organization of KPC*. Retrieved from https://www.kpc.or.kr/eng/Info/Organization.asp.

KT. 2015. *KT Integrated Report 2015*. Retrieved from: http://www.kt.com/sustainability/disclosure.jsp.

KT. 2016 *History of KT*. Retrieved from: http://www.kt.com/eng/corp/history_01.jsp.

Lan, Mai Thanh. (2016). Public Management and Strategic Management in Vietnam State-Owned Enterprises (SOEs). *International Business Research*. 9(4). 58-65.

Lee, Jinjoo, Zong-Tae Bae, and Dong-Kyu Choi. 1998. Technology Development Processes: A Model for a Developing Country with a Global Perspective. *R&D Management*. 18(3). 235-250.

Le Quan. (2016) *Leadership and management competency framework in the public administration sector*. Vietnam National University Press.

Lucas, R. E. 1988. On the mechanics of economic development. *Journal of Monetary Economics*. 22(1). 3-42.

McLagan, P. A., and D. Suhadolnik. 1989. *Models for HRD Practice: The Research Report*. American Society for Training and Development.

Michie, J. (2001). *The Impact of Foreign Direct Investment on Human Capital Enhancement in Developing Countries*. Available at: https://www.researchgate.net/publication/228919929_The_Impact_of_Foreign_Direct_Investment_on_Human_Capital_Enhancement_in_Developing_Countries.

Ministry of Finance and Strategy and KDI. (2011). *Supporting the Establishment of Vietnam's 2011~20 Socio-economic Development Strategy*. KSP.

Ministry of Labor (2015). *Act on the Development of Workplace Skills of Workers.* Retrieved from https://elaw.klri.re.kr/eng_service/lawView.do?lang=ENG&hseq=33587

Ministry of Science and Technology. 2014. Data from 65 scientific and technological enterprises by the Departments of Science and Technology in 2013 statistical report. Hanoi, Vietnam: Author.

Ministry of Science, ICT and Future Planning. *Survey of Research and Development in Korea(each year)*

Mogaka, D. O. (2011). *Public enterprises and the new constitution: towards a better system for corporate governance* (Unpublished doctoral dissertation). University of Nairobi, Kenya.

MOST. (2012). Conference on *Human Resources Development Policies for Sciences and Technology*. Hanoi.

Nankervis, Alan, Chris Rowley, and Noorziah Mohd Salleh. 2016. *Asia Pacific Human Resource Management and Organizational Effectiveness: Impacts on Practice.* Oxford, UK: Chandos Publishing.

Nguyen, Nhu-Ty, Thanh-TuyenTran, and Chia-NanWang. 2015. Management Styles and Organizational Effectiveness in Vietnam: A Comparison in Terms of Management Practices between State-Owned and Foreign Enterprises. *Research in World Economy.* 6(1). 85-98.

Nguyen, T. H. G. 2011. *Human Resource Management in Vietnamese Businesses.* Retrieved from: https://www.ukessays.com/essays/business/human-resource-management-in-vietnamese-businesses-business-essay.php.

Nguyen, T. H. N. and J. Kretschmann. 2013). *The risk management system in*

German hard coal companies and the transference to Southeast Asia (Doctoral dissertation). Hochschulbibliothek der Rheinisch-Westfälischen Technischen Hochschule Aachen.

Nguyen, Thanh Trung. 2015. *Building human resources Vietnam in management and scientific research in order to develop science and technology in the period of accelerated industrialization and modernization of the country* (Doctoral thesis). Hanoi.

Nguyen, Thi Ngoc Diep, Terri Mylett, and Stephen T. T. Teo. 2013. *A repertory grid approach in exploring the roles of HR departments in Vietnam.* Available at: http://aut.researchgateway.ac.nz/bitstream/handle/10292/6643/BAM2013%20RepGrid%20HR%20roles%20in%20Vietnam.pdf;sequence=2.

Nguyen, Van Anh. 2013. A number of mechanisms and policies for S&T enterprises today. The Journal of Information of Political Science and Administration, Center for Science Information. Ho Chi Minh National Academy of Politics. No. 1.

Nguyen, Vo Hung. 2014. Roles of the State in Emerging Process of Innovation System. *JSTPM*. 3(2).

Nonghyup. 2016. *What Nonghyup Does.* Retrieved from http://www.nonghyup.com/Html/Nhnonghyup/ustatus/nhwork/Index.aspx.

NSF. (2014). *Science and Engineering Indicators 2014*, Appendix 2

Organization for Economic Co-operation and Development and the World Bank. 2014. *Science, Technology and Innovation in Vietnam.* OECD Reviews of Innovation Policy. Retrieved from http://www.oecd.org

Organization for Economic Co-operation and Development and the World Bank.

2014. *Science, Technology and Innovation in Vietnam.* OECD Publishing: Paris.

Ohno, K. 2014. *Learning to Industrialize: From Given Growth to Policy-Aided Value Creation.* New York: Routledge.

Park, S. J., J. K. Park, and K. Y. Shin. 2012. *Operation of Agricultural Cooperative for Rural Development.* Knowledge Sharing Program: KSP Modularization, Seoul, Korea.

Park, S. M.2013. *Public Management.* Seoul, Korea: DayongMoonhwasa Publishing.

Parry, S. B. (1996). Just What Is a Competency?(And Why Should You Care?). *Training*, 35(6), 58

Pham, L. 2011. Impact of Applying Human Resource Management Practices on Equitized State Owned Enterprises' Financial Performance in Vietnam. *Journal of International Business Research.* 10(2). 79-90.

Phong, T. 2012, March 7. *As Lucky as SOE officials.* Vietnamnet. Retrieved from http://english.vietnamnet.vn/fms/special-reports/24000/as-lucky-as-soe-officials.html.

Poon, Yeow, Nguyen Khac Hung, and Do Xuan Truong.2009. *The Reform of the Civil Service System as Vietnam moves into the Middle-Income Country Category.* Hanoi, Vietnam: United Nations Development Programme. Available at: http://www.undp.org/content/dam/vietnam/docs/Project%20Documents/25525_3_CivilServiceReform.pdf.

Quan, Le. 2016. *Leadership and Management Competency Framework in the Public Administration Sector.* Vietnam National University Press.

Quang, T., and H. K. Dung. 1998. Human resource development in state-owned enterprises in Vietnam. *Research and Practice in Human Resource Management.* 6(1). 85-103.

Rothwell, W.J., C. K. Hohne, and S. B. King. 2000. *Human Performance Improvement.* Houston, TX: Gulf.

Ruiz, P., C. Ruiz, and R. Martínez. 2011. Improving the "leader-follower" relationship: Top manager or supervisor? The ethical leadership trickle-down effect on follower job response. *Journal of Business Ethics* 99(4). 587-608.

SaKong, I., Koh, Y. 2010. *The Korean Economy: Six Decades of Growth and Development*(Vol. 2). Seoul, Korea: Korea Development Institute.

Selstad, T. 1990. The rise of the quaternary sector. The regional dimension of knowledge-based services in Norway, 1970-1985. *Norwegian Journal of Geography.* 44(1). 21-37.

Sjoholm, F. 2006. *State-owned enterprises and equitization in Vietnam.* New York: United Nations Development Program.

Socio-economic development strategy for period 2011 - 2020

Strategic Risk. 2014. Asia Risk Report: The Top Concerns of Asian Risk Managers, www.strategic-risk-global.com/asia.

Taek Soo Chung & In joong Ju. 2000. The way to activate Training by Position Level. KRIVET.

Thang, N. N. and T. Quang. 2011. The impact of training on firm performance in a transitional economy: Evidence from Vietnam. *Research & Practice in Human Resource Management.* 19(1). 11-24.

The Economist Intelligence Unit & Asian Development Bank. 2014. *Creative*

Productivity Index: Analyzing Creativity and Innovation in Asia. Retrieved from: http://www.adb.org/publications/creative-productivity-index-analysing-creativity-and-innovation-asia.

The Prime Minister. (2010). Decision 49/2010 / QD-TTg of July 19, 2010 by the Prime Minister on approving the list of high technology in priority development and sales of products of high-tech is encouraged. Hanoi.

The Prime Minister. (2010). Decree 96/2010 / ND-CP of September 20, 2010 of the Government, amending and supplementing some articles of Decree No. 115/2005 / ND-CP dated 5.9. 2005 regulates the mechanism of autonomy and self-responsibility of S & T public organization and Decree No. 80/2007 / ND-CP dated 05/19/2007 on science and technology enterprises;

The Prime Minister. (2011). Decision No. 1244 / QD-TTg of July 25, 2011 on the approval of the direction, objectives and tasks of science and technology for the period 2011 to 2015;

The Prime Minister. (2012). Decision No. 418 / QD-TTg of April 11, 2012 approving the strategy for development of science and technology phase 2011-2020;

The Prime Minister. (2012). Decision No. 592 / QD-TTg dated 22/05/2012 on approving the Program supports development of S&T business and S & T public institutions in implementation of autonomy, self-responsibility.

Thomson, R. and C. Mabey. 1994.*Developing Human Resources.* Oxford, UK: Butterworth-Heinemann.

Tong cuc Thong ke (General Statistical Office – GSO). 2016. So lieu thong ke,tai khoan quoc gia, Retrieved from https://www.gso.vn

Torrington, D. and Tan, C. H. (1994) *Human Resource Management for South East Asia*, Singapore: Prentice Hall

Tran, Bao Tran, Bernice Ong, and Scott. Weldon. 2015. Vietnam Banking Industry Report.

United Nations, Economic and Social Commission for Asia and the Pacific. (2005). *Strengthening Institutional Capacity to Promote Investment and Transfer of Technology with Special Emphasis on Information and Communication Technology.* New York: United Nations.

Utterback, James M. 1994. *Mastering the Dynamics of Innovation.* Boston: Harvard Business School Press.

Vietnam Government (2011a). *On The 2011 - 2015 Socio-Economic Development Plan*. Retrieved from http://www2.chinhphu.vn/portal/page/portal/English/strategies/Strategies%20details?articleId=10057591

Vietnam Government (2011b). *Vietnam's Socio-Economic Development Strategy for The Period of 2011-2020*. Retrieved from http://www.economica.vn/portals/0/maubieu/1d3f7ee0400e42152bdcaa439bf62686.pdf

Vinacomin Business School. 2014. Function – Tasks of VBS. Retrieved from: http://vbs.edu.vn/en/about/Functions-Tasks.html.

Vinacomin Business School. 2014. History and Development of VBS. Retrieved from: http://vbs.edu.vn/en/tin-tuc/Short-courses/Training-Courses-1.html.

Vinacomin Business School. 2014. Mission – Vision of VBS. Retrieved from: http://vbs.edu.vn/en/about/Mission-Vision.html.

Vinacomin Business School.2015. History of Vinacomin. Retrieved from: http://www.vinacomin.vn/introduction/history-201507151622403603.htm

Vinacomin Business School. 2016. Mission – Vision of Vinacomin. Retrieved from: http://vbs.edu.vn/en/about/Mission-Vision.html.

Vinacomin Business School.2016. Training Courses of VINACOMIN, In VINACOMIN BUSINESS SCHOOL website. Retrieved from http://vbs.edu.vn/en/tin-tuc/Short-courses/Training-Courses-1.html.

VCCI. (2015). *Global Entrepreneurship Monitor: Vietnam Report 2014*Hanoi, Vietnam: Vietnam News Agency Publishing House.

Vietnam Raises Minimum Wage for Public Sector, First Time in 3 Years. 2016, May 6.*Thanh Nien News.* Retrieved from http://www.thanhniennews.com/society/vietnam-raises-minimum-wage-for-public-sector-first-time-in-3-years-61850.html.

Vietnam's Public Wages Too Low, Cover a Third of Basic Needs: Official. 2015, March 10. *Thanh Nien News.* Retrieved from http://www.thanhniennews.com/politics/vietnams-public-wages-too-low-cover-a-third-of-basic-needs-official-39612.html.

VNPT. 2011. Online Learning System for VNPT E- learning. Retrieved from http://www.khoahocphothong.com.vn/news/detail/9670/he-thong-hoc-truc-tuyen-e-learning-cua-vnpt.html

VNPT. 2016. e-learning of VNPT. Retrieved from In http://elearning.vnpt.vn.

VNPT. 2016. *Vietnam Telecommunications Report.* Hanoi, Vietnam: Author.

Vo, Anne Ngoc. 2009. *The Transformation of Human Resource Management and Labour Relations in Vietnam.* Oxford, UK: Chandos Publishing.

Warner, M. 2013. Comparing Human Resource Management in China and Vietnam: An Overview. *Human System Management.* 32. 217-229.

Watkins, K. E. 2001. Philosophical metaphors for HRD theory and practice. In Richard A. Swanson and Elwood F. Holton, III, *Foundations of Human Resource Development*(pp. 70-83). San Francisco, CA: Berrett-Koehler Publishers.

Werner, Jon M., and Randy L. DeSimone. 2006. *Human Resource Development: Foundation, Framework and Application*. Mason, OH: South-Western Cengage learning.

Werner, Jon M., and Randy L. DeSimone. 2009. Evaluating HRD programs. Human Resource Development, 5.

World Intellectual Property Organization. 2015. Statistics database. Retrieved from http://ipstats.wipo.int/ipstatv2/index.htm

Wonhyuk Lim and Tai Hee Lee. 2011. *2010 Modularization of Korea's Development Experience: Productivity Improvement* (GPR No. 11-1051000-000140-01). Ministry of Strategy and Finance, Republic of Korea.

World Bank. 2013. Strategic Approaches to Science and Technology in Development. World Bank Policy Research Paper.

World Bank. 2014. Science, Technology and Innovation in Vietnam: Driving Sustained Growth.

World Bank. 2014. World Governance Indicators, 2014 update. (http://info.worldbank.org/governance/wgi/index.aspx#home)

World Bank. 2015. report on the evaluation of science, technology and innovation in Vietnam. Hanoi.

World Bank. 2016. Vietnam 2035: Toward Prosperity Creativity, Equity, and Democracy.

World Economic Forum. (2012). *The Financial Development Report 2012*. New

York: World Economic Forum USA.

World Economic Forum. (2015). *The Global Competitiveness Report 2015-2016.* Geneva: World Economic Forum.

INDEX

"3 X 3 Model" 23

A

advanced human resource development (AHRD) 17
advancement of HRD system 19
Agribank 23, 294
AHRD 293
AHRD Agency 124
AHRD philosophy 22
AHRD System 140
AHR Planning 114
AHR Rotation 116
AHR Training 116
A Process 133
Assessment 133

C

career development program (CDP) 199
CCO 299
Central Committee for Organizations 299
Central Committee for Organizations (CCO) 29
central government 300
collaboration 287
competitiveness 299
Comprehensive AHRD 124, 140
Comprehensive AHRD Program 132
Cultural and Legal Values 112

D

Department of Organization and Human Resource Managemen 93
Department of Organization and Human Resource Management 299
Designing AHRD Content 134
Developing Quality of Trainers 298
DHRM 299
Distribution of R&D personnel by organizations 243
Dual System 112

E

economic growth, 17
economic modernization 292
Economic Prosperity 19

enhancing quality of government 17
Evaluation 134

F

FDI 260
Flipped Learning 234
fragmented innovation system 258

G

government 16, 19, 21, 293
government research institutes 298
government research institutes (GRI) 28
GRI 298

H

HCMA 16
High Level Government 19
High Level Management 19
Ho Chi Minh National Academy of Politics (HCMA) 174
HR 24, 293
HRD 23, 293
HR 'imperatives' 21
HRM 23
HR Professionals 29, 298
Human capital 161
Human Resource Development Institute of Vietnam (NAHRDI) 28
Human resource management 19
human resources 292
Human Resources Development(HRD) 161
Hybrid Recruitment System 148

I

Implementation 134
inclusive growth 17
innovative capacity 292
innovativeness 299
institutional capacity 299
Institutionalized HRM/D Systems 147
instructional design 164
Integrated HRD Agency 129
Interactive HRD Programs 137
invention patent 249
ISD (Instructional Systems Design) 172

K

KMA (Korea Management Association) 232
KOCOAL 23, 294

KOICA 16

Korea Coal Corporation (KOCOAL) 165

Korean public HRD 22

KPC 23

KT (Korea Telecom) 165

L

level of competencies (advancement of competencies) 17

level of HRD system (advancement of competencies) 17

level of management (middle and top managers) 17

LMS (Learning Management System) 232

Local Government Officials Development Institute (LOGODI) 125

M

Majungmul Effect 162

Management Training Program (MTP) 172

merit-based human resource system 27

merit-based personnel system 296

meritocracy 293, 296

Meritocracy 27, 296

meta-resources 161

Ministry of Home Affairs 299

Ministry of Home Affairs (MOHA) 29

modularization-centered approach of training 163

MOHA 299

MOOC (Massive Open Online Course) 232

N

NAHRDI 296, 298

National Advanced Human Resource Development Institute of Vietnam 298

National Human Resource Development Institute [NHI]) 124

National Institute for Science and Technology Policy and Strategy Studies(NISTPASS) 261

National Strategic Leadership 100

Needs analysis 164

nepotism-based 27, 297

Nonghyup (National Agricultural Cooperative Federation) 165

non-merit factors 27, 296, 297

O

OCW (Open Course Ware) 234

P

Performance and Career Management 120
performance-related pay (PRP) system 113
Pilot Testing 133
position-based system 25, 293
problem-based training programs 31, 300
promotion of various competencies 17
Provincial Department of Home Affairs 29, 299
provincial governments 300
public corporation 19

Q

Quality of Trainers 29

R

R&D 16, 19, 292, 293
R&D Personnel 19

S

Saemaeul Movement(SMU) 191
science and technology (S&T) 21
science, technology and innovation 285
SEDP 2016-2020 298
SEDS 19
SEDS 2016-2020 18
select and concentrate strategy 285
seniority-based 27, 297
seniority-based personnel system 296
skill-based 31, 300
Social Economic Development Strategy 19
socio-economic development plans (SEDPs) 168
SOEs 292, 293
State Capacity Building 19
state-owned enterprises 16
state-owned enterprises (SOE) 21
state-owned enterprises(SOEs) 160
sustainable development 16

T

target of AHRD 18
technical-vocational education and

training (TVET) 168
technological 292
Technology transfers 260
the Korea Productivity Center (KPC) 188
The Ministry of Education and Training 86
the Ministry of Education and Training (MOET) 169
The Ministry of Home Affairs (MOHA) 92
the Ministry of Labour and Social Affairs (MOLISA) 169
the National Strategy for Science and Technology Development 2011-2020 (SSTD) 254
The Senior Civil Service System 144
the Vietnam Bank for Agriculture and Rural Development (Agribank) 175
The Vietnam National Coal and Mineral Industries group (VINACOMIN) 174
Training Curricula 29, 298
Training Program for High Ranking Officials 136

V

Vietnam 2035 292, 298
Vietnam Bank for Agriculture and Rural Development (Agribank) 183
Vietnam Posts and Telecommunications(VNPT) 174
Vietnam Productivity Center for SOEs 298
Vietnam Productivity Center for SOEs (VPCS) 28
Vietnam version of Korean Institute of Science and Technology 298
Vietnam Vision 2035 18
VINACOMIN 23, 294
V-KIST 298
V-KIST (Vietnam version of Korean Institute of Science and Technology) 28
VNPT 23, 294, 299
VPC 296
VPCS 298

AUTHORS

M. Jae Moon

Professor, Department of Public Administration, Yonsei University

Director, Institute for Future Government, Yonsei University

Fellow of National Academy of Public Administration (NAPA)

Ilhyun Jo

Professor, Department of Educational Technology, Ewha Womans University

Dean, Career Development Center, Ewha Womans University

Former President, Korea Society of Learning and Performance

Sam Youl Lee

Professor & Chair, Department of Public Administration

Chair, Science, Technology, and Policy (STP) Major, Underwood Int'l College (UIC), Yonsei University

Former Senior Research, Korean Information Society Development Institute

Sung Min Park

Professor, Graduate School of Governance,
Sungkyunkwan University (SKKU)
Director, SKKU Center for Public Human
Resource Development (CPHRD), SKKU
Managing Editor, International Review
of Public Administration (IRPA)
Former Assistant Professor, University of Nevada-Las Vegas

Jung Wook Lee

Professor, Department of Public
Administration, Yonsei University
Associate Dean of Academic Affairs,
University College, Yonsei University
Former Faculty, College of Public Affairs and
Administration, University of Illinois at Springfield